C-2396   CAREER EXAMINATION SERIES

This is your
PASSBOOK for...

Director of Fire Safety

Test Preparation Study Guide
Questions & Answers

NATIONAL LEARNING CORPORATION®

COPYRIGHT NOTICE

This book is SOLELY intended for, is sold ONLY to, and its use is RESTRICTED to individual, bona fide applicants or candidates who qualify by virtue of having seriously filed applications for appropriate license, certificate, professional and/or promotional advancement, higher school matriculation, scholarship, or other legitimate requirements of education and/or governmental authorities.

This book is NOT intended for use, class instruction, tutoring, training, duplication, copying, reprinting, excerption, or adaptation, etc., by:

1) Other publishers
2) Proprietors and/or Instructors of "Coaching" and/or Preparatory Courses
3) Personnel and/or Training Divisions of commercial, industrial, and governmental organizations
4) Schools, colleges, or universities and/or their departments and staffs, including teachers and other personnel
5) Testing Agencies or Bureaus
6) Study groups which seek by the purchase of a single volume to copy and/or duplicate and/or adapt this material for use by the group as a whole without having purchased individual volumes for each of the members of the group
7) Et al.

Such persons would be in violation of appropriate Federal and State statutes.

PROVISION OF LICENSING AGREEMENTS – Recognized educational, commercial, industrial, and governmental institutions and organizations, and others legitimately engaged in educational pursuits, including training, testing, and measurement activities, may address request for a licensing agreement to the copyright owners, who will determine whether, and under what conditions, including fees and charges, the materials in this book may be used them. In other words, a licensing facility exists for the legitimate use of the material in this book on other than an individual basis. However, it is asseverated and affirmed here that the material in this book CANNOT be used without the receipt of the express permission of such a licensing agreement from the Publishers. Inquiries re licensing should be addressed to the company, attention rights and permissions department.

All rights reserved, including the right of reproduction in whole or in part, in any form or by any means, electronic or mechanical, including photocopying, recording, or by any information storage and retrieval system, without permission in writing from the Publisher.

Copyright © 2025 by
National Learning Corporation

212 Michael Drive, Syosset, NY 11791
(516) 921-8888 • www.passbooks.com
E-mail: info@passbooks.com

PASSBOOK® SERIES

THE *PASSBOOK® SERIES* has been created to prepare applicants and candidates for the ultimate academic battlefield – the examination room.

At some time in our lives, each and every one of us may be required to take an examination – for validation, matriculation, admission, qualification, registration, certification, or licensure.

Based on the assumption that every applicant or candidate has met the basic formal educational standards, has taken the required number of courses, and read the necessary texts, the *PASSBOOK® SERIES* furnishes the one special preparation which may assure passing with confidence, instead of failing with insecurity. Examination questions – together with answers – are furnished as the basic vehicle for study so that the mysteries of the examination and its compounding difficulties may be eliminated or diminished by a sure method.

This book is meant to help you pass your examination provided that you qualify and are serious in your objective.

The entire field is reviewed through the huge store of content information which is succinctly presented through a provocative and challenging approach – the question-and-answer method.

A climate of success is established by furnishing the correct answers at the end of each test.

You soon learn to recognize types of questions, forms of questions, and patterns of questioning. You may even begin to anticipate expected outcomes.

You perceive that many questions are repeated or adapted so that you can gain acute insights, which may enable you to score many sure points.

You learn how to confront new questions, or types of questions, and to attack them confidently and work out the correct answers.

You note objectives and emphases, and recognize pitfalls and dangers, so that you may make positive educational adjustments.

Moreover, you are kept fully informed in relation to new concepts, methods, practices, and directions in the field.

You discover that you are actually taking the examination all the time: you are preparing for the examination by "taking" an examination, not by reading extraneous and/or supererogatory textbooks.

In short, this PASSBOOK®, used directedly, should be an important factor in helping you to pass your test.

DIRECTOR OF FIRE SAFETY

DUTIES
Administers department programs in the areas of fire training, mutual aid, emergency service dispatching, and fire education; performs related work as required.

SCOPE OF THE WRITTEN TEST
The written test will be designed to test for knowledge, skills, and/or abilities in the following areas:
1. Reading comprehension;
2. Special problems;
3. Combat techniques;
4. Fire command;
5. Pumpers;
6. Extinguishers;
7. Training;
8. Fire inspection;
9. Records and reports;
10. Combat equipment;
11. Hydraulics;
12. Fire chemistry;
13. Supervision;
14. Planning;
15. NBFU standards;
16. Fire hazards;
17. Public relations;
18. Education;
19. Fire training;
20. Budget;
21. Personnel; and
22. Administration.

HOW TO TAKE A TEST

I. YOU MUST PASS AN EXAMINATION

A. WHAT EVERY CANDIDATE SHOULD KNOW

Examination applicants often ask us for help in preparing for the written test. What can I study in advance? What kinds of questions will be asked? How will the test be given? How will the papers be graded?

As an applicant for a civil service examination, you may be wondering about some of these things. Our purpose here is to suggest effective methods of advance study and to describe civil service examinations.

Your chances for success on this examination can be increased if you know how to prepare. Those "pre-examination jitters" can be reduced if you know what to expect. You can even experience an adventure in good citizenship if you know why civil service exams are given.

B. WHY ARE CIVIL SERVICE EXAMINATIONS GIVEN?

Civil service examinations are important to you in two ways. As a citizen, you want public jobs filled by employees who know how to do their work. As a job seeker, you want a fair chance to compete for that job on an equal footing with other candidates. The best-known means of accomplishing this two-fold goal is the competitive examination.

Exams are widely publicized throughout the nation. They may be administered for jobs in federal, state, city, municipal, town or village governments or agencies.

Any citizen may apply, with some limitations, such as the age or residence of applicants. Your experience and education may be reviewed to see whether you meet the requirements for the particular examination. When these requirements exist, they are reasonable and applied consistently to all applicants. Thus, a competitive examination may cause you some uneasiness now, but it is your privilege and safeguard.

C. HOW ARE CIVIL SERVICE EXAMS DEVELOPED?

Examinations are carefully written by trained technicians who are specialists in the field known as "psychological measurement," in consultation with recognized authorities in the field of work that the test will cover. These experts recommend the subject matter areas or skills to be tested; only those knowledges or skills important to your success on the job are included. The most reliable books and source materials available are used as references. Together, the experts and technicians judge the difficulty level of the questions.

Test technicians know how to phrase questions so that the problem is clearly stated. Their ethics do not permit "trick" or "catch" questions. Questions may have been tried out on sample groups, or subjected to statistical analysis, to determine their usefulness.

Written tests are often used in combination with performance tests, ratings of training and experience, and oral interviews. All of these measures combine to form the best-known means of finding the right person for the right job.

II. HOW TO PASS THE WRITTEN TEST

A. NATURE OF THE EXAMINATION

To prepare intelligently for civil service examinations, you should know how they differ from school examinations you have taken. In school you were assigned certain definite pages to read or subjects to cover. The examination questions were quite detailed and usually emphasized memory. Civil service exams, on the other hand, try to discover your present ability to perform the duties of a position, plus your potentiality to learn these duties. In other words, a civil service exam attempts to predict how successful you will be. Questions cover such a broad area that they cannot be as minute and detailed as school exam questions.

In the public service similar kinds of work, or positions, are grouped together in one "class." This process is known as *position-classification*. All the positions in a class are paid according to the salary range for that class. One class title covers all of these positions, and they are all tested by the same examination.

B. FOUR BASIC STEPS

1) Study the announcement

How, then, can you know what subjects to study? Our best answer is: "Learn as much as possible about the class of positions for which you've applied." The exam will test the knowledge, skills and abilities needed to do the work.

Your most valuable source of information about the position you want is the official exam announcement. This announcement lists the training and experience qualifications. Check these standards and apply only if you come reasonably close to meeting them.

The brief description of the position in the examination announcement offers some clues to the subjects which will be tested. Think about the job itself. Review the duties in your mind. Can you perform them, or are there some in which you are rusty? Fill in the blank spots in your preparation.

Many jurisdictions preview the written test in the exam announcement by including a section called "Knowledge and Abilities Required," "Scope of the Examination," or some similar heading. Here you will find out specifically what fields will be tested.

2) Review your own background

Once you learn in general what the position is all about, and what you need to know to do the work, ask yourself which subjects you already know fairly well and which need improvement. You may wonder whether to concentrate on improving your strong areas or on building some background in your fields of weakness. When the announcement has specified "some knowledge" or "considerable knowledge," or has used adjectives like "beginning principles of…" or "advanced … methods," you can get a clue as to the number and difficulty of questions to be asked in any given field. More questions, and hence broader coverage, would be included for those subjects which are more important in the work. Now weigh your strengths and weaknesses against the job requirements and prepare accordingly.

3) Determine the level of the position

Another way to tell how intensively you should prepare is to understand the level of the job for which you are applying. Is it the entering level? In other words, is this the position in which beginners in a field of work are hired? Or is it an intermediate or advanced level? Sometimes this is indicated by such words as "Junior" or "Senior" in the class title. Other jurisdictions use Roman numerals to designate the level – Clerk I, Clerk II, for example. The word "Supervisor" sometimes appears in the title. If the level is not indicated by the title, check the description of duties. Will you be working under very close supervision, or will you have responsibility for independent decisions in this work?

4) Choose appropriate study materials

Now that you know the subjects to be examined and the relative amount of each subject to be covered, you can choose suitable study materials. For beginning level jobs, or even advanced ones, if you have a pronounced weakness in some aspect of your training, read a modern, standard textbook in that field. Be sure it is up to date and has general coverage. Such books are normally available at your library, and the librarian will be glad to help you locate one. For entry-level positions, questions of appropriate difficulty are chosen – neither highly advanced questions, nor those too simple. Such questions require careful thought but not advanced training.

If the position for which you are applying is technical or advanced, you will read more advanced, specialized material. If you are already familiar with the basic principles of your field, elementary textbooks would waste your time. Concentrate on advanced textbooks and technical periodicals. Think through the concepts and review difficult problems in your field.

These are all general sources. You can get more ideas on your own initiative, following these leads. For example, training manuals and publications of the government agency which employs workers in your field can be useful, particularly for technical and professional positions. A letter or visit to the government department involved may result in more specific study suggestions, and certainly will provide you with a more definite idea of the exact nature of the position you are seeking.

III. KINDS OF TESTS

Tests are used for purposes other than measuring knowledge and ability to perform specified duties. For some positions, it is equally important to test ability to make adjustments to new situations or to profit from training. In others, basic mental abilities not dependent on information are essential. Questions which test these things may not appear as pertinent to the duties of the position as those which test for knowledge and information. Yet they are often highly important parts of a fair examination. For very general questions, it is almost impossible to help you direct your study efforts. What we can do is to point out some of the more common of these general abilities needed in public service positions and describe some typical questions.

1) General information

Broad, general information has been found useful for predicting job success in some kinds of work. This is tested in a variety of ways, from vocabulary lists to questions about current events. Basic background in some field of work, such as sociology or economics, may be sampled in a group of questions. Often these are principles which have become familiar to most persons through exposure rather than through formal training. It is difficult to advise you how to study for these questions; being alert to the world around you is our best suggestion.

2) Verbal ability

An example of an ability needed in many positions is verbal or language ability. Verbal ability is, in brief, the ability to use and understand words. Vocabulary and grammar tests are typical measures of this ability. Reading comprehension or paragraph interpretation questions are common in many kinds of civil service tests. You are given a paragraph of written material and asked to find its central meaning.

3) Numerical ability

Number skills can be tested by the familiar arithmetic problem, by checking paired lists of numbers to see which are alike and which are different, or by interpreting charts and graphs. In the latter test, a graph may be printed in the test booklet which you are asked to use as the basis for answering questions.

4) Observation

A popular test for law-enforcement positions is the observation test. A picture is shown to you for several minutes, then taken away. Questions about the picture test your ability to observe both details and larger elements.

5) Following directions

In many positions in the public service, the employee must be able to carry out written instructions dependably and accurately. You may be given a chart with several columns, each column listing a variety of information. The questions require you to carry out directions involving the information given in the chart.

6) Skills and aptitudes

Performance tests effectively measure some manual skills and aptitudes. When the skill is one in which you are trained, such as typing or shorthand, you can practice. These tests are often very much like those given in business school or high school courses. For many of the other skills and aptitudes, however, no short-time preparation can be made. Skills and abilities natural to you or that you have developed throughout your lifetime are being tested.

Many of the general questions just described provide all the data needed to answer the questions and ask you to use your reasoning ability to find the answers. Your best preparation for these tests, as well as for tests of facts and ideas, is to be at your physical and mental best. You, no doubt, have your own methods of getting into an exam-taking mood and keeping "in shape." The next section lists some ideas on this subject.

IV. KINDS OF QUESTIONS

Only rarely is the "essay" question, which you answer in narrative form, used in civil service tests. Civil service tests are usually of the short-answer type. Full instructions for answering these questions will be given to you at the examination. But in case this is your first experience with short-answer questions and separate answer sheets, here is what you need to know:

1) Multiple-choice Questions

Most popular of the short-answer questions is the "multiple choice" or "best answer" question. It can be used, for example, to test for factual knowledge, ability to solve problems or judgment in meeting situations found at work.

A multiple-choice question is normally one of three types—
- It can begin with an incomplete statement followed by several possible endings. You are to find the one ending which *best* completes the statement, although some of the others may not be entirely wrong.
- It can also be a complete statement in the form of a question which is answered by choosing one of the statements listed.

- It can be in the form of a problem – again you select the best answer.

Here is an example of a multiple-choice question with a discussion which should give you some clues as to the method for choosing the right answer:

When an employee has a complaint about his assignment, the action which will *best* help him overcome his difficulty is to
- A. discuss his difficulty with his coworkers
- B. take the problem to the head of the organization
- C. take the problem to the person who gave him the assignment
- D. say nothing to anyone about his complaint

In answering this question, you should study each of the choices to find which is best. Consider choice "A" – Certainly an employee may discuss his complaint with fellow employees, but no change or improvement can result, and the complaint remains unresolved. Choice "B" is a poor choice since the head of the organization probably does not know what assignment you have been given, and taking your problem to him is known as "going over the head" of the supervisor. The supervisor, or person who made the assignment, is the person who can clarify it or correct any injustice. Choice "C" is, therefore, correct. To say nothing, as in choice "D," is unwise. Supervisors have and interest in knowing the problems employees are facing, and the employee is seeking a solution to his problem.

2) True/False Questions

The "true/false" or "right/wrong" form of question is sometimes used. Here a complete statement is given. Your job is to decide whether the statement is right or wrong.

SAMPLE: A roaming cell-phone call to a nearby city costs less than a non-roaming call to a distant city.

This statement is wrong, or false, since roaming calls are more expensive.

This is not a complete list of all possible question forms, although most of the others are variations of these common types. You will always get complete directions for answering questions. Be sure you understand *how* to mark your answers – ask questions until you do.

V. RECORDING YOUR ANSWERS

Computer terminals are used more and more today for many different kinds of exams.

For an examination with very few applicants, you may be told to record your answers in the test booklet itself. Separate answer sheets are much more common. If this separate answer sheet is to be scored by machine – and this is often the case – it is highly important that you mark your answers correctly in order to get credit.

An electronic scoring machine is often used in civil service offices because of the speed with which papers can be scored. Machine-scored answer sheets must be marked with a pencil, which will be given to you. This pencil has a high graphite content which responds to the electronic scoring machine. As a matter of fact, stray dots may register as answers, so do not let your pencil rest on the answer sheet while you are pondering the correct answer. Also, if your pencil lead breaks or is otherwise defective, ask for another.

Since the answer sheet will be dropped in a slot in the scoring machine, be careful not to bend the corners or get the paper crumpled.

The answer sheet normally has five vertical columns of numbers, with 30 numbers to a column. These numbers correspond to the question numbers in your test booklet. After each number, going across the page are four or five pairs of dotted lines. These short dotted lines have small letters or numbers above them. The first two pairs may also have a "T" or "F" above the letters. This indicates that the first two pairs only are to be used if the questions are of the true-false type. If the questions are multiple choice, disregard the "T" and "F" and pay attention only to the small letters or numbers.

Answer your questions in the manner of the sample that follows:

32. The largest city in the United States is
    A. Washington, D.C.
    B. New York City
    C. Chicago
    D. Detroit
    E. San Francisco

1) Choose the answer you think is best. (New York City is the largest, so "B" is correct.)
2) Find the row of dotted lines numbered the same as the question you are answering. (Find row number 32)
3) Find the pair of dotted lines corresponding to the answer. (Find the pair of lines under the mark "B.")
4) Make a solid black mark between the dotted lines.

VI. BEFORE THE TEST

Common sense will help you find procedures to follow to get ready for an examination. Too many of us, however, overlook these sensible measures. Indeed, nervousness and fatigue have been found to be the most serious reasons why applicants fail to do their best on civil service tests. Here is a list of reminders:

- Begin your preparation early – Don't wait until the last minute to go scurrying around for books and materials or to find out what the position is all about.
- Prepare continuously – An hour a night for a week is better than an all-night cram session. This has been definitely established. What is more, a night a week for a month will return better dividends than crowding your study into a shorter period of time.
- Locate the place of the exam – You have been sent a notice telling you when and where to report for the examination. If the location is in a different town or otherwise unfamiliar to you, it would be well to inquire the best route and learn something about the building.
- Relax the night before the test – Allow your mind to rest. Do not study at all that night. Plan some mild recreation or diversion; then go to bed early and get a good night's sleep.
- Get up early enough to make a leisurely trip to the place for the test – This way unforeseen events, traffic snarls, unfamiliar buildings, etc. will not upset you.
- Dress comfortably – A written test is not a fashion show. You will be known by number and not by name, so wear something comfortable.

- Leave excess paraphernalia at home – Shopping bags and odd bundles will get in your way. You need bring only the items mentioned in the official notice you received; usually everything you need is provided. Do not bring reference books to the exam. They will only confuse those last minutes and be taken away from you when in the test room.
- Arrive somewhat ahead of time – If because of transportation schedules you must get there very early, bring a newspaper or magazine to take your mind off yourself while waiting.
- Locate the examination room – When you have found the proper room, you will be directed to the seat or part of the room where you will sit. Sometimes you are given a sheet of instructions to read while you are waiting. Do not fill out any forms until you are told to do so; just read them and be prepared.
- Relax and prepare to listen to the instructions
- If you have any physical problem that may keep you from doing your best, be sure to tell the test administrator. If you are sick or in poor health, you really cannot do your best on the exam. You can come back and take the test some other time.

VII. AT THE TEST

The day of the test is here and you have the test booklet in your hand. The temptation to get going is very strong. Caution! There is more to success than knowing the right answers. You must know how to identify your papers and understand variations in the type of short-answer question used in this particular examination. Follow these suggestions for maximum results from your efforts:

1) Cooperate with the monitor

The test administrator has a duty to create a situation in which you can be as much at ease as possible. He will give instructions, tell you when to begin, check to see that you are marking your answer sheet correctly, and so on. He is not there to guard you, although he will see that your competitors do not take unfair advantage. He wants to help you do your best.

2) Listen to all instructions

Don't jump the gun! Wait until you understand all directions. In most civil service tests you get more time than you need to answer the questions. So don't be in a hurry. Read each word of instructions until you clearly understand the meaning. Study the examples, listen to all announcements and follow directions. Ask questions if you do not understand what to do.

3) Identify your papers

Civil service exams are usually identified by number only. You will be assigned a number; you must not put your name on your test papers. Be sure to copy your number correctly. Since more than one exam may be given, copy your exact examination title.

4) Plan your time

Unless you are told that a test is a "speed" or "rate of work" test, speed itself is usually not important. Time enough to answer all the questions will be provided, but this does not mean that you have all day. An overall time limit has been set. Divide the total time (in minutes) by the number of questions to determine the approximate time you have for each question.

5) Do not linger over difficult questions

If you come across a difficult question, mark it with a paper clip (useful to have along) and come back to it when you have been through the booklet. One caution if you do this – be sure to skip a number on your answer sheet as well. Check often to be sure that you have not lost your place and that you are marking in the row numbered the same as the question you are answering.

6) Read the questions

Be sure you know what the question asks! Many capable people are unsuccessful because they failed to *read* the questions correctly.

7) Answer all questions

Unless you have been instructed that a penalty will be deducted for incorrect answers, it is better to guess than to omit a question.

8) Speed tests

It is often better NOT to guess on speed tests. It has been found that on timed tests people are tempted to spend the last few seconds before time is called in marking answers at random – without even reading them – in the hope of picking up a few extra points. To discourage this practice, the instructions may warn you that your score will be "corrected" for guessing. That is, a penalty will be applied. The incorrect answers will be deducted from the correct ones, or some other penalty formula will be used.

9) Review your answers

If you finish before time is called, go back to the questions you guessed or omitted to give them further thought. Review other answers if you have time.

10) Return your test materials

If you are ready to leave before others have finished or time is called, take ALL your materials to the monitor and leave quietly. Never take any test material with you. The monitor can discover whose papers are not complete, and taking a test booklet may be grounds for disqualification.

VIII. EXAMINATION TECHNIQUES

1) Read the general instructions carefully. These are usually printed on the first page of the exam booklet. As a rule, these instructions refer to the timing of the examination; the fact that you should not start work until the signal and must stop work at a signal, etc. If there are any *special* instructions, such as a choice of questions to be answered, make sure that you note this instruction carefully.

2) When you are ready to start work on the examination, that is as soon as the signal has been given, read the instructions to each question booklet, underline any key words or phrases, such as *least, best, outline, describe* and the like. In this way you will tend to answer as requested rather than discover on reviewing your paper that you *listed without describing*, that you selected the *worst* choice rather than the *best* choice, etc.

3) If the examination is of the objective or multiple-choice type – that is, each question will also give a series of possible answers: A, B, C or D, and you are called upon to select the best answer and write the letter next to that answer on your answer paper – it is advisable to start answering each question in turn. There may be anywhere from 50 to 100 such questions in the three or four hours allotted and you can see how much time would be taken if you read through all the questions before beginning to answer any. Furthermore, if you come across a question or group of questions which you know would be difficult to answer, it would undoubtedly affect your handling of all the other questions.

4) If the examination is of the essay type and contains but a few questions, it is a moot point as to whether you should read all the questions before starting to answer any one. Of course, if you are given a choice – say five out of seven and the like – then it is essential to read all the questions so you can eliminate the two that are most difficult. If, however, you are asked to answer all the questions, there may be danger in trying to answer the easiest one first because you may find that you will spend too much time on it. The best technique is to answer the first question, then proceed to the second, etc.

5) Time your answers. Before the exam begins, write down the time it started, then add the time allowed for the examination and write down the time it must be completed, then divide the time available somewhat as follows:
   - If 3-1/2 hours are allowed, that would be 210 minutes. If you have 80 objective-type questions, that would be an average of 2-1/2 minutes per question. Allow yourself no more than 2 minutes per question, or a total of 160 minutes, which will permit about 50 minutes to review.
   - If for the time allotment of 210 minutes there are 7 essay questions to answer, that would average about 30 minutes a question. Give yourself only 25 minutes per question so that you have about 35 minutes to review.

6) The most important instruction is to *read each question* and make sure you know what is wanted. The second most important instruction is to *time yourself properly* so that you answer every question. The third most important instruction is to *answer every question*. Guess if you have to but include something for each question. Remember that you will receive no credit for a blank and will probably receive some credit if you write something in answer to an essay question. If you guess a letter – say "B" for a multiple-choice question – you may have guessed right. If you leave a blank as an answer to a multiple-choice question, the examiners may respect your feelings but it will not add a point to your score. Some exams may penalize you for wrong answers, so in such cases *only*, you may not want to guess unless you have some basis for your answer.

7) Suggestions
   a. Objective-type questions
      1. Examine the question booklet for proper sequence of pages and questions
      2. Read all instructions carefully
      3. Skip any question which seems too difficult; return to it after all other questions have been answered
      4. Apportion your time properly; do not spend too much time on any single question or group of questions

5. Note and underline key words – *all, most, fewest, least, best, worst, same, opposite*, etc.
6. Pay particular attention to negatives
7. Note unusual option, e.g., unduly long, short, complex, different or similar in content to the body of the question
8. Observe the use of "hedging" words – *probably, may, most likely,* etc.
9. Make sure that your answer is put next to the same number as the question
10. Do not second-guess unless you have good reason to believe the second answer is definitely more correct
11. Cross out original answer if you decide another answer is more accurate; do not erase until you are ready to hand your paper in
12. Answer all questions; guess unless instructed otherwise
13. Leave time for review

  b. Essay questions
1. Read each question carefully
2. Determine exactly what is wanted. Underline key words or phrases.
3. Decide on outline or paragraph answer
4. Include many different points and elements unless asked to develop any one or two points or elements
5. Show impartiality by giving pros and cons unless directed to select one side only
6. Make and write down any assumptions you find necessary to answer the questions
7. Watch your English, grammar, punctuation and choice of words
8. Time your answers; don't crowd material

8) Answering the essay question

Most essay questions can be answered by framing the specific response around several key words or ideas. Here are a few such key words or ideas:

M's: manpower, materials, methods, money, management
P's: purpose, program, policy, plan, procedure, practice, problems, pitfalls, personnel, public relations

  a. Six basic steps in handling problems:
1. Preliminary plan and background development
2. Collect information, data and facts
3. Analyze and interpret information, data and facts
4. Analyze and develop solutions as well as make recommendations
5. Prepare report and sell recommendations
6. Install recommendations and follow up effectiveness

  b. Pitfalls to avoid
1. *Taking things for granted* – A statement of the situation does not necessarily imply that each of the elements is necessarily true; for example, a complaint may be invalid and biased so that all that can be taken for granted is that a complaint has been registered

2. *Considering only one side of a situation* – Wherever possible, indicate several alternatives and then point out the reasons you selected the best one
3. *Failing to indicate follow up* – Whenever your answer indicates action on your part, make certain that you will take proper follow-up action to see how successful your recommendations, procedures or actions turn out to be
4. *Taking too long in answering any single question* – Remember to time your answers properly

IX. AFTER THE TEST

Scoring procedures differ in detail among civil service jurisdictions although the general principles are the same. Whether the papers are hand-scored or graded by machine we have described, they are nearly always graded by number. That is, the person who marks the paper knows only the number – never the name – of the applicant. Not until all the papers have been graded will they be matched with names. If other tests, such as training and experience or oral interview ratings have been given, scores will be combined. Different parts of the examination usually have different weights. For example, the written test might count 60 percent of the final grade, and a rating of training and experience 40 percent. In many jurisdictions, veterans will have a certain number of points added to their grades.

After the final grade has been determined, the names are placed in grade order and an eligible list is established. There are various methods for resolving ties between those who get the same final grade – probably the most common is to place first the name of the person whose application was received first. Job offers are made from the eligible list in the order the names appear on it. You will be notified of your grade and your rank as soon as all these computations have been made. This will be done as rapidly as possible.

People who are found to meet the requirements in the announcement are called "eligibles." Their names are put on a list of eligible candidates. An eligible's chances of getting a job depend on how high he stands on this list and how fast agencies are filling jobs from the list.

When a job is to be filled from a list of eligibles, the agency asks for the names of people on the list of eligibles for that job. When the civil service commission receives this request, it sends to the agency the names of the three people highest on this list. Or, if the job to be filled has specialized requirements, the office sends the agency the names of the top three persons who meet these requirements from the general list.

The appointing officer makes a choice from among the three people whose names were sent to him. If the selected person accepts the appointment, the names of the others are put back on the list to be considered for future openings.

That is the rule in hiring from all kinds of eligible lists, whether they are for typist, carpenter, chemist, or something else. For every vacancy, the appointing officer has his choice of any one of the top three eligibles on the list. This explains why the person whose name is on top of the list sometimes does not get an appointment when some of the persons lower on the list do. If the appointing officer chooses the second or third eligible, the No. 1 eligible does not get a job at once, but stays on the list until he is appointed or the list is terminated.

X. HOW TO PASS THE INTERVIEW TEST

The examination for which you applied requires an oral interview test. You have already taken the written test and you are now being called for the interview test – the final part of the formal examination.

You may think that it is not possible to prepare for an interview test and that there are no procedures to follow during an interview. Our purpose is to point out some things you can do in advance that will help you and some good rules to follow and pitfalls to avoid while you are being interviewed.

What is an interview supposed to test?

The written examination is designed to test the technical knowledge and competence of the candidate; the oral is designed to evaluate intangible qualities, not readily measured otherwise, and to establish a list showing the relative fitness of each candidate – as measured against his competitors – for the position sought. Scoring is not on the basis of "right" and "wrong," but on a sliding scale of values ranging from "not passable" to "outstanding." As a matter of fact, it is possible to achieve a relatively low score without a single "incorrect" answer because of evident weakness in the qualities being measured.

Occasionally, an examination may consist entirely of an oral test – either an individual or a group oral. In such cases, information is sought concerning the technical knowledges and abilities of the candidate, since there has been no written examination for this purpose. More commonly, however, an oral test is used to supplement a written examination.

Who conducts interviews?

The composition of oral boards varies among different jurisdictions. In nearly all, a representative of the personnel department serves as chairman. One of the members of the board may be a representative of the department in which the candidate would work. In some cases, "outside experts" are used, and, frequently, a businessman or some other representative of the general public is asked to serve. Labor and management or other special groups may be represented. The aim is to secure the services of experts in the appropriate field.

However the board is composed, it is a good idea (and not at all improper or unethical) to ascertain in advance of the interview who the members are and what groups they represent. When you are introduced to them, you will have some idea of their backgrounds and interests, and at least you will not stutter and stammer over their names.

What should be done before the interview?

While knowledge about the board members is useful and takes some of the surprise element out of the interview, there is other preparation which is more substantive. It *is* possible to prepare for an oral interview – in several ways:

1) Keep a copy of your application and review it carefully before the interview

This may be the only document before the oral board, and the starting point of the interview. Know what education and experience you have listed there, and the sequence and dates of all of it. Sometimes the board will ask you to review the highlights of your experience for them; you should not have to hem and haw doing it.

2) Study the class specification and the examination announcement

Usually, the oral board has one or both of these to guide them. The qualities, characteristics or knowledges required by the position sought are stated in these documents. They offer valuable clues as to the nature of the oral interview. For example, if the job involves supervisory responsibilities, the announcement will usually indicate that knowledge of modern supervisory methods and the qualifications of the candidate as a supervisor will be tested. If so, you can expect such questions, frequently in the form of a hypothetical situation which you are expected to solve. NEVER go into an oral without knowledge of the duties and responsibilities of the job you seek.

3) Think through each qualification required

Try to visualize the kind of questions you would ask if you were a board member. How well could you answer them? Try especially to appraise your own knowledge and background in each area, *measured against the job sought*, and identify any areas in which you are weak. Be critical and realistic – do not flatter yourself.

4) Do some general reading in areas in which you feel you may be weak

For example, if the job involves supervision and your past experience has NOT, some general reading in supervisory methods and practices, particularly in the field of human relations, might be useful. Do NOT study agency procedures or detailed manuals. The oral board will be testing your understanding and capacity, not your memory.

5) Get a good night's sleep and watch your general health and mental attitude

You will want a clear head at the interview. Take care of a cold or any other minor ailment, and of course, no hangovers.

What should be done on the day of the interview?

Now comes the day of the interview itself. Give yourself plenty of time to get there. Plan to arrive somewhat ahead of the scheduled time, particularly if your appointment is in the fore part of the day. If a previous candidate fails to appear, the board might be ready for you a bit early. By early afternoon an oral board is almost invariably behind schedule if there are many candidates, and you may have to wait. Take along a book or magazine to read, or your application to review, but leave any extraneous material in the waiting room when you go in for your interview. In any event, relax and compose yourself.

The matter of dress is important. The board is forming impressions about you – from your experience, your manners, your attitude, and your appearance. Give your personal appearance careful attention. Dress your best, but not your flashiest. Choose conservative, appropriate clothing, and be sure it is immaculate. This is a business interview, and your appearance should indicate that you regard it as such. Besides, being well groomed and properly dressed will help boost your confidence.

Sooner or later, someone will call your name and escort you into the interview room. *This is it.* From here on you are on your own. It is too late for any more preparation. But remember, you asked for this opportunity to prove your fitness, and you are here because your request was granted.

What happens when you go in?

The usual sequence of events will be as follows: The clerk (who is often the board stenographer) will introduce you to the chairman of the oral board, who will introduce you to the other members of the board. Acknowledge the introductions before you sit down. Do not be surprised if you find a microphone facing you or a stenotypist sitting by. Oral interviews are usually recorded in the event of an appeal or other review.

Usually the chairman of the board will open the interview by reviewing the highlights of your education and work experience from your application – primarily for the benefit of the other members of the board, as well as to get the material into the record. Do not interrupt or comment unless there is an error or significant misinterpretation; if that is the case, do not hesitate. But do not quibble about insignificant matters. Also, he will usually ask you some question about your education, experience or your present job – partly to get you to start talking and to establish the interviewing "rapport." He may start the actual questioning, or turn it over to one of the other members. Frequently, each member undertakes the questioning on a particular area, one in which he is perhaps most competent, so you can expect each member to participate in the examination. Because time is limited, you may also expect some rather abrupt switches in the direction the questioning takes, so do not be upset by it. Normally, a board member will not pursue a single line of questioning unless he discovers a particular strength or weakness.

After each member has participated, the chairman will usually ask whether any member has any further questions, then will ask you if you have anything you wish to add. Unless you are expecting this question, it may floor you. Worse, it may start you off on an extended, extemporaneous speech. The board is not usually seeking more information. The question is principally to offer you a last opportunity to present further qualifications or to indicate that you have nothing to add. So, if you feel that a significant qualification or characteristic has been overlooked, it is proper to point it out in a sentence or so. Do not compliment the board on the thoroughness of their examination – they have been sketchy, and you know it. If you wish, merely say, "No thank you, I have nothing further to add." This is a point where you can "talk yourself out" of a good impression or fail to present an important bit of information. Remember, *you close the interview yourself.*

The chairman will then say, "That is all, Mr. _____, thank you." Do not be startled; the interview is over, and quicker than you think. Thank him, gather your belongings and take your leave. Save your sigh of relief for the other side of the door.

How to put your best foot forward

Throughout this entire process, you may feel that the board individually and collectively is trying to pierce your defenses, seek out your hidden weaknesses and embarrass and confuse you. Actually, this is not true. They are obliged to make an appraisal of your qualifications for the job you are seeking, and they want to see you in your best light. Remember, they must interview all candidates and a non-cooperative candidate may become a failure in spite of their best efforts to bring out his qualifications. Here are 15 suggestions that will help you:

1) Be natural – Keep your attitude confident, not cocky

If you are not confident that you can do the job, do not expect the board to be. Do not apologize for your weaknesses, try to bring out your strong points. The board is interested in a positive, not negative, presentation. Cockiness will antagonize any board member and make him wonder if you are covering up a weakness by a false show of strength.

2) Get comfortable, but don't lounge or sprawl

Sit erectly but not stiffly. A careless posture may lead the board to conclude that you are careless in other things, or at least that you are not impressed by the importance of the occasion. Either conclusion is natural, even if incorrect. Do not fuss with your clothing, a pencil or an ashtray. Your hands may occasionally be useful to emphasize a point; do not let them become a point of distraction.

3) Do not wisecrack or make small talk

This is a serious situation, and your attitude should show that you consider it as such. Further, the time of the board is limited – they do not want to waste it, and neither should you.

4) Do not exaggerate your experience or abilities

In the first place, from information in the application or other interviews and sources, the board may know more about you than you think. Secondly, you probably will not get away with it. An experienced board is rather adept at spotting such a situation, so do not take the chance.

5) If you know a board member, do not make a point of it, yet do not hide it

Certainly you are not fooling him, and probably not the other members of the board. Do not try to take advantage of your acquaintanceship – it will probably do you little good.

6) Do not dominate the interview

Let the board do that. They will give you the clues – do not assume that you have to do all the talking. Realize that the board has a number of questions to ask you, and do not try to take up all the interview time by showing off your extensive knowledge of the answer to the first one.

7) Be attentive

You only have 20 minutes or so, and you should keep your attention at its sharpest throughout. When a member is addressing a problem or question to you, give him your undivided attention. Address your reply principally to him, but do not exclude the other board members.

8) Do not interrupt

A board member may be stating a problem for you to analyze. He will ask you a question when the time comes. Let him state the problem, and wait for the question.

9) Make sure you understand the question

Do not try to answer until you are sure what the question is. If it is not clear, restate it in your own words or ask the board member to clarify it for you. However, do not haggle about minor elements.

10) Reply promptly but not hastily

A common entry on oral board rating sheets is "candidate responded readily," or "candidate hesitated in replies." Respond as promptly and quickly as you can, but do not jump to a hasty, ill-considered answer.

11) Do not be peremptory in your answers

A brief answer is proper – but do not fire your answer back. That is a losing game from your point of view. The board member can probably ask questions much faster than you can answer them.

12) Do not try to create the answer you think the board member wants

He is interested in what kind of mind you have and how it works – not in playing games. Furthermore, he can usually spot this practice and will actually grade you down on it.

13) Do not switch sides in your reply merely to agree with a board member

Frequently, a member will take a contrary position merely to draw you out and to see if you are willing and able to defend your point of view. Do not start a debate, yet do not surrender a good position. If a position is worth taking, it is worth defending.

14) Do not be afraid to admit an error in judgment if you are shown to be wrong

The board knows that you are forced to reply without any opportunity for careful consideration. Your answer may be demonstrably wrong. If so, admit it and get on with the interview.

15) Do not dwell at length on your present job

The opening question may relate to your present assignment. Answer the question but do not go into an extended discussion. You are being examined for a *new* job, not your present one. As a matter of fact, try to phrase ALL your answers in terms of the job for which you are being examined.

Basis of Rating

Probably you will forget most of these "do's" and "don'ts" when you walk into the oral interview room. Even remembering them all will not ensure you a passing grade. Perhaps you did not have the qualifications in the first place. But remembering them will help you to put your best foot forward, without treading on the toes of the board members.

Rumor and popular opinion to the contrary notwithstanding, an oral board wants you to make the best appearance possible. They know you are under pressure – but they also want to see how you respond to it as a guide to what your reaction would be under the pressures of the job you seek. They will be influenced by the degree of poise you display, the personal traits you show and the manner in which you respond.

ABOUT THIS BOOK

This book contains tests divided into Examination Sections. Go through each test, answering every question in the margin. We have also attached a sample answer sheet at the back of the book that can be removed and used. At the end of each test look at the answer key and check your answers. On the ones you got wrong, look at the right answer choice and learn. Do not fill in the answers first. Do not memorize the questions and answers, but understand the answer and principles involved. On your test, the questions will likely be different from the samples. Questions are changed and new ones added. If you understand these past questions you should have success with any changes that arise. Tests may consist of several types of questions. We have additional books on each subject should more study be advisable or necessary for you. Finally, the more you study, the better prepared you will be. This book is intended to be the last thing you study before you walk into the examination room. Prior study of relevant texts is also recommended. NLC publishes some of these in our Fundamental Series. Knowledge and good sense are important factors in passing your exam. Good luck also helps. So now study this Passbook, absorb the material contained within and take that knowledge into the examination. Then do your best to pass that exam.

EXAMINATION SECTION

SAFETY
EXAMINATION SECTION
TEST 1

DIRECTIONS: Each question or incomplete statement is followed by several suggested answers or completions. Select the one that BEST answers the question or completes the statement. *PRINT THE LETTER OF THE CORRECT ANSWER IN THE SPACE AT THE RIGHT.*

1. Which one of the following is an INCORRECT safety guideline? 1.____

   A. All working conditions and equipment should be considered carefully before beginning an operation.
   B. Aisles should be lighted properly.
   C. Personnel should be provided with protective clothing essential to safe performance of a task.
   D. In manual lifting, the worker must keep his knees straight and lift with the arm muscles.

2. Of the following, the supply item with the GREATEST susceptibility to spontaneous heating is 2.____

   A. alcohol, ethyl   B. kerosene
   C. candles   D. turpentine

Questions 3-7.

DIRECTIONS: Questions 3 through 7 are descriptions of accidents that occurred in a warehouse. For each accident, choose the letter in front of the safety measure that is MOST likely to prevent a repetition of the accident indicated.

SAFETY MEASURE

   A. Posting warning signs
   B. Redesign of layout or facilities
   C. Repairing, improving or replacing supplies, tools or equipment
   D. Training the staff in safe practices

3. After a new all-glass door was installed at the entrance to the warehouse, one of the employees banged his head into the door causing a large lump on his forehead when he failed to realize that the door was closed. 3.____

4. While tieing up a package with manila rope, an employee got several small rope splinters in his right hand and he had to have medical treatment to remove the splinters. 4.____

5. An employee discovered a small fire in a wastepaper basket but was unable to prevent it from spreading because all the nearby fire extinguishers were inaccessible due to skids of material being stacked in front of the extinguishers. 5.____

6. When a laborer attempted to drop the tailgate of a delivery truck while the truck was being backed into the loading dock, he had his fingers crushed when the truck continued to move while he was working on lowering the tailgate. 6.____

1

7. An employee carrying a carton with both hands tripped over a broom which had been left 7.____
lying in an aisle by another employee after the latter had swept the aisle.

8. Safety experts agree that accidents can probably BEST be prevented by 8.____

   A. developing safety consciousness among employees
   B. developing a program which publicizes major accidents
   C. penalizing employees the first time they do not follow safety procedures
   D. giving recognition to employees with accident-free records

9. The accident records of many agencies indicate that most on-the-job injuries are caused 9.____
by the unsafe acts of their employees.
Which one of the following statements pinpoints the MOST probable cause of this safety problem?

   A. Responsibility for preventing on-the-job accidents has not been delegated.
   B. Lack of proper supervision has permitted these unsafe actions to continue.
   C. No consideration has been given to eliminating environmental job hazards.
   D. Penalties for causing on-the-job accidents are not sufficiently severe.

10. Which of the following methods is LEAST essential to the success of an accident preven- 10.____
tion program?

    A. Determining corrective measures by analyzing the causes of accidents and making recommendations to eliminate them
    B. Educating employees as to the importance of safe working conditions and methods
    C. Determining accident causes by seeking out the conditions from which each accident has developed
    D. Holding each supervisor responsible for accidents occurring during the on-the-job performance of his immediate subordinates

11. The effectiveness of a public relations program in a public agency is BEST indicated by 11.____
the

    A. amount of mass media publicity favorable to the policies of the agency
    B. morale of those employees who directly serve the patrons of the agency
    C. public's understanding and support of the agency's program and policies
    D. number of complaints received by the agency from patrons using its facilities

12. Buttered bread and coffee dropped on an office floor in a terminal are 12.____

    A. minor hazards which should cause no serious injury
    B. unattractive, but not dangerous
    C. the most dangerous types of office hazards
    D. hazards which should be corrected immediately

13. A laborer was sent upstairs to get a 20-pound sack of rock salt. While going downstairs 13.____
and reading the printing on the sack, he fell, and the sack of rock salt fell and broke his toe.
Which of the following is MOST likely to have been the MOST important cause of the accident?
The

A. stairs were beginning to become worn
B. laborer was carrying too heavy a sack of rock salt
C. rock salt was in a place that was too inaccessible
D. laborer was not careful about the way he went down the stairs

14. A COMMONLY recommended safe distance between the foot of an extension ladder and the wall against which it is placed is

   A. 3 feet for ladders less than 18 feet in height
   B. between 3 feet and 6 feet for ladders less than 18 feet in length
   C. 1/8 the length of the extended ladder
   D. 1/4 the length of the extended ladder

14.____

15. The BEST type of fire extinguisher for electrical fires is the _____ extinguisher.

   A. dry chemical
   B. foam
   C. carbon monoxide
   D. baking soda-acid

15.____

16. A Class A extinguisher should be used for fires in

   A. potassium, magnesium, zinc, sodium
   B. electrical wiring
   C. oil, gasoline
   D. wood, paper, and textiles

16.____

17. The one of the following which is NOT a safe practice when lifting heavy objects is:

   A. Keep the back as nearly upright as possible
   B. If the object feels too heavy, keep lifting until you get help
   C. Spread the feet apart
   D. Use the arm and leg muscles

17.____

18. In a shop, it would be MOST necessary to provide a fitted cover on the metal container for

   A. old paint brushes
   B. oily rags and waste
   C. sand
   D. broken glass

18.____

19. Safety shoes usually have the unique feature of

   A. extra hard heels and soles to prevent nails from piercing the shoes
   B. special leather to prevent the piercing of the shoes by falling objects
   C. a metal guard over the toes which is built into the shoes
   D. a non-slip tread on the heels and soles

19.____

20. Of the following, the MOST important factor contributing to a helper's safety on the job is for him to

   A. work slowly
   B. wear gloves
   C. be alert
   D. know his job well

20.____

21. If it is necessary for you to lift one end of a piece of heavy equipment with a crowbar in order to allow a maintainer to work underneath it, the BEST of the following procedures to follow is to

    A. support the handle of the bar on a box
    B. insert temporary blocks to support the piece
    C. call the supervisor to help you
    D. wear heavy gloves

22. Of the following, the MOST important reason for not letting oily rags accumulate in an open storage bin is that they

    A. may start a fire by spontaneous combustion
    B. will drip oil onto other items in the bin
    C. may cause a foul odor
    D. will make the area messy

23. Of the following, the BEST method to employ in putting out a gasoline fire is to

    A. use a bucket of water
    B. smother it with rags
    C. use a carbon dioxide extinguisher
    D. use a carbon tetrachloride extinguisher

24. When opening an emergency exit door set in the sidewalk, the door should be raised slowly to avoid

    A. a sudden rush of air from the street
    B. making unnecessary noise
    C. damage to the sidewalk
    D. injuring pedestrians

25. The BEST reason to turn off lights when cleaning lampshades on electrical fixtures is to

    A. conserve energy
    B. avoid electrical shock
    C. prevent breakage of lightbulbs
    D. prevent unnecessary eye strain

KEY (CORRECT ANSWERS)

1. D
2. D
3. A
4. D
5. B

6. D
7. D
8. A
9. B
10. D

11. C
12. D
13. D
14. D
15. A

16. D
17. B
18. B
19. C
20. C

21. B
22. A
23. C
24. D
25. B

TEST 2

DIRECTIONS: Each question or incomplete statement is followed by several suggested answers or completions. Select the one that BEST answers the question or completes the statement. *PRINT THE LETTER OF THE CORRECT ANSWER IN THE SPACE AT THE RIGHT.*

1. The MOST important reason for roping off a work area in a terminal is to

   A. protect the public
   B. protect the repair crew
   C. prevent distraction of the crew by the public
   D. prevent delays to the public

   1.___

2. Shoes which have a sponge rubber sole should NOT be worn around a work area because such a sole

   A. will wear quickly
   B. is not waterproof
   C. does not keep the feet warm
   D. is easily punctured by steel objects

   2.___

3. When repair work is being done on an elevated structure, canvas spreads are suspended under the working area MAINLY to

   A. reduce noise   B. discourage crowds
   C. protect the structure D. protect pedestrians

   3.___

4. It is poor practice to hold a piece of wood in the hands or lap when tightening a screw in the wood.
   This is for the reason that

   A. sufficient leverage cannot be obtained
   B. the screwdriver may bend
   C. the wood will probably split
   D. personal injury is likely to result

   4.___

5. Steel helmets give workers the MOST protection from

   A. falling objects   B. eye injuries
   C. fire   D. electric shock

   5.___

6. It is POOR practice to wear goggles

   A. when chipping stone
   B. when using a grinder
   C. while climbing or descending ladders
   D. when handling molten metal

   6.___

7. When using a brace and bit to bore a hole completely through a partition, it is MOST important to

   7.___

A. lean heavily on the brace and bit
B. maintain a steady turning speed all through the job
C. have the body in a position that will not be easily thrown off balance
D. reverse the direction of the bit at frequent intervals

8. Gloves should be used when handling

    A. lanterns
    B. wooden rules
    C. heavy ropes
    D. all small tools

Questions 9-16.

DIRECTIONS: Questions 9 through 16, inclusive, are based on the ladder safety rules given below. Read these rules fully before answering these items.

LADDER SAFETY RULES

When a ladder is placed on a slightly uneven supporting surface, use a flat piece of board or small wedge to even up the ladder feet. To secure the proper angle for resting a ladder, it should be placed so that the distance from the base of the ladder to the supporting wall is 1/4 the length of the ladder. To avoid overloading a ladder, only one person should work on a ladder at a time. Do not place a ladder in front of a door. When the top rung of a ladder rests against a pole, the ladder should be lashed securely. Clear loose stones or debris from the ground around the base of a ladder before climbing. While on a ladder, do not attempt to lean so that any part of the body, except arms or hands, extends more than 12 inches beyond the side rail. Always face the ladder when ascending or descending. When carrying ladders through buildings, watch for ceiling globes and lighting fixtures. Avoid the use of rolling ladders as scaffold supports.

9. A small wedge is used to

    A. even up the feet of a ladder resting on an uneven surface
    B. lock the wheels of a roller ladder
    C. secure the proper resting angle for a ladder
    D. secure a ladder against a pole

10. An 8 foot ladder resting against a wall should be so inclined that the distance between the base of the ladder and the wall is _____ feet.

    A. 2   B. 5   C. 7   D. 9

11. A ladder should be lashed securely when

    A. it is placed in front of a door
    B. loose stones are on the ground near the base of the ladder
    C. the top rung rests against a pole
    D. two people are working from the same ladder

12. Rolling ladders

    A. should be used for scaffold supports
    B. should not be used for scaffold supports
    C. are useful on uneven ground
    D. should be used against a pole

13. When carrying a ladder through a building, it is necessary to   13.___
    A. have two men to carry it
    B. carry the ladder vertically
    C. watch for ceiling globes
    D. face the ladder while carrying it

14. It is POOR practice to   14.___
    A. lash a ladder securely at any time
    B. clear debris from the base of a ladder before climbing
    C. even up the feet of a ladder resting on slightly uneven ground
    D. place a ladder in front of a door

15. A person on a ladder should NOT extend his head beyond the side rail by more than _____ inches.   15.___
    A. 12   B. 9   C. 7   D. 5

16. The MOST important reason for permitting only one person to work on a ladder at a time is that   16.___
    A. both could not face the ladder at one time
    B. the ladder will be overloaded
    C. time would be lost going up and down the ladder
    D. they would obstruct each other

17. Many portable electric power tools, such as electric drills, have a third conductor in the power lead which is used to connect the case of the tool to a grounded part of the electric outlet.
    The reason for this extra conductor is to   17.___
    A. have a spare wire in case one power wire should break
    B. strengthen the power lead so it cannot easily be damaged
    C. prevent the user of the tool from being shocked
    D. enable the tool to be used for long periods of time without overheating

18. Protective goggles should NOT be worn when   18.___
    A. standing on a ladder drilling a steel beam
    B. descending a ladder after completing a job
    C. chipping concrete near a third rail
    D. sharpening a cold chisel on a grinding stone

19. When the foot of an extension ladder, placed against a high wall, rests on a sidewalk or another such similar surface, it is advisable to tie a rope between the bottom rung of the ladder and a point on the wall opposite this rung.
    This is done to prevent   19.___
    A. people from walking under the ladder
    B. another worker from removing the ladder
    C. the ladder from vibrating when ascending or descending
    D. the foot of the ladder from slipping

20. In construction work, practically all accidents can be blamed on the 20.____
    A. failure of an individual to give close attention to the job assigned to him
    B. use of improper tools
    C. lack of cooperation among the men in a gang
    D. fact that an incompetent man was placed in a key position

21. If it is necessary for you to do some work with your hands under a piece of heavy equipment while a fellow worker lifts up and holds one end of it by means of a pinch bar, one important precaution you should take is to 21.____

    A. wear gloves
    B. watch the bar to be ready if it slips
    C. insert a temporary block to support the piece
    D. work as fast as possible

22. Employees of the transit system whose work requires them to enter upon the tracks in the subway are cautioned not to wear loose fitting clothing. 22.____
    The MOST important reason for this caution is that loose fitting clothing may

    A. interfere when men are using heavy tools
    B. catch on some projection of a passing train
    C. tear more easily than snug fitting clothing
    D. give insufficient protection against subway dust

23. The MOST important reason for insisting on neatness in maintenance quarters is that it 23.____

    A. keeps the men busy in slack periods
    B. prevents tools from becoming rusty
    C. makes a good impression on visitors and officials
    D. decreases the chances of accidents to employees

24. Maintenance workers whose duties require them to do certain types of work generally work in pairs. 24.____
    The LEAST likely of the following possible reasons for this practice is that

    A. some of the work requires two men
    B. the men can help each other in case of accident
    C. there is too much equipment for one man to carry
    D. it protects against vandalism

25. A foreman reprimands a helper for actions in violation of the rules and regulations. 25.____
    The BEST reaction of the helper in this situation is to

    A. tell the foreman that he was careful and that he did not take any chances
    B. explain that he took this action to save time
    C. keep quiet and accept the criticism
    D. demand that the foreman show him the rule he violated

KEY (CORRECT ANSWERS)

1. A
2. D
3. D
4. D
5. A

6. C
7. C
8. C
9. A
10. A

11. C
12. B
13. C
14. D
15. A

16. B
17. C
18. B
19. D
20. A

21. C
22. B
23. D
24. D
25. C

EXAMINATION SECTION
TEST 1

DIRECTIONS: Each question or incomplete statement is followed by several suggested answers or completions. Select the one that BEST answers the question or completes the statement. *PRINT THE LETTER OF THE CORRECT ANSWER IN THE SPACE AT THE RIGHT.*

1. The first aid procedure of not moving a person unless absolutely necessary is MOST important in the case of a person who has

    A. broken a finger
    B. fainted
    C. collapsed from the heat
    D. fractured his leg

    1.____

2. In treating a cut finger, the FIRST action should be to

    A. wash it
    B. bandage it
    C. request sick leave
    D. apply antiseptic

    2.____

3. When administering first aid to a person suffering from shock as a result of an accident, it is MOST important to

    A. keep him moving
    B. prop him up in a sitting position
    C. apply artificial respiration
    D. cover the person and keep him warm

    3.____

4. A shop employee is involved in an accident and severely injures his ankle. If a tourniquet were used, it would be to

    A. keep the ankle warm
    B. prevent infection
    C. prevent the ankle from moving
    D. stop the loss of blood

    4.____

5. First aid instructions are given to some employees to

    A. eliminate the need for calling a doctor
    B. prepare them to give emergency aid
    C. collect blood for the blood bank
    D. reduce the number of accidents

    5.____

6. According to the LATEST recommended first-aid practice, a cut finger should be cleaned with

    A. soap and water
    B. phenol
    C. mercurochrome
    D. iodine

    6.____

7. The preferred first-aid treatment for a person who has a badly bleeding forearm is to

    A. apply a splint
    B. apply a tourniquet
    C. apply an antiseptic
    D. wash with soap and water

    7.____

8. It is LEAST advisable to move an injured man before the arrival of a doctor if the man has

   A. first degree burns
   B. been internally injured
   C. a severe nosebleed
   D. been overcome from smoke

9. The CHIEF purpose of administering artificial respiration in first aid is to

   A. exert regular pressure on the heart
   B. force the blood into circulation by pressure
   C. force air into the lungs
   D. keep the person warm by keeping his body in motion

10. When severe shock occurs, it is IMPORTANT for the person being treated to have

    A. sedatives and cold drinks
    B. warmth and low head position
    C. hot drinks and much activity
    D. sedatives and sitting position

11. When administering first aid, a tourniquet is used to

    A. sterilize the injured area
    B. hold the splints in place
    C. hold the dressing in place
    D. stop the loss of blood.

12. Artificial respiration should be started immediately on a trackman who has suffered an electric shock by coming in contact with the third rail if he is

    A. conscious but badly burned
    B. unconscious and breathing heavily
    C. conscious but in a daze
    D. unconscious and not breathing

13. When administering first aid for the accidental swallowing of poison, water is given CHIEFLY to

    A. increase energy
    B. quiet the nerves
    C. weaken the poison
    D. prevent choking

14. The recommended first aid procedure for a person who has fainted is to lay him down with his head lower than his body. Such a position is used because it

    A. quickly relieves exhaustion
    B. speeds the return of blood to the head
    C. retards rapid breathing
    D. is the most comfortable position

15. The BEST immediate first aid treatment for an eye burn caused by acid is to

    A. flush the eye with water
    B. bandage the eye
    C. dry the eye
    D. rub the eye

16. If a trackman suffers a deep puncture in his hand or foot, the BEST immediate first aid treatment would be to

    A. stop all bleeding
    B. encourage bleeding by exerting pressure around the injured area
    C. prevent air from reaching the wound
    D. probe the wound for foreign matter

17. Proper first aid treatment for a man who has suffered electrical shock is to

    A. keep him warm and permit no movement whatever
    B. give him approved stimulants by mouth
    C. apply artificial respiration if he is not breathing
    D. massage his neck to restore circulation

18. In a small wound which is not bleeding, it is desirable to encourage some bleeding by squeezing toward the wound MAINLY because this

    A. helps to form a blood clot
    B. helps to locate the wound exactly for further treatment
    C. washes out some of the germs
    D. will show whether the wound is near an artery or vein

19. As a dressing to be applied directly over a wound or burn, it is

    A. more desirable to use cotton, rather than gauze, because cotton is cheaper and just as good
    B. more desirable to use cotton, rather than gauze, because cotton is more absorbent
    C. less desirable to use cotton, rather than gauze, because cotton is not sterile
    D. less desirable to use cotton, rather than gauze, because cotton sticks and is hard to remove

20. Water or other liquid should NOT be administered to an unconscious person. The MOST probable reason for this is that

    A. an unconscious person would probably consume more of the liquid than would be good for him
    B. an untrained person would not know the proper way to administer such liquid to an unconscious person
    C. someone untrained in first aid might administer a liquid that would be harmful
    D. the liquid might enter the windpipe of the unconscious person and strangle him

21. In a case of stomach poisoning, it is MOST important to clean out the stomach. For this purpose, it is LEAST effective to administer

    A. lukewarm water   B. milk of magnesia
    C. ipecac   D. stomach pump

22. The PRIMARY purpose of a tourniquet is to

    A. prevent infection   B. serve as a sling
    C. set a broken bone   D. stop bleeding

23. Aromatic spirits of ammonia should properly be administered to

    A. a person who has swallowed poison
    B. clean a wound
    C. deaden pain
    D. revive a person who has fainted

24. The symptoms of heat exhaustion are

    A. pale, clammy skin, low temperature, weak pulse
    B. rapid and strong pulse, dry skin, high temperature
    C. headache, red face, unconsciousness
    D. abdominal cramps, red skin, profuse sweating

25. Arterial pressure points

    A. are best located by taking the pulse
    B. lie close to bones near the surface of the body
    C. are used to cut off all blood circulation
    D. are deepseated and require great pressure

KEY (CORRECT ANSWERS)

1.	D	11.	D
2.	A	12.	D
3.	D	13.	C
4.	D	14.	B
5.	B	15.	A
6.	A	16.	B
7.	B	17.	C
8.	B	18.	C
9.	C	19.	D
10.	D	20.	D

21. B
22. D
23. D
24. A
25. B

TEST 2

DIRECTIONS: Each question or incomplete statement is followed by several suggested answers or completions. Select the one that BEST answers the question or completes the statement. *PRINT THE LETTER OF THE CORRECT ANSWER IN THE SPACE AT THE RIGHT.*

1. In administering first aid care to a youngster suffering from convulsion, the CORRECT procedure to follow is to

    A. provide mild exercise such as walking
    B. apply hot wet-packs to the forehead
    C. provide a light body covering
    D. have the victim rest with feet elevated

    1.____

2. Floor or scuff "burns" are examples of _____ wounds.

    A. abrasion   B. puncture   C. laceration   D. incision

    2.____

3. When applying an arm sling in cases of injury to the hand or lower forearm, the sling should be adjusted so that the hand is

    A. completely covered
    B. four inches above the level of the elbow
    C. on the same level as the elbow
    D. six inches below the level of the elbow

    3.____

4. The first aid procedure recommended by the American Red Cross in the case of a poisonous sting on the finger is to

    A. use the cut and suction technique
    B. keep the hand in an elevated position
    C. apply a constricting band at the base of the finger
    D. apply heat to the area

    4.____

5. Modern practice advises *strongly* AGAINST use of emetics in cases of poisoning by

    A. sleep inducing drugs   B. acids and alkalies
    C. strychnine   D. foods

    5.____

6. The INITIAL action taken by a first aider in treating a case of severe bleeding is to

    A. apply pressure to the point nearest the injured part
    B. apply direct pressure on the wound
    C. apply a tourniquet
    D. elevate the injured part

    6.____

7. The subclavian pressure point is used to control bleeding from the

    A. shoulder   B. lungs
    C. chest   D. lower leg

    7.____

8. The first aid procedure for strains is to

    A. massage the affected part vigorously
    B. apply warm, moist applications

    8.____

C. immediately immobilize the affected part
D. bandage tightly to restrict movement

9. If a fellow worker has stopped breathing after an electric shock, the BEST first aid treatment is

   A. artificial respiration
   B. to massage his chest
   C. an application of cold compresses
   D. a hot drink

10. The Transit Authority gives some of its maintenance employees instruction in first aid. The MOST likely reason for doing this is to

    A. eliminate the need for calling a doctor in case of accident
    B. reduce the number of accidents
    C. lower the cost of accidents to the Transit Authority
    D. provide temporary first aid

11. If you had to telephone for an ambulance because of an accident, the MOST important information for you to give the person who answered the telephone would be the

    A. exact time of the accident
    B. place where the ambulance is needed
    C. cause of the accident
    D. names and addresses of those injured

12. Inhalation of smelling salts is NOT generally recommended as a first aid treatment for a victim who has been exposed to the fumes of

    A. freon
    B. chlorine
    C. sulfur dioxide
    D. hydrogen sulfide

13. The application of cold or iced water to burned skin areas is a first aid practice that is GENERALLY recommended provided that it is

    A. delayed for several minutes and the water is then poured onto the affected areas heavily
    B. done immediately and the water is poured onto the affected areas heavily
    C. delayed for several minutes and the water is then poured slowly over the affected areas
    D. done immediately and the water is poured slowly over the affected areas

14. For rescue breathing to have any chance of success, it is vital that the lapse of time between the cessation of breathing and the start of this procedure be no more than

    A. 2 minutes
    B. 4 minutes
    C. 6 minutes
    D. 8 minutes

15. Recognition of shock in a victim and administration of proper first aid measures may be the means of saving a life.
    The one of the following which is the MOST complete and accurate description of the shock condition is:

A. Pale and cool skin later becoming bluish, lackluster look of the eyes, veins of the hands barely visible
B. Pale and cool skin later becoming bluish, lackluster look of the eyes, veins of the hand bulging and readily visible
C. Pink skin, warm perspiration about the head, veins of the hand barely visible
D. Pink skin, warm perspiration about the head, veins of the hand bulging and readily visible

16. Extensive loss of blood can be a threat to a person's survival. To control severe bleeding, a tourniquet is sometimes used.
Of the following statements regarding the use of a tourniquet, the LEAST appropriate is that the

   A. use of a tourniquet may be considered when all other methods have failed
   B. decision to apply a tourniquet is really a decision to risk sacrificing a limb in order to save a life
   C. tourniquet should be loosened every half hour until the arrival of a physician or qualified medical personnel
   D. tourniquet should be placed immediately above the joint if the wound is in a joint area

17. The one of the following statements that is MOST accurate and complete is that when a person is found unconscious, cardiac massage is to be started if there is

   A. no pulse
   B. no pulse or breathing
   C. no pulse or breathing and the pupils do not contract when the eyelid is opened
   D. no pulse or breathing, the pupils do not contract when the eyelid is opened, and the lips are blue

18. A fireman discovers a man bleeding moderately from a gash wound about 1 1/2" long in his right arm.
Of the following, the FIRST action this fireman should take is to

   A. apply a tourniquet between the wound and the heart
   B. give the injured man a blood transfusion
   C. apply pressure at the nearest pressure point between the wound and the heart
   D. apply pressure directly to the wound with compress

19. In treating burns, the LEAST important of the following goals is to

   A. prevent blistering   B. prevent infection
   C. relieve pain   D. prevent shock

20. During a firefighting operation, a fireman's eye is accidentally burned by a chemical. The one of the following USUALLY recommended as first aid procedure in such a case is

   A. covering the eye with pads dipped in sodium bicarbonate
   B. wrapping ice in a sterile bandage and placing it over the eye
   C. flushing the eye with fresh clean water
   D. taking no action other than removing the member from the scene

21. When firefighters give first aid to an unconscious person, there are several things to check for. Which of the following is NOT one of them?

    A. Are the person's legs twisted in a way which might show that bones may be broken?
    B. Is the person breathing?
    C. Is there an open container of poison nearby?
    D. Did the person try to commit suicide?

22. The LEAST likely result of a severe electrical shock is

    A. unconsciousness
    B. a burn
    C. stoppage of breathing
    D. bleeding

23. The BEST immediate first aid if electrolyte splashes into the eyes when filling a storage battery is to

    A. bandage the eyes to keep out light
    B. wipe the eyes dry with a soft towel
    C. induce tears to flow by staring at a bright light
    D. bathe the eyes with plenty of clean water

24. An unconscious civilian is discovered by two firemen at a fire with the following symptoms: he is not breathing, his pulse cannot be felt, and his pupils are wide and dilated. The one of the following courses of treatment which would be BEST under these circumstances would be to apply

    A. mouth-to-mouth resuscitation until breathing is restored and then cardiac massage
    B. cardiac massage until the pulse can be felt and then mouth-to-mouth breathing
    C. mouth-to-mouth resuscitation and cardiac massage alternately
    D. mouth-to-mouth resuscitation and cardiac massage simultaneously

25. A fireman incurs a severe head injury and appears to be in a state of shock. After medical help has been summoned, a proper step in handling the injured fireman is to

    A. make the fireman lie down, cover him and have his head level or slightly raised
    B. make the fireman lie down, cover him and keep his head lower than his body
    C. wrap the prone fireman in blankets so that he perspires heavily and keep the head low
    D. keep the prone fireman's head level, wrap him warmly and give him stimulants

KEY (CORRECT ANSWERS)

1. C
2. A
3. B
4. C
5. B

6. B
7. A
8. B
9. A
10. D

11. B
12. D
13. D
14. B
15. A

16. C
17. C
18. D
19. A
20. C

21. D
22. D
23. D
24. D
25. A

EXAMINATION SECTION
TEST 1

DIRECTIONS: Each question or incomplete statement is followed by several suggested answers or completions. Select the one that BEST answers the question or completes the statement. *PRINT THE LETTER OF THE CORRECT ANSWER IN THE SPACE AT THE RIGHT.*

1. Assume that you are making an inspection at a plastics manufacturing factory. The plant manager discusses fire safety procedures with you and tells you that he will be having small-scale bench tests made in order to measure various properties of plastics exposed to fire. The manager tells you he expects to gain certain information from these tests. Of the following, you would be correct in telling him that these tests will be MOST effective in evaluating the

   A. tendency of the plastic to melt and drip
   B. relative combustibility of plastics
   C. composition of products of combustion
   D. methods of installation of plastic parts

1.____

2. Assume that your division commander has asked you to prepare a report on minimizing the hazard of dust explosions. This is one in a series of reports to be used to guide industrial plant managers in your division on fire safety precautions.
Of the following, it would be MOST appropriate for you to point out that generally

   A. a high level of moisture in the air will be effective in raising the ignition temperature of most dusts and reducing the deflagration once ignition has occurred
   B. relatively small amounts of inert solid powder will be effective in preventing explosions by reducing the combustibility of a dust through heat absorption
   C. removal of high-temperature sources of ignition will be effective in reducing the possibility of explosion because common ignition sources generally do not provide ignition temperatures required for dust explosions
   D. inert gas will be effective in preventing explosions because it dilutes the oxygen to a concentration too low to support combustion

2.____

3. The selection of smoke removal and venting procedures in hi-rise buildings depends to a large extent on the factors which affect smoke movement in these structures, such as the *stack effect*.
Which one of the following statements about the stack effect is MOST NEARLY correct?

   A. When the outside temperature is much lower than the inside temperature and a fire occurs some distance below the neutral pressure plane, the stack effect will not overcome the fire pressure.
   B. The stack effect will cause smoke and toxic gases to flow through stairwells and elevator shafts, except when the doors of these shafts remain closed.
   C. When the outside temperature is greater than the inside temperature, a reverse stack effect occurs with the upper building opening becoming the inlet and the lower opening the outlet.
   D. The magnitude of the stack effect is a function of building height, air leakage between floors, and the differences between inside and outside temperatures, but is not affected by the air leakage through exterior walls.

3.____

21

4. Warehouse fires often present a severe challenge to firefighters. A fire officer inspecting a storage warehouse should be aware of proper indoor storage practices and the use of racks and pallets in such storage.
   Which one of the following statements regarding storage practices in warehouses is generally CORRECT?

   A. The arrangement of commodities stored in racks generally provides greater flue spaces both horizontally and vertically than palletized general storage.
   B. Storage of empty plastic pallets within warehouses should be in piles limited to eight feet in height.
   C. Stacking idle pallets in piles is unlikely to promote rapid spread of fire, heat release, and complete combustion.
   D. Storage of empty wood pallets in an unsprinklered warehouse containing other storage should be limited to buildings of fireproof construction.

5. The Fire Code provides that, in a dry cleaning establishment, each room where a washing tank is located must be provided with an approved fire extinguishing system.
   The type of system which is specified is a(n) _____ system.

   A. steam
   B. carbon dioxide
   C. foam
   D. ordinary sprinkler

6. According to the Fire Code, the MAXIMUM quantity of calcium carbide which may be lawfully stored without a permit is _____ lbs.

   A. 60   B. 80   C. 100   D. 120

7. A Class C refrigerating system, as defined in the Fire Code, is one in which the quantity of refrigerant does NOT exceed _____ lbs.

   A. 20   B. 25   C. 30   D. 35

8. According to the Building Code, a tank used to provide the required primary water supply to a standpipe system may also be used as a supply for an automatic sprinkler system

   A. in all cases where both have been installed
   B. where there are other acceptable sources of water supply for the sprinkler system
   C. only when the standpipe system has a direct connection to the public water system
   D. provided that its capacity is at least five thousand gallons greater than that required for the sprinkler system

9. For computing the capacity of water supplies other than the fire pump, the Building Code assumes that the average discharge, in gallons per minute, from a standard one-half inch sprinkler head is

   A. 20   B. 25   C. 30   D. 35

10. The door that can be closed to separate the bedrooms from the rest of the apartment is the door between the

    A. entrance hall and the bedroom hall
    B. living room and the entrance hall
    C. kitchen and the living room
    D. dining room and the living room

Questions 11-25.

DIRECTIONS: Questions 11 through 25 are to be answered SOLELY on the basis of the following facts and Building Inspection Form. Each box on the form is numbered. Read the facts and review the form before answering the questions.

Firefighters are required to inspect all buildings within their assigned area of the city. They check conditions within the building for violations of fire safety laws. While inspecting a building, they must fill out a Building Inspection Form as a record of the conditions they observed.

On June 12, 2015, Firefighter Edward Gold, assigned to Engine Company 82, is ordered by Captain John Bailey to inspect the building at 1400 Compton Place as part of the engine company's monthly building inspection duty. The building is a one-story brick warehouse where books of the S & G Publishing Company are stored before shipment to stores.

Firefighter Gold enters the warehouse through the main entrance door in the front of the building. Though an exit sign is present above the door, the sign is unlit because of a burned-out bulb. There is a small office to one side of the main entrance area where Firefighter Gold goes to meet the warehouse manager, Mr. Stevens. The firefighter explains the purpose of the inspection.

Firefighter Gold tells the manager that he will check the automatic sprinkler system first because if a fire got started in a warehouse full of stored books, the fire could spread rapidly. He asks Mr. Stevens for the Certificate of Fitness issued to the company employee certified to maintain the sprinkler system in working order. The certificate is dated June 1, 2002, and Gold observes that it has expired. The manager promises to have the certificate renewed as soon as possible.

The firefighter wants to locate the main control valve of the sprinkler system. He asks Mr. Stevens to go with him and show him its location. Gold and the manager leave through an office door which leads into the main working area of the warehouse. They locate the main sprinkler control valve on the wall in a corner of the work area behind high shelves stocked with books. The firefighter observes that the main control valve is sealed in the open position. Gold next climbs a ladder lying against the storage shelves and measures the distance between the top of the stack of books on the highest shelf and the sprinkler heads suspended on pipes below the ceiling. The distance is three feet.

Firefighter Gold next inspects the remaining exits from the building. A large fire door leads out to the loading dock in the rear of the warehouse. A small door on the side of the warehouse that is used by employees when they leave for the day is partially obstructed by cartons. Lighted exit signs can be clearly seen above both doors. During working hours, only the main entrance door and the fire door to the loading dock are unlocked. Mr. Stevens says he keeps the side door locked to keep employees from leaving early and only unlocks it at closing time.

Firefighter Gold and the manager then walk through the main work area. Gold observes that fireproof rubbish receptacles are placed at frequent intervals. However, they are not covered and the contents are overflowing, resulting in several piles of litter on the floor. *No Smok-*

ing signs are on the walls of the work area, but are difficult to see behind the rows of high storage shelves.

The two fire extinguishers in the work area are found lying on the floor rather than hung on wall racks. The two other fire extinguishers in the warehouse, one in the office and one in the employee lounge, are both correctly hung on wall racks. All four fire extinguishers are fully charged. According to their tags, they were last inspected on March 11, 2015.

Firefighter Gold continues the inspection by checking on the electrical wiring, which appears to be generally in good condition. However, four switch boxes lack covers. The main junction box has a cover, but it cannot be closed because the cover is corroded.

The inspection is now complete, so Firefighter Gold thanks Mr. Stevens for his cooperation and leaves the building. Gold checks that all required information is entered on the Building Inspection Form, including information concerning building violations. Firefighter Gold signs and dates the Building Inspection Form and then submits it to Captain Bailey for his review. After reviewing Firefighter Gold's report, Captain Bailey signs the Building Inspection Form.

5 (#1)

BUILDING INSPECTION FORM

DIVISION (1)		BATTALION (2)		COMPANY (3)	
BUILDING INFORMATION	Name of Business (4)			Address (5)	
	Type of Business (6)			Occupancy Code Number (7)	
CONDITION OF EXITS	Number of Exits (8)		Exits Obstructed (9)		Exits unlocked (10)
	Exit Signs (11)		Exit Sign Lights (12)		Fire Doors (13)
HOUSEKEEPING CONDITIONS	Rubbish Receptacles (14)			No Smoking Signs (15)	
	Clearance of stock in Feet from Sprinkler Heads (16)				
	Electrical Wiring (17)		Switches (18)		Junction Box (19)
CONDITION OF FIRE EXTINGUISHERS	Charged (20)		Placement (21)		Date of Last Inspection (22)
CONDITION OF AUTOMATIC SPRINKLER SYSTEM	Color of Siamese (23)		Main Control Valve (24)		Shut-off sign (25)
	Certificate of Fitness (26)			Date of Last Inspection (27)	
SPECIAL CONDITIONS	Rubbish/Obstructions (28)			Certificate of Occupancy (29)	
				Heavy Load Signs (30)	
FIRE DEPARTMENT INFORMATION	Inspector Name _____ Signature _____ (31)			Rank (32)	Date (33)
	Officer Name _____ (34) Signature _____			Rank (35)	Date (36)

6 (#1)

11. Which one of the following should be entered in Box 3? 11.____

    A. Ladder Company 79   B. Engine Company 12
    C. Ladder Company 140   D. Engine Company 82

12. Which one of the following should be entered in Box 4? _____ Company. 12.____

    A. G & R Printing   B. S & G Printing
    C. R & G Publishing   D. S & G Publishing

13. Which one of the following should be entered in Box 8? 13.____

    A. 2   B. 3   C. 4   D. 5

14. Which one of the following should be entered in Box 9? _____ door. 14.____

    A. Office   B. Side   C. Main   D. Fire

15. Which one of the following should be entered in Box 10? _____ door and _____ door. 15.____

    A. Fire; main   B. Side; office
    C. Fire; side   D. Main; cellar

16. The entry in Box 12 should show that replacement bulbs are needed for _____ light(s). 16.____

    A. one   B. two   C. three   D. all

17. The entry in Box 14 should show that covers are missing from _____ of the rubbish receptacles. 17.____

    A. two   B. three   C. four   D. all

18. Which one of the following should be entered in Box 16? 18.____

    A. One and one-half   B. Two
    C. Two and one-half   D. Three

19. Which one of the following should be entered in Box 19? 19.____

    A. Faulty circuits   B. Exposed wiring
    C. Corroded cover   D. Good condition

20. Which one of the following entries about the placement of fire extinguishers should appear in Box 21? 20.____

    A. One on the floor; three hung on wall racks
    B. Two on the floor; two hung on wall racks
    C. Three on the floor; one hung on wall rack
    D. Four hung on wall racks

21. Which one of the following should be entered in Box 22? 21.____

    A. June 1, 2012   B. May 21, 2014
    C. March 11, 2015   D. May 1, 2015

22. The entry in Box 24 should show that the position of the main control valve is 22.____

    A. open   B. half open
    C. one-third closed   D. closed

23. Which one of the following should be entered in Box 26?   23._____

    A. Expired   B. Missing from file
    C. Never issued   D. Current

24. Which one of the following should be entered in Box 28?   24._____

    A. Ceiling plaster cracked
    B. Rubbish piles litter work floor
    C. Second floor stairway blocked
    D. Open paint cans on loading dock

25. Which one of the following should be entered in Box 34?   25._____

    A. John Bailey   B. Edward Gold
    C. John Gold   D. Edward Bailey

KEY (CORRECT ANSWERS)

1.	D	11.	D
2.	A	12.	D
3.	D	13.	B
4.	C	14.	B
5.	A	15.	A
6.	D	16.	A
7.	A	17.	D
8.	D	18.	D
9.	A	19.	C
10.	A	20.	B

21. C
22. A
23. A
24. B
25. A

TEST 2

DIRECTIONS: Each question or incomplete statement is followed by several suggested answers or completions. Select the one that BEST answers the question or completes the statement. *PRINT THE LETTER OF THE CORRECT ANSWER IN THE SPACE AT THE RIGHT.*

1. The materials of which a building are constructed and the opportunities for the spread of fire are important, but the GREATEST single hazard is usually that of

    A. occupancy
    B. location
    C. fire protective measures
    D. construction

2. A warehouse with a leaky roof contains a large amount of building material. The one of the following materials which is MOST likely to set fire to the warehouse is

    A. gasoline
    B. crude oil
    C. lime
    D. kerosene

3. For the most effective results in conducting a Fire Prevention Week campaign, it would be DESIRABLE to emphasize fire prevention

    A. in its broader community aspects
    B. as a means of lowering insurance rates
    C. as it applies to the individuals' own homes
    D. as a means of lowering operating costs of the fire department

4. Floor or wall openings sometimes prevent the banking up of heated air. This condition, with respect to sprinklers, is considered

    A. advantageous
    B. unimportant
    C. detrimental
    D. good ventilation

5. The BEST all-round fireproofing material, due to its high resistance to heat, its lightness, its great strength, its adaptability to any shape, and which is also very easily repaired when damaged by a severe fire, is

    A. brick
    B. hollow clay tile
    C. gypsum
    D. concrete

6. Commercial storage and industrial occupancies are classified in the Fire Code as

    A. highly hazardous
    B. moderately hazardous
    C. lightly hazardous
    D. all of the above

7. An unusually large number of fires of *unknown cause* is characteristic of the fires involving

    A. restaurants
    B. warehouses
    C. mercantile stores
    D. hospitals

8. It is obvious that where a division wall is not continued through the roof, and where the roof is combustible on both sides of the wall, fire is almost certain to spread beyond the wall if the fire is of any duration. According to the above statement, there is NEED of

    A. parapets
    B. more resistive division walls
    C. fire-stopping of roof spaces
    D. fire-stopping division walls

9. The hazard of flammable gases is generally _____ to that of flammable liquids.

    A. opposite
    B. dissimilar
    C. similar
    D. identical

10. The MOST important factor that would materially decrease large-loss supermarket fires is

    A. education of the general public
    B. separating the utility area from the rest of the building by a fire-resistive wall
    C. maintenance of an adequate supply of fire extinguishers
    D. keeping all aisles clear of merchandise and storage

11. The PRIMARY difference between the large number of small fires that produces a small percentage of total losses, and the smaller number of large fires that accounts for 95 percent of the total loss in the United States is usually

    A. the nature of the material involved in the fire
    B. the type of structure involved
    C. early discovery
    D. availability of personnel to fight the fire

12. From the fire prevention standpoint, air conditioning and air blower systems are of concern MAINLY because they

    A. provide a means for the spread of fire through the building served
    B. severely limit adequate ventilation in case of fire
    C. intensify fires from other sources by providing abnormally large amounts of air
    D. characteristically accumulate hazardous quantities of dust and lints which are subject to spontaneous ignition

13. At what interval of time should rubbish and waste materials be removed from piers, docks, and wharves?

    A. At least daily
    B. Once per week
    C. As often as needed to prevent dangerous condition
    D. As fast as accumulated

14. Of the various rooms found in the average school building, which two places deserve MORE consideration from a point of view of preventing personal injuries that may result from panic?
    The

    A. auditorium and the boiler room
    B. classroom on the highest floor and the room in the lowest (basement) part of the building
    C. auditorium and the cafeteria
    D. classroom nearest the auditorium exit and the auditorium itself

15. The underlying reason behind routine periodic and frequent fire prevention inspection is: 15.____

    A. Occupants, hazards, and code compliances may vary considerably in given buildings over a short period
    B. The need for favorable public opinion
    C. A large city usually has many new buildings being constructed
    D. Most individuals continually and consciously try to evade the fire regulations

16. The FIRST objective of all fire prevention is 16.____

    A. safeguarding life against fire
    B. reducing insurance rates
    C. preventing property damage
    D. confining fire to a limited area

17. Which one of the following is the cause of the GREATEST number of fires? 17.____

    A. Electrical wiring   B. Spontaneous ignition
    C. Sparks on roofs   D. Smoking and matches

18. The type of occupancy in which the LARGEST number of fires occurs is 18.____

    A. restaurants and other mercantile establishments
    B. hospitals, theatres, and other public buildings
    C. dwellings, including apartments and hotels
    D. bakeries, cleaning establishments, and other manufacturing plants

19. Which one of the following factors generally should be given the GREATEST right in estimating the fire risk in a general or mixed public warehouse? 19.____

    A. Availability of water hydrants to the warehouse
    B. Location of warehouse with respect to other buildings in the area
    C. Intensity and direction of prevailing winds in the area
    D. Kind of merchandise stored in the warehouse

20. Of the following, the one which is perhaps the MOST important year-round element in fire prevention in residences is 20.____

    A. proper and regular disposal of combustible waste
    B. care in the operation of heating systems
    C. periodic inspections by members of the fire department
    D. radio announcements calling attention to fire hazards in the home

21. The fire prevention and fire protection problem resolves itself into three phases, each of which must receive attention. The possibility of human or mechanical failure makes it unsafe to place sole reliance on any one method. If two of these phases are preventing the outbreak of fire and preventing the serious spread of fire, then the third phase would be providing for 21.____

    A. extensive research in the cause and prevention of non-incendiary fires
    B. the specialized training of fire department personnel at all levels
    C. the prompt detecting and extinguishing of fire
    D. ample modern firefighting equipment

22. The LARGEST cause of apartment and tenement house fires is

    A. smoking and matches
    B. electrical
    C. gas stoves and explosions
    D. heating equipment

23. Fire loss statistics show that 90 percent of the losses occur at _____ percent of the fires.

    A. 10   B. 15   C. 20   D. 30

24. To best analyze the fire prevention and protection problem in a certain section of the city, the MOST basic thing that is necessary to know is the _____ the area.

    A. number of fire companies in
    B. structural and occupancy data of
    C. number of people living in
    D. available water supply for

25. Of the following, the GREATEST fire hazard in furniture and cabinet shops is

    A. spontaneous ignition
    B. heating systems in buildings
    C. exposure
    D. misuse of electricity

KEY (CORRECT ANSWERS)

1. A	11. C
2. C	12. A
3. C	13. A
4. C	14. C
5. B	15. A
6. D	16. A
7. B	17. D
8. A	18. C
9. C	19. D
10. B	20. A

21. C
22. A
23. A
24. B
25. A

TEST 3

DIRECTIONS: Each question or incomplete statement is followed by several suggested answers or completions. Select the one that BEST answers the question or completes the statement. *PRINT THE LETTER OF THE CORRECT ANSWER IN THE SPACE AT THE RIGHT.*

1. On inspection of a 5-story building, you find that only half of the required stairways serving the top floor continue to the roof.
   This condition is legal if the building is a(n)

   A. warehouse
   B. school
   C. office building
   D. department store

   1.____

2. In order to determine whether a building in a county is within the fire limits, one of the sources you should check is the maps that are part of the

   A. Administrative Code
   B. most recent zoning resolution
   C. zoning resolution in force
   D. Sanborn maps

   2.____

3. During inspection of a motion picture theatre, you find 6 reels of safety film in closed containers in the manager's office.
   This condition is

   A. *legal* because the film is safety film
   B. *illegal* because film may not be kept in an office
   C. *legal* because there is less than 25,000 feet of film
   D. *illegal* because the film must be kept in a vented metal cabinet

   3.____

4. A two-story, two-family dwelling has been converted to three-family use. There is only one stairway to the street. There is no fire escape. The stairs are not enclosed with fire-regarded partitions. The doors to the apartments are self-closing, but are not fireproof.
   Of the following statements, the one that is MOST complete and accurate is that the condition described

   A. *conforms* to the requirements of the Multiple Dwelling Law
   B. *does not conform* to the requirements of the Multiple Dwelling Law because the apartment doors should be fireproof
   C. *does not conform* to the requirements of the Multiple Dwelling Law because the apartment doors should be fireproof and the stair hall should be enclosed
   D. *does not conform* to the requirements of the Multiple Dwelling Law because the apartment doors should be fireproof, the stair hall should be enclosed, and a second means of egress should be provided

   4.____

5. On fire prevention inspection, you find a revolving door being used as a required means of egress from the lobby of a hospital.
   This condition is

   A. *illegal*
   B. *legal* only if the door is a type A revolving door
   C. *legal* only if the door is a type B revolving door
   D. *legal* only if all other required means of egress are swinging doors

   5.____

6. The time of day when the GREATEST number of fires occur is from   6._____

   A. Midnight to 6 A.M.   B. 6 A.M. to 12 Noon
   C. 12 Noon to 6 P.M.   D. 6 P.M. to Midnight

7. Of the following types of industrial organizations, the one in which the GREATEST number of fires occur is   7._____

   A. newspaper and printing shops
   B. carpet and rug factories
   C. foundries, metal works, and machine shops
   D. paint, oil, and varnish factories

8. The fire department and the United States Coast Guard have agreed on a program for coordinating their fire prevention activities on the city waterfront.   8._____
   Part of this agreement provides for notification of the other party whenever

   A. any violation is discovered
   B. any serious violation is discovered
   C. any violation is discovered and is not abated within 10 days
   D. any violation is discovered involving a matter under the jurisdiction of the other party

9. A company on AFID makes a complete inspection of a 12-story commercial building occupied as follows: 9._____
       Alpha Co. - floors 1 through 5 and half of 6
       Beta Co. - half of 6 and all of 7
       Delta Co. - part of 8
       Gamma Co. - part of 8
       Epsilon Co. - part of 8
   All other floors - each occupied by single companies According to Regulations, the number of inspections to be recorded on reports for statistical purposes is MOST NEARLY

   A. 12   B. 13   C. 16   D. 18

10. The division coordinator is authorized to discontinue the use of individual inspectors for inspections generally performed by companies on AFID. This action is to be taken when the company   10._____

    A. is up to date on its inspection schedule for the year
    B. is 10 percent ahead of its inspection schedule for the year
    C. has completed sufficient number of inspections to assure completion of its schedule for the year
    D. has completed its regular inspection schedule for the year

Questions 11-15.

DIRECTIONS: Column I lists five properties of fire extinguishers. Column II lists various types of fire extinguishers. For each property in Column I, select the fire extinguisher from Column II having that property and place the letter next to the extinguisher in the properly numbered space.

COLUMN I	COLUMN II	
11. Contains aluminum sulphate in solution	A. Water gas cartridge expelled	11._____
12. Water in extinguishing agent will cause corrosion of container	B. Antifreeze (water mixed with antifreeze chemical)	12._____
13. Usually contains sodium chloride	C. Carbon dioxide	13._____
	D. Foam	
14. Produces a mass of bubbles filled with CO_2 gas	E. Carbon tetrachloride	14._____
15. Inspection check by weighing extinguisher only		15._____

16. Of the following categories by means of which structured fires were extended during the last few years, the MOST common involved was   16._____

    A. cocklofts
    B. partitions
    C. stairways
    D. doors

17. The one of the following which is NOT required by the housing maintenance code for the protection of openings into public halls in old-law tenements less than four stories high is that *every*   17._____

    A. door opening into the public hall shall be fireproof, having a fire-resisting rating of at least one hour
    B. door opening into the public hall shall be self-closing
    C. glazed panel in a door opening into a public hall shall be glazed with wire glass
    D. transom opening upon any public hall shall be glazed with wire glass and firmly secured in a closed position

18. Firestopping of the space above a hung ceiling into areas not exceeding 3,000 square feet is REQUIRED when the   18._____

    A. structural members within the concealed space are individually protected with materials having the required fire resistance
    B. concealed space is sprinklered
    C. ceiling contributes to the required fire resistance of the floor or roof assembly
    D. ceiling is not an essential part of the fire-resistive assembly

19. When a deluge sprinkler system is provided around the perimeter of a theater stage, manual operating devices as well as automatic controls are required by the building code.
The MOST complete and accurate statement concerning these manual operating devices is that they should be located   19._____

    A. at the emergency control station
    B. adjacent to one exit from the stage
    C. at the emergency control station and adjacent to one exit from the stage
    D. at the emergency control station, adjacent to one exit from the stage, and at the deluge valve

20. Yellow painted Siamese caps on office buildings will indicate that the Siamese serves ONLY 20.____

    A. the standpipe in pressurized stairs
    B. the sprinklers in sub-basement locations
    C. a combination standpipe and sprinkler system
    D. as a supply line to the fire pump for the upper level standpipe outlets

21. A fireman, on his way to work, is stopped by a citizen who complains that the employees of a nearby store frequently pile empty crates and boxes in a doorway, blocking passage. The one of the following which would be the MOST appropriate action for the fireman to take is to 21.____

    A. assure the citizen that the fire department's inspectional activities will eventually *catch up* with the store
    B. obtain the address of the store and investigate to determine whether the citizen's complaint is justified
    C. obtain the address of the store and report the complaint to his superior officer
    D. ask the citizen for specific dates on which this practice has occurred to determine whether the complaint is justified

22. In the Halon coding system, each digit represents the number of atoms while the position of the digit in the number represents a specific chemical element.
    For Halon number 1202, the number 1 indicates that the molecule contains one atom of 22.____

    A. bromine   B. carbon   C. chlorine   D. fluorine

23. A street vault incident described in a department safety bulletin explains how two persons were asphyxiated when they descended into the vault.
    Tests of the atmosphere of the vault showed that the hazard was due to 23.____

    A. light smoke and flames generated by burning synthetic insulation
    B. gasoline vapors from a leaking underground tank
    C. replacement of oxygen by carbon dioxide
    D. natural gas entering the vault

24. It is sometimes necessary to make a simple field test to determine the flammability of decorative materials.
    Of the following, the one that generally produces the LEAST reliable results when tested by exposure to a small flame is 24.____

    A. all-glass fabric
    B. untreated cotton cloth
    C. flame-retardant treated paper
    D. flexible plastic film

25. The one of the following substances with the LEAST tendency to spontaneous heating is 25.____

    A. fish meal   B. lamp black
    C. scrap rubber   D. soap powder

KEY (CORRECT ANSWERS)

1.	B	11.	D
2.	C	12.	E
3.	B	13.	B
4.	A	14.	D
5.	A	15.	C
6.	C	16.	B
7.	C	17.	A
8.	B	18.	C
9.	C	19.	C
10.	C	20.	C

21. C
22. B
23. D
24. D
25. B

TEST 4

DIRECTIONS: Each question or incomplete statement is followed by several suggested answers or completions. Select the one that BEST answers the question or completes the statement. *PRINT THE LETTER OF THE CORRECT ANSWER IN THE SPACE AT THE RIGHT.*

1. Every applicant for a certificate of license to install underground gasoline storage tanks is required to   1._____

    A. be a resident of the city and maintain a place of business in the city
    B. file a bond and evidence of liability insurance
    C. be a resident of the city or maintain a place of business in the city
    D. pass a written examination given by the fire department

2. After firing a blast, the licensed blaster at a construction site discovered that one charge had not detonated and the exact direction of the drill hole could not be determined. The licensed blaster under the supervision and orders of the walking boss used a metal scraper to remove the tamping, after which the hole was reloaded and fired. This action   2._____

    A. complies with the Fire Prevention Code
    B. violates the Code because a metal scraper was used
    C. violates the Code because the Fire Commissioner's approval is required before charges are removed
    D. violates the Code because no notification was given to the Division of Fire Prevention concerning the incident

3. The Fire Prevention Code specifies that a special permit is required for each of the following EXCEPT   3._____

    A. refining petroleum collected from oil separators or manufacturing plants
    B. loading of small arms ammunition by hand in a retail store selling ammunition
    C. operating a wholesale drug or chemical house
    D. generating acetylene gas

4. The one of the following that is the MOST acceptable statement concerning the fire protection for the truck loading rack in a bulk oil terminal is that the rack must be equipped with a   4._____

    A. water spray system, automatically controlled
    B. foam system, remote manually controlled
    C. water spray system, remote manually controlled
    D. foam system, automatically controlled

5. A fire insurance inspector suggested to the manager of a fireproof warehouse that bags of flour be stacked on skids (wooden platforms 6" high, 6x6 feet in area).
Of the following, the BEST justification for this suggestion is that, in the event of a fire, the bags on skids are LESS likely to   5._____

    A. topple
    B. be damaged by water used in extinguishment
    C. catch fire
    D. be ripped by fire equipment

6. Permitting piles of scrap paper cuttings to accumulate in a factory building is a bad practice CHIEFLY because they may

   A. ignite spontaneously
   B. interfere with fire extinguishment operations
   C. catch fire from a spark
   D. interfere with escape of occupants if a fire occurs

7. Firefighters are inspecting a furniture factory. During the inspection, they find employees smoking cigarettes in various areas.
   In which area does smoking pose the GREATEST danger of causing a fire?

   A. Employee lounge   B. Woodworking shop
   C. A private office   D. A rest room

8. The MAXIMUM quantity of paints which may be manufactured or stored without a permit, according to the Fire Prevention Code, is _____ gallons.

   A. 20   B. 25   C. 30   D. 50

9. Oil separators are required by the Administrative Code before issuance of a permit to a garage for the storage of volatile inflammable oil if the garage accommodates _____ or more motor vehicles.

   A. four   B. five   C. six   D. ten

10. *The term cellar, as used in the Building Code, shall mean a story having _____ of its height, measured from finished floor to finished ceiling, below the curb level at the center of the street front.*
    The one of the following which, when filled in the blank space, BEST completes the sentence is

    A. more than one-half
    B. no more than one-half
    C. more than three-quarters
    D. no more than three-quarters

11. The Oil Burner Rules of the Board of Standards and Appeals state, *No movable combustible materials shall be stored or maintained within _____ feet of heating apparatus, except where same is protected by fire-retarding material.*
    The one of the following numbers which, when inserted in the blank space above, MOST accurately completes the sentence is

    A. 2   B. 3   C. 4   D. 5

12. As used in the Building Code, the term *horizontal exit* refers to a(n)

    A. exit door on the ground floor which is at the same level as the street grade
    B. corridor or hallway leading to the exit stairs
    C. fire escape with the balcony at the same level as the floor
    D. connection between two floor areas through a fire wall

13. According to the Building Code, a required exit stairway enclosure in a public building MUST have a fire resistance rating of _____ hour(s).

    A. 1   B. 2   C. 3   D. 4

14. A recently enacted section of the Fire Prevention Code places limitations on the use of kerosene-burning equipment.
When all the provisions of this section of the Code are in full effect, the one of the following uses of kerosene-burning equipment which will NOT be permitted is equipment used exclusively for

    A. cooking purposes
    B. lighting purposes
    C. demonstration and sales purposes
    D. heating purposes in any building in an area not supplied with permanent piped gas

14.____

15. The provisions of the Building Code require that in a building more than two stories high, the required stairways must all continue to the roof EXCEPT in a(n)

    A. office building
    B. school building
    C. theater
    D. storage warehouse

15.____

16. The definition of *non-combustible* in the Building Code was recently amended with regard to acoustical and thermal insulation.
Which one of the following would be *non-combustible* according to the Code?
Insulation with a flame-spread rating not greater than _____, smoke-developed rating not greater than _____.

    A. 25; 50   B. 50; 50   C. 50; 75   D. 75; 100

16.____

17. A new school dormitory is two stories and less than thirty feet in height. Inspection reveals that there is only one stairway from the second floor and the maximum travel distance to the stair enclosure is 80 feet. The stair enclosure and corridors are provided with automatic sprinkler protection.
With respect to the provisions of the Building Code as it applies to this situation, it would be MOST appropriate to state that this building

    A. complies with the Code
    B. does not comply with the Code because the maximum travel distance is excessive
    C. does not comply with the Code because two exits remote from each other on each story are lacking
    D. does not comply with the Code because the sprinkler system was not extended into the rooms

17.____

18. Of the following statements, the one that is LEAST in accord with the material and equipment requirements for oil spill control at bulk storage plants and petroleum product pipelines is that

    A. all material and equipment must be of a type acceptable to the Fire Commissioner
    B. dispersants should be used only when directed by the fire department, Coast Guard, or Corps of Engineers
    C. pipeline operators shall provide at least one vacuum truck
    D. the minimum amount of absorbent material at any plant shall be 2,000 pounds

18.____

19. In a high-rise office building over 100 feet in height, the doors opening into interior stair enclosures may NOT be locked from either side at intervals of four stories or less EXCEPT where

   A. the building is equipped with an approved automatic sprinkler system
   B. the doors are equipped with an automatic fail-safe system for opening doors
   C. the second means of egress is a standard fire tower
   D. every floor of the building has a fire warden on duty

20. The Rules of the Board of Standards and Appeals require that combustible materials used for decorative purposes within special occupancy structures be made flameproof. Approval of flameproof materials is

   A. valid for an indefinite period
   B. limited to a period of 6 months
   C. limited to a period of 1 year
   D. limited to a period of 2 years

21. A multiple dwelling, according to the Multiple Dwelling Law, is a dwelling occupied as the residence of _____ or more families living independently of each other.
    The one of the following numbers which, when inserted in the blank space above, MOST accurately completes the sentence is

   A. 2   B. 3   C. 4   D. 5

22. The one of the following statements that is MOST accurate is that in multiple dwellings, windows at grade levels at sidewalks, yards, or courts may

   A. not have bars
   B. have bars provided that they are easily removed from the inside of the window
   C. have bars but at least one window in each room must be without bars
   D. have bars but at least one window in each apartment must be without bars

23. The number of extra sprinkler heads which must be kept in the premises of a building with an automatic sprinkler system, according to the Building Code, is

   A. 10
   B. 10 percent of the number of sprinkler heads in the entire system
   C. 6
   D. 6 percent of the number of sprinkler heads in the entire system

24. The Building Code requires that standpipe systems be equipped with pressure reducing valves where the normal hydrostatic pressure at a 2 1/2" hose outlet valve exceeds _____ lbs. per square inch.

   A. 50   B. 55   C. 60   D. 65

25. Walls of structures used for public entertainment may be covered with combustible wall coverings, according to the Building Code, provided that the

   A. wall covering is pasted or cemented directly to the plaster surfaces of the wall
   B. wall covering does not extend more than six feet in height
   C. building is a Class 1 fireproof structure
   D. building has a seating capacity of 600 people or less

KEY (CORRECT ANSWERS)

1.	C	11.	D
2.	A	12.	D
3.	D	13.	C
4.	C	14.	D
5.	B	15.	B
6.	C	16.	A
7.	B	17.	A
8.	A	18.	B
9.	B	19.	B
10.	A	20.	C

21. B
22. D
23. C
24. B
25. A

EXAMINATION SECTION
TEST 1

DIRECTIONS: Each question or incomplete statement is followed by several suggested answers or completions. Select the one that BEST answers the question or completes the statement. *PRINT THE LETTER OF THE CORRECT ANSWER IN THE SPACE AT THE RIGHT.*

1. Of the following materials, the one which has the HIGHEST tendency to spontaneous heating is

   A. lanolin
   B. linseed oil
   C. coconut oil
   D. turpentine

   1.____

2. The one of the following fabrics used in the manufacture of clothing that is MOST flammable is

   A. wool   B. acetate   C. cotton   D. linen

   2.____

3. Which of the following substances has the LOWEST boiling point?

   A. Turpentine
   B. Benzene
   C. Mineral spirits
   D. Cellosolve

   3.____

4. Which of the following non-solid fuels has the HIGHEST ignition temperature?

   A. Acetone
   B. Carbon monoxide
   C. Ethylene
   D. Methyl alcohol

   4.____

5. Assume that the cellar of a building is 100 feet long, 100 feet wide, and 10 feet high. If natural gas were distributed evenly throughout the cellar, and all openings from the cellar are closed, which one of the following volumes of natural gas would create an explosive atmosphere if suddenly released into this cellar?
   _____ cubic feet.

   A. 2,500   B. 7,500   C. 17,500   D. 25,000

   5.____

6. A lighted cigarette is LEAST likely to start a fire if dropped and left

   A. on a kapok pillow
   B. on cotton bed clothes
   C. in an explosive vapor-air mixture
   D. on dry grass

   6.____

7. A fire marshal inspecting a number of buildings where explosions are suspected as having been caused by dynamite would find that the scene of the dynamite explosion is MOST likely the one where

   A. a large section of wall has toppled, with its mortar remaining intact
   B. there are fragments of shattered cast iron
   C. a window frame has been pushed out from the wall surface, with some or all of the windows remaining intact
   D. the light bulbs in the building have remained unbroken

   7.____

8. During apparatus field inspection of a restaurant located in a building erected in 1972, a fireman finds that the filters for the cooking equipment exhaust system are cleaned every three months and the entire system is cleaned once a year.
   This maintenance procedure is

   A. *correct*
   B. *incorrect,* because the filters should be discarded at least every three months and the system cleaned at least once a year
   C. *incorrect,* because the filters should be discarded at least once a year and the system cleaned at least once a year
   D. *incorrect,* because both the filters and the entire system should be cleaned at least every three months

9. A group home is a facility for the care and maintenance of not less than three nor more than twelve children and is classified by the building code in the same occupancy group as a one-family dwelling.
   This much of the definition of a group home GENERALLY is

   A. *correct*
   B. *incorrect,* because a group home may not have less than seven children
   C. *incorrect,* because a group home is for adults, not children
   D. *incorrect,* because a group home is classified in the same occupancy group as a rooming house

10. A fifty-foot high, five-story multiple dwelling built in 1974 has a floor area of 7,000 square feet on each floor. It is equipped with a non-automatic dry standpipe system. During apparatus field inspection duty, a member discovers that a control valve on the standpipe is in closed position with no placard indicating that this was the normal position of the valve. Further investigation reveals that there is no one in the building who has a certificate of fitness to maintain the standpipe system. Of the following statements concerning the above situation, the one that is CORRECT is that the situation as described is

    A. *legal*
    B. *illegal,* because an individual with a certificate of fitness must be on the premises
    C. *illegal,* because an automatic system is required
    D. *illegal,* because the control valve must be in the open position

11. A tank truck with a capacity of 4,400 gallons is delivering #4 fuel oil to a multiple dwelling. According to the specifications for tank trucks, the person in control of the truck and supervising this delivery

    A. *does not* require a certificate of fitness because the capacity of the tank is less than 5,000 gallons
    B. *does not* require a certificate of fitness because the tank has light oil
    C. *does not* require a certificate of fitness because the delivery is being made to a non-commercial occupancy
    D. *requires* a certificate of fitness because a fire department permit is needed for all tank trucks delivering #4 fuel oil

12. The multiple dwelling law states that sprinkler systems in lodging houses shall have a supervisory and maintenance service satisfactory to the fire department. The fire department requires a valid inspection of the sprinkler control valve AT LEAST once

A.	daily	B.	semi-weekly
C.	weekly	D.	monthly

13. Anhydrous ammonia is being used in a duplicating machine located in a school office. There is no one in the school with a certificate of fitness for the storage and use of ammonia or for the servicing of the duplicating machine. In this situation, a certificate of fitness is GENERALLY

    A. *not* required because the machine is considered office equipment
    B. *not* required unless the quantity of anhydrous ammonia being stored on the premises is more than two 150-lb. cylinders
    C. *not* required because schools, with regular supervised fire drills, are exempt from certain requirements of the fire prevention code
    D. *required* whether or not a permit is needed under the fire prevention code

14. According to the labor law, fire drills are required to be conducted in certain factory buildings.
    Which of the following statements is CORRECT with respect to such fire drills?

    A. Fire drills are required to be conducted in every factory building in which there are more than 75 persons above or below the street floor.
    B. Fire drills are not required to be conducted in factory buildings less than 100 feet in height.
    C. Fire drills are required to be conducted in every factory building over two stories in height in which more than twenty-five persons are employed above the ground floor unless the sprinkler system and number of occupants of the building are in accordance with the other provisions of the labor law.
    D. The sprinklering of a factory building is not a factor in determining whether or not a building is required to conduct fire drills.

15. An officer tells members during a drill that a red light and a placard should serve to locate the Siamese hose connection of a temporary standpipe system in a building under construction.
    The officer's instructions are

    A. *correct,* because both the red light and a placard are required
    B. *incorrect,* because only the red light is required
    C. *incorrect,* because only a placard is required
    D. *incorrect,* because neither the red light nor a placard is required

16. During apparatus field inspection duty, a fireman inspecting a 40-story office building occupied by 1,000 people is unable to find a fire safety director or deputy fire safety director in the building. The manager of the building states that the fire safety director is out to lunch, that there is no deputy fire safety director, and that he, the manager, is acting as the fire safety director pending the return of the fire safety director. Because the manager does not have a fire safety director certificate of fitness, the fireman issues a violation to him.
    The fireman's action in this situation is

A. *correct*, because local law requires a fire safety director with a certificate of fitness in a building this high to be on duty whenever the building is occupied by more than 500 people
B. *incorrect*, because local law permits the fire safety director to be temporarily relieved, for short intervals, by responsible individuals who do not have the required certificate of fitness
C. *correct*, because local law requires a fire safety director with a certificate of fitness to be on duty in a building this high, regardless of the occupancy of the building
D. *incorrect*, because whenever local law is not complied with, a referral report should be forwarded, and no violation issued

17. A commercial vehicle without a fire department permit is transporting 500 pounds of dynamite from a neighboring outside county through the city to another out-of-town county without stopping to make any deliveries enroute. There is no department pumping engine escort. The situation as described is

    A. *legal*, because the shipment contains less than 1,000 pounds of dynamite
    B. *illegal*, because a pumping engine escort is required whenever explosives are transported without a fire department permit through the city
    C. *legal*, even though a fire department permit has not been issued, because the shipment does not contain any blasting caps
    D. *illegal*, because dynamite may not be transported through the city from one out-of-town location to another

18. Of the following exit doors in buildings erected in 1976, the one that does NOT have to swing outward is a(n)

    A. corridor door from a room used for office purposes with an occupancy of 80 persons
    B. corridor door from a lecture room in a school building where the room has an occupancy of 80 persons
    C. exterior street-floor exit door from a space 2,000 square feet in area in a business building, where the space is occupied by fewer than 50 persons and the maximum travel distance to the door is 50 feet
    D. exterior street-floor exit door from a lobby in a hotel, where the lobby will not be occupied by more than 50 persons and the maximum travel distance to the door is 50 feet

19. During apparatus field inspection duty, a fireman inspecting a 90-foot high apartment house erected in 1972 finds that the standpipe hose is missing from every hose rack in the building. Of the following statements concerning this situation, the one that is CORRECT is that

    A. the situation as described may be legal but the fire-man needs additional information to make a final decision
    B. all such buildings, regardless of when erected, must have the standpipe hose racks equipped with hose
    C. all such buildings, if erected under the new building code, must have their standpipe hose racks equipped with hose
    D. the situation as described would be acceptable for an office building but not for an apartment house

20. A permit is required to store empty combustible packing boxes in a building whenever the   20.____

    A. boxes occupy more than two thousand cubic feet
    B. storage space is less than 50 feet from the nearest wall of a building occupied as a hospital, school, or theater
    C. boxes are of cardboard or similarly combustible material
    D. building is of non-fireproof construction

21. An inspector, taking some clothing to a dry cleaner in his neighborhood, noticed that   21.____
    inflammable cleaning fluid was stored in a way which created a fire hazard. The fireman called this to the attention of the proprietor, explaining the danger involved.
    This method of handling the situation was

    A. *bad;* the fireman should not have interfered in a matter which was not his responsibility
    B. *good;* the proprietor would probably remove the hazard and be more careful in the future
    C. *bad;* the fireman should have reported the situation to the fire inspector's office without saying anything to the proprietor
    D. *good;* since the fireman was a customer, he should treat the proprietor more leniently than he would treat other violators

22. According to the Building Code, a vertical iron ladder to an escape manhole opening in   22.____
    the sidewalk is required from a cellar room when the room is being used as a

    A. coal storage room   B. restaurant kitchen
    C. boiler room   D. factory

23. In a building of public assembly, the provisions of the Fire Prevention Code prohibit the   23.____
    use of decorations, drapes, or scenery made of combustible material which have not been rendered fireproof.
    Of the following types of occupancies, the one that is exempt from the provisions of this section is a

    A. school   B. hospital   C. church   D. museum

24. As used in the Building Code, a *4-hour fire rating* of a wall means that in a standard fire   24.____
    test of four hours duration, the

    A. wall will not collapse
    B. unexposed side of the wall will not char or smolder
    C. temperature on the unexposed side of the wall will not rise
    D. temperature on the unexposed side of the wall will not rise more than a predetermined amount

25. The prohibition against smoking in retail stores applies   25.____

    A. to all stores
    B. only to stores employing more than 25 persons
    C. only to stores accommodating more than 300 persons
    D. only to stores employing more than 25 persons or accommodating more than 300 persons

KEY (CORRECT ANSWERS)

1.	C	11.	D
2.	D	12.	C
3.	B	13.	D
4.	D	14.	C
5.	C	15.	A
6.	C	16.	D
7.	A	17.	B
8.	D	18.	C
9.	B	19.	A
10.	D	20.	A

21. B
22. C
23. C
24. D
25. A

TEST 2

DIRECTIONS: Each question or incomplete statement is followed by several suggested answers or completions. Select the one that BEST answers the question or completes the statement. *PRINT THE LETTER OF THE CORRECT ANSWER IN THE SPACE AT THE RIGHT.*

1. The one of the following which is NOT required by the Code for the protection of openings into public halls in old-law tenements less than four stories high is that every   1.____

    A. door opening into the public hall shall be fireproof, having a fire-resisting rating of at least one hour
    B. door opening into the public hall shall be self-closing
    C. glazed panel in a door opening into a public hall shall be glazed with wire glass
    D. transom opening upon any public hall shall be glazed with wire glass and firmly secured in a closed position

2. Firestopping of the space above a hung ceiling into areas not exceeding 3,000 square feet is REQUIRED when the   2.____

    A. structural members within the concealed space are individually protected with materials having the required fire resistance
    B. concealed space is sprinklered
    C. ceiling contributes to the required fire resistance of the floor or roof assembly
    D. ceiling is not an essential part of the fire-resistive assembly

3. When a deluge sprinkler system is provided around the perimeter of a theater stage, manual operating devices as well as automatic controls are required by the Building Code.
The MOST complete and accurate statement concerning these manual operating devices is that they should be located   3.____

    A. at the emergency control station
    B. adjacent to one exit from the stage
    C. at the emergency control station and adjacent to one exit from the stage
    D. at the emergency control station, adjacent to one exit from the stage, and at the deluge valve

4. Yellow painted Siamese caps on office buildings will indicate that the Siamese serves ONLY   4.____

    A. the standpipe in pressurized stairs
    B. the sprinklers in sub-basement locations
    C. a combination standpipe and sprinkler system
    D. as a supply line to the fire pump for the upper level standpipe outlets

5. Of the following buildings, the one that MUST have emergency smoke-venting equipment is a   5.____

    A. new office building, 275 feet high, equipped throughout with automatic sprinklers
    B. new office building, 175 feet high, without an air conditioning system

C. new office building, 75 feet high, without sprinklers and with a central air conditioning system serving more than the floor on which the equipment is located
D. one-story building, classified in occupancy group B-1, greater in depth than 100 feet from a frontage space

6. A factory building was erected in 1912 and was occupied continuously as such until 1950 when it became completely vacant. After many years, it was reoccupied with factory occupancies.
This structure

   A. must comply with the State Labor Law affecting factory buildings erected after October 1, 1913
   B. may be reoccupied as a factory building without changing its classification as one erected before October 1, 1913
   C. may be reoccupied as a factory building erected before October 1, 1913 provided an automatic sprinkler system is installed
   D. cannot be reoccupied as a factory unless it is of fireproof construction

7. A five-story fireproof factory building erected in 1909 has the following occupancies:
   First floor - dress manufacturing
   Second floor - tannery
   Third floor - artificial flower manufacturing
   Fourth floor - machine shop
   Fifth floor - vacant
Under the State Labor Law, an automatic extinguishing system is

   A. *not required* because the building is classed as fireproof
   B. *required* for the artificial flower factory and all floors above
   C. *not required* if the tannery is moved to the fifth floor
   D. *required* throughout

8. Which one of the following statements does NOT correctly describe the protection requirements for vertical separation of openings?
In buildings classified in occupancy group

   A. E exceeding three stories or 40 feet in height, openings located vertically above one another in exterior walls except in stairway enclosures required to have a fire resistance rating of one hour or more shall be separated by a spandrel wall at least three feet high between the top of one opening and the bottom of the opening immediately above
   B. D exceeding three stories or 40 feet in height, openings located vertically above one another in exterior walls except in stairway enclosures shall have each such opening above the lower one protected against fire by an opening protective
   C. C exceeding three stories or 40 feet in height, openings located vertically above one another in exterior walls except in stairway enclosures shall be protected by a fire canopy of non-combustible materials extending out at least two feet horizontally from the wall and at least as long as the width of the lower opening
   D. B, spandrels and fire canopies shall be constructed to provide at least the fire-resistance rating required for the exterior wall, but in no event less than one hour

9. It is MOST complete and accurate to state that, according to the Manual of Fire Communications, in the event the officer in command of a fire or emergency operation requires additional manpower, in lieu of transmitting additional alarms or special calls, he may

   A. telephone the Office of the Chief of Department, specifying the kind of aid required and when it should be sent
   B. notify the dispatcher by radio of the assistance required, specifying the number of officers and fire-men, and the location to which they shall report
   C. telephone the dispatcher specifying the assistance required, including the number of officers and fire-men needed, location to which they shall report, and the expected time additional manpower will be released
   D. notify the Office of the Chief of Department, specifying the assistance required, the location to which they shall report, the reason for calling additional manpower, and the amount of time they can be expected to be detained

10. While inspecting a sprinklered building, a fire officer is asked by the building manager for his opinion about painting the wooden water tank on the roof. The manager explains it is his understanding that painting the tank will extend its useful life.
    Of the following, it would probably be MOST appropriate for the fire officer to indicate that

    A. painting the interior of the tank below water level will prolong the life of the tank, but painting the exterior may tend to hide structural defects
    B. painting a wooden tank may be desirable from the standpoint of appearance, but it is of questionable value in increasing the life of the tank
    C. the use of paint is undesirable for any purpose on either the exterior or interior of the tank
    D. the manager should consult a painting contractor to find out what his experience and recommendations are

11. In a large warehouse facility, the GREATEST fire hazard potential will result if rubber automotive tires are stored on the

    A. side in stacked piles   B. tread in racks
    C. side on pallets   D. tread in stacked piles

12. During a fire prevention inspection, a firefighter may find a condition which could be the immediate cause of death in the event of a fire.
    Which one of the following conditions in a restaurant is the MOST dangerous?

    A. Blocked exit doors
    B. A crack in the front door
    C. A window that does not open
    D. A broken air conditioning system

13. Firefighters must regularly inspect office buildings to determine whether fire prevention laws have been obeyed. Some of these fire prevention laws are as follows: DOORS: Doors should be locked as follows:
    I. Doors on the ground floor may be locked on the street side to prevent entry into the stairway.
    II. Doors in office buildings that are less than 100 feet in height may be locked on the stairway side on each floor above the ground floor.
    III. Doors in office buildings that are 100 feet or more in height may be locked on the stairway side except for every fourth floor.

    The doors in an office building which is less than 100 feet in height may be locked on the stairway side

    A. on all floors including the ground floor
    B. on all floors above the ground floor
    C. except for every fourth floor
    D. on all floors above the fourth floor

14. SIGNS: Signs concerning stairways should be posted in the following manner:
    I. A sign shall be posted near the elevator on each floor, stating, *IN CASE OF FIRE, USE STAIRS UNLESS OTHERWISE INSTRUCTED.* The sign shall contain a diagram showing the location of the stairs and the letter identification of the stairs.
    II. Each stairway shall be identified by an alphabetical letter on a sign posted on the hallway side of the stair door.
    III. Signs indicating the floor number shall be attached to the stairway side of each door.
    IV. Signs indicating whether re-entry can be made into the building, and the floors where re-entry can be made, shall be posted on the stairway side of each door.

    Which one of the following CORRECTLY lists the information which should be posted on the stairway side of a door?

    A sign will indicate the
    A. floor number, whether re-entry can be made into the building, and the floors where re-entry can be made
    B. alphabetical letter of the stairway, whether re-entry can be made into the building, and the floors where re-entry can be made
    C. alphabetical letter of the stairway and the floor number
    D. alphabetical letter of the stairway, the floor number, whether re-entry can be made into the building, and the floors where re-entry can be made

15. The Fire Department now uses companies on fire duty, with their apparatus, for fire prevention inspection in commercial buildings.
    The one of the following changes which was MOST important in making this inspection procedure practicable was the

    A. reduction of hours of work of firemen
    B. use of two-way radio equipment
    C. use of enclosed cabs on fire apparatus
    D. increase in property values during the post-war period

16. The MAXIMUM length of unlined linen hose which shall be permitted at any standpipe hose outlet valve is 16.____

    A. 50' B. 75' C. 100' D. 125'

17. The State Labor Law requires that fire drills be conducted monthly in factory buildings over two stories in height in which more than 25 persons are employed above the ground floor. 17.____
    The one of the following statements that is MOST complete and accurate is that the law provides for automatic exemption from this requirement to factory buildings which are

    A. completely sprinklered
    B. completely sprinklered by a system having two adequate sources of water supply
    C. completely sprinklered by a system having two adequate sources of water supply and a maximum number of occupants of any one floor not more than 50 percent above the capacity of the exits required for the same building if unsprinklered
    D. completely sprinklered by a system having two adequate sources of water supply, a maximum number of occupants of any one floor not more than 50 percent above the capacity of the exits required for the same building if unsprinklered and an interior fire alarm system

18. Automatic sprinkler systems installed in the public halls of converted multiple dwellings with a required Siamese are subjected to a hydrostatic pressure test before acceptance. The test pressure for such systems is to be NOT less than 18.____

    A. 30 pounds per square inch
    B. 30 pounds per square inch in excess of the normal pressure required for such systems when in service
    C. 200 pounds per square inch
    D. 200 pounds per square inch in excess of the normal pressure required for such systems when in service

19. According to the rules of the Board of Standards and Appeals, when flameproofed materials are subjected to prescribed tests, they shall meet established standards for each of the following properties EXCEPT 19.____

    A. flashing   B. duration of flame
    C. duration of glow   D. temperature of flame

20. Each year many children die in fires which they have started while playing with matches. Of the following measures, the one that would be MOST effective in preventing such tragedies is to 20.____

    A. warn the children of the dangers involved
    B. punish parents who are found guilty of neglecting their children
    C. keep matches out of the reach of children
    D. use only safety matches

21. Sparks given off by welding torches are a serious fire hazard.
The BEST of the following methods of dealing with this hazard is to conduct welding operations

    A. only in fireproof buildings protected by sprinkler systems
    B. only out-of-doors on a day with little wind blowing
    C. only on materials certified to be non-combustible by recognized testing laboratories
    D. only after loose combustible materials have been cleared from the area and with a man standing by with a hose line

22. A two-story, Class 3, non-fireproof building was originally occupied as a store on the first floor and one apartment on the second floor. Upon inspection, you find that the second floor is now being used for offices. The building is 20' x 50'. There is one stairway made of wood, enclosed with fire-retarded stud partitions, leading directly to the street from the second floor.
The one of the following statements that is MOST complete and accurate is that the situation as described

    A. complies with applicable laws
    B. is illegal because the stair should be of incombustible material
    C. is illegal because there should be two means of egress
    D. is illegal because there should be two means of egress and the stair should be of incombustible material

Questions 23-25.

DIRECTIONS: Questions 23 through 25 are to be answered SOLELY on the basis of the following passage.

Automatic sprinkler systems are installed in many buildings. They extinguish or keep from spreading 96% of all fires in areas they protect. Sprinkler systems are made up of pipes which hang below the ceiling of each protected area and sprinkler heads which are placed along the pipes. The pipes are usually filled with water, and each sprinkler head has a heat sensitive part. When the heat from the fire reaches the sensitive part of the sprinkler head, the head opens and showers water upon the fire in the form of spray. The heads are spaced so that the fire is covered by overlapping showers of water from the open heads.

23. Automatic sprinkler systems are installed in buildings to

    A. prevent the build-up of dangerous gases
    B. eliminate the need for fire insurance
    C. extinguish fires or keep them from spreading
    D. protect 96% of the floor space

24. If more than one sprinkler head opens, the area sprayed will be

    A. flooded with hot water
    B. overlapped by showers of water
    C. subject to less water damage
    D. about 1 foot per sprinkler head

25. A sprinkler head will open and shower water when   25._____
    A. it is reached by heat from a fire
    B. water pressure in the pipes gets too high
    C. it is reached by sounds from a fire alarm
    D. water temperature in the pipes gets too low

KEY (CORRECT ANSWERS)

1.	A	11.	B
2.	C	12.	A
3.	C	13.	B
4.	C	14.	A
5.	D	15.	B
6.	B	16.	D
7.	D	17.	C
8.	A	18.	C
9.	B	19.	D
10.	B	20.	C

21. D
22. A
23. C
24. B
25. A

TEST 3

DIRECTIONS: Each question or incomplete statement is followed by several suggested answers or completions. Select the one that BEST answers the question or completes the statement. *PRINT THE LETTER OF THE CORRECT ANSWER IN THE SPACE AT THE RIGHT.*

1. The one of the following which is the MOST valid statement in the Fire Prevention Code regarding height restrictions on combustible fiber storage is that

   A. a clearance of at least 18 inches shall be maintained below the sprinkler head
   B. storage shall be no higher than 20 feet above the floor
   C. storage shall be no higher than 2/3 of the distance from floor to ceiling
   D. storage shall be piled to a height not greater than 6 inches below the top of the enclosing wall

   1.___

2. The one of the following which is NOT among the Fire Prevention Code protection requirements for the storage of television special effects is that

   A. partitions in the storage room shall have at least a one-hour fire resistive rating
   B. the roof of the storage room shall have at least a 1 1/2 hour fire resistive rating
   C. there shall be one sprinkler head for each 80 square feet of floor space in the storage room
   D. there shall be mechanical ventilation providing at least four air changes per hour

   2.___

3. According to the Fire Prevention Code, of the following containers, the ones which are NOT legal for the transportation of gasoline are

   A. 5-gallon cans with metal seals
   B. glass bottles not exceeding 4 ounces each
   C. 55-gallon steel barrels or drums
   D. 10-gallon safety cans

   3.___

4. The following conditions have been found during an inspection:
   I. 10,000 small arms cartridges in a store authorized to sell gunpowder
   II. 500 small arms cartridges in a pawn shop
   III. 200 small arms cartridges in a liquor store
   IV. 100 small arms cartridges in a drug store

   Which of the following choices lists ONLY those of the above conditions that comply with the Fire Prevention Code either because a permit may be issued or because a pernit is not required?

   A. I, II, III   B. I, II, IV
   C. I, III, IV   D. II, III, IV

   4.___

5. While inspecting a building, an officer notices that a standard enclosure having a three-hour fire resistance rating has been constructed above ground on the lowest floor of the building.
   According to the Building Code, the MAXIMUM size fuel oil storage tank that can be placed in this enclosure is one with a capacity of _____ gallons.

   A. 1,100   B. 2,500   C. 10,000   D. 20,000

   5.___

6. The one of the following which is NOT a Class B multiple dwelling is a 6.____

   A. hotel B. boarding school
   C. clubhouse D. hospital

7. When inspecting an industrial plant, an officer discovers a conveyor passing through a 7.____
   fire wall with no fire shutter for the opening.
   The MOST valid of the following statements concerning alternate forms of protection is that

   A. no alternate is acceptable; a shutter having fire resistance equal to the wall fire resistance is required
   B. a sprinkler head located in the opening to provide at least 3 gallons per square foot per minute is acceptable
   C. two sprinkler heads to provide a water curtain for the entire opening is acceptable
   D. four water spray nozzles on each side of the opening controlled by an automatic valve actuated by a heat detector is acceptable

8. A new restaurant in a multiple-story building of Class I construction has a false front on 8.____
   the outside of the building representing an English castle.
   The one of the following which meets the Building Code requirement for this condition to be legal is that the false front is of

   A. fire retardant treated wood not over 40 feet high
   B. fire retardant treated wood covering less than 2,000 square feet of surface
   C. slow burning plastic, not over 25 feet high, covering not over 1,000 square feet of surface
   D. slow burning plastic, not over 40 feet high, covering less than 5% of the building surface

9. At a recent fire on the third floor of a building, firemen could not open the locked windows 9.____
   nor could they break the plastic glazing.
   For such conditions, the Building Code requires that

   A. keys to the windows be available in the lobby
   B. one window for each 50 feet of street front be openable from the inside or outside
   C. all plastic glazing be replaced by glass
   D. all locks be removed and replaced with spring latches

10. Showroom spaces located in office buildings over 100 feet high are required to be sprin- 10.____
    klered when the

    A. building air conditioning system serves more than the floor in which the equipment is located, and the showroom space exceeds 7,500 square feet in area and is located more than 40 feet above curb level
    B. showroom space is over 1,000 square feet in area and is located more than 40 feet above curb level
    C. showroom space is over 7,500 square feet in area, is not equipped with an approved smoke detection alarm system, and is served by a one-floor mechanical ventilation system
    D. showroom space exceeds 2,500 square feet in area and is located more than 75 feet above curb level

11. In a building classified as occupancy group E, occupied or arranged to be occupied for an occupant load of more than one hundred persons above or below the street level or more than a total of five hundred persons in the entire building, a building evacuation supervisor performs his training activities under the direction of

    A. the battalion chief on duty
    B. the building fire safety director
    C. the building fire brigade supervisor
    D. someone other than any of the above

12. The one of the following which BEST identifies where a Class E fire alarm signal system will sound continuously upon operation of a manual station is only on the floor where

    A. actuated
    B. actuated and the floor above
    C. actuated and the next two floors above
    D. actuated, the floor above, and the floor below

13. The ONLY one of the following occupancies in which portable kerosene space heaters approved by the Board of Standards and Appeals may be used in the event of failure of the central heating unit is in

    A. private dwellings
    B. multiple dwellings
    C. places of public assembly
    D. schools

14. The one of the following which is NOT a requirement relating to oxygen and acetylene torch operations in a building under demolition is that there be

    A. one fire guard in the area of torch operation equipped with a 2 1/2" hose line
    B. one fire guard for each torch operator and an addi-tional fire guard on the floor or level below
    C. fire guards to make an inspection of the exposed area one half hour after completion of torch operations
    D. fire guards to make an inspection of the exposed area one hour after completion of torch operations

15. Upon responding to an alarm of fire in a building, an officer notes that the Siamese connections are painted yellow.
    This color coding indicates that

    A. the sprinkler system protects only showrooms located not over 40 feet above the curb line
    B. the standpipe riser is only four inches in size
    C. a floor control valve is provided for the sprinkler system on each floor
    D. the Siamese connection supplies a high-expansion foam system

16. The one of the following which does NOT correctly describe what can happen during manual operation of an elevator with the keyed switch in the *Fireman Service* position is that the

    A. doors will open on all floors but the fire floor
    B. direction of travel can be changed after a floor selection has been made

C. doors will open only in response to the *Door Open* button in the car
D. doors can be automatically reclosed while in the process of opening

17. The Building Code places restrictions on the suspension of new ceilings below existing suspended ceilings in construction group II in order to restrict the travel of fire in hidden spaces.
 The one of the following requirements which BEST describes the nature of this restriction is that the

   A. concealed space shall be provided with firestops to divide the space into sections not exceeding 3,000 square feet each
   B. new ceiling shall be supported directly from the ceiling carrying channels and shall have no openings from the concealed space to the area below
   C. new ceiling shall be of non-combustible construction or have a flame spread rating of 25 or less, and a smoke developed rating of 50 or less
   D. existing ceiling shall be completely removed before the new ceiling is suspended

17.____

18. While inspecting a 125-foot-high factory building constructed in 1912 within 20 feet of an adjacent one-story fireproof garage 12 feet in height, an officer notices that the fire windows in the factory wall facing the garage are glazed with wireglass only to the fourth floor or 65-foot level. Windows above that level are 60 feet higher vertically than the roof of the garage and are glazed with inch plate glass lights 400 square inches in area.
 The one of the following which is the PROPER conclusion for the officer to draw is that

   A. such windows comply with the State Labor Law
   B. a violation exists since all fire windows in the wall of a factory building facing any building within 30 feet must be glazed with wireglass
   C. a violation exists since the fire windows in all factory buildings erected before 1913 must have wireglass
   D. none of the fire windows in the factory wall need be wireglass if there are no openings in the garage wall facing it

18.____

19. An officer submits for review a referral report containing statements about the exterior screened stairway of a factory building he has recently inspected which he considers to be in violation of the State Labor Law.
 Of the officer's observations listed below, the one that is NOT a violation of the State Labor Law is:

   A. No balcony connecting with the stairs at the fourth floor
   B. Door connecting with the balcony at the third floor opens inward
   C. Stair terminates in rear yard not communicating to a street
   D. Access to balcony at second floor via sliding door

19.____

20. A five story non-fireproof factory building erected in 1908 has an area on all floors of 900 square feet with two exits remote from each other on all floors, except for the fourth floor which is used entirely as a raw material storeroom. No one is regularly employed on that floor. For security reasons, the fourth floor has only one exit.
 It would be CORRECT to say that, according to the State Labor Law,

   A. this arrangement is expressly forbidden, as every floor must have two exits
   B. one exit from the fourth floor would be acceptable provided it is protected by an automatic sprinkler system

20.____

C. the one exit from the fourth floor is acceptable provided it conforms to the criteria for a factory exit
D. one exit from the fourth floor is acceptable provided the longest distance to the exit from any point on the floor does not exceed 75 feet

21. Buildings which have been vacated by order of the fire department are kept under surveillance.
When such buildings have been boarded up, surveillance may, with approval, be reduced to once each

    A. week   B. month
    C. quarter-year   D. half-year

22. Overly detailed fire prevention inspections are to be avoided CHIEFLY because they

    A. unduly interfere with the normal activities of the occupancy, causing public resentment
    B. require excessive time which could be used to better advantage inspecting other occupancies
    C. tend to result in oversight of some fundamental hazards
    D. are beyond the capabilities of many firemen who are not specifically trained in inspectional techniques

23. Requests for sprinkler re-evaluation are accepted by the fire department, and a re-inspection made, if the petitioner states that substantial changes have been made in the sprinkler system.
The one of the following statements that is MOST accurate and complete is that such re-inspections are made by the division commander

    A. in all instances
    B. except when he has endorsed the original sprinkler order
    C. except when he has endorsed the original sprinkler order or when his workload is excessive
    D. except when he has endorsed the original sprinkler order, his workload is excessive, or the re-evaluation is extremely complex

24. Department regulations require the forwarding of reports to the Fire Commissioner relating to demolition work adjacent to or adjoining company quarters.
The one of the following statements that is MOST accurate and complete is that such reports should be forwarded when notice of the proposed demolition is

    A. received
    B. received and when the work is completed
    C. received, when the work actually starts, and when the work is completed
    D. received, when the work actually starts, when any interruption of work occurs, and when the work is completed

25. The one of the following statements that is MOST complete and accurate is that when a building inspector issues a Violation Order, the time allowed for compliance

    A. must be the specific number of days indicated on the Standard Form of Orders
    B. may be less than the specific number of days indicated on the Standard Form of Orders

C. may be more than the specific number of days indicated on the Standard Form of Orders
D. may be more or less than the specific number of days indicated on the Standard Form of Orders, depending upon the circumstances

---

KEY (CORRECT ANSWERS)

1.	C	11.	B
2.	D	12.	B
3.	D	13.	D
4.	C	14.	A
5.	D	15.	C
6.	D	16.	A
7.	D	17.	D
8.	C	18.	A
9.	B	19.	D
10.	A	20.	C

21. C
22. B
23. D
24. A
25. B

TEST 4

DIRECTIONS: Each question or incomplete statement is followed by several suggested answers or completions. Select the one that BEST answers the question or completes the statement. *PRINT THE LETTER OF THE CORRECT ANSWER IN THE SPACE AT THE RIGHT.*

1. Of the following substances, the one that would MOST appropriately be protected with a sprinkler installation is   1.___

    A. cellulose acetate
    B. quicklime
    C. magnesium powder
    D. calcium carbide

2. Providing clearance around unprotected steel columns in storage occupancies is a practice which is GENERALLY   2.___

    A. *desirable,* chiefly because the quantity of combustibles stored is reduced
    B. *undesirable,* chiefly because flue-like conditions will prevail
    C. *desirable,* chiefly because it will allow water from sprinklers to keep the column wet
    D. *undesirable,* chiefly because stock can topple if not supported

3. National fire records indicate that over the years restaurant fires have increased in number and in total dollar loss despite technological improvements.   3.___
The large increase in the number of restaurant fires is PRIMARILY attributable to

    A. fires of incendiary origin
    B. duct fires
    C. the use of open flames for cooking
    D. careless handling of smoking materials

4. When serving a summons for a violation of the Building Code, it is most important that proper procedure be followed.   4.___
Of the following statements, the one that is MOST acceptable is that a summons may be

    A. mailed to the residence of the building's owner if he is not on the premises
    B. given to a superintendent to be forwarded to the owner if he is not on the premises
    C. placed on the desk or in the immediate vicinity of the owner if he refuses to accept it
    D. made out with the initials of the owner if the full name is not known

5. A dry-pipe sprinkler system is generally not considered acceptable protection for an occupancy utilizing flammable liquids MAINLY because   5.___

    A. corrosion tends to weaken these systems
    B. water is a poor extinguishing agent for flammable liquids
    C. the systems are too expensive for the purpose
    D. a fast spreading fire may be out of control by the time water arrives

6. In order to enforce the fire safety laws, firefighters must inspect buildings and stores.   6.___
It is NOT a good idea for firefighters to let owners of buildings and stores know when they are coming because

A. firefighters will waste valuable time if the owner breaks the appointment
B. owners might try to hide fire hazards from the fire-fighters
C. firefighters can make the inspection faster without an appointment
D. owners would be angry if the firefighters were unable to keep the appointment

7. Many older buildings are modernized to give a blank wall appearance by being *wrapped*. It is INACCURATE to state, with reference to *wrapped* buildings, that

   A. the use of expanded metal panels reduces the hazard from exposure fires
   B. they are essentially windowless buildings
   C. solid metal panels may be blown loose and scale a considerable distance
   D. expanded metal panels may be hung or mounted a foot or more from the original exterior wall

8. According to the Administrative Code, it is unlawful to manufacture within the city all of the following EXCEPT

   A. blank cartridges
   B. railroad track torpedoes
   C. flashlight compositions
   D. ship signal rockets

9. A newly appointed firefighter is assigned to go with an experienced firefighter to inspect a paint store. The paint store owner refuses to allow the inspection, saying that he is closing the store early that day and going on vacation. The new firefighter demands rudely that the inspection be allowed, even though it would be permissible to delay it.
Of the following, it would be BEST for the experienced firefighter to

   A. repeat the demand that the inspection be allowed and quote the law to the store owner
   B. tell the new firefighter that it would be best to schedule the inspection after the store owner's vacation
   C. tell the store owner to step aside, and instruct the new firefighter to enter the store and begin the inspection
   D. tell the new firefighter to forget about the inspection because the store owner is uncooperative

10. One person shall be permitted to supervise more than one interior fire alarm system. The one of the following that is NOT in accord with the restrictions placed on this permission is that

    A. the buildings in which the interior fire alarm systems are located must be within an area whose diameter does not exceed six hundred feet
    B. the interior fire alarms in all buildings in the group can be tested within thirty minutes of commencing work daily
    C. the addresses of all buildings shall be listed on the one certificate of fitness
    D. records and logbooks must be kept on each premises

11. The one of the following which is NOT in accord with the Regulations for Use of Halon 1301, Extinguishing Agent, is that

    A. maximum concentration shall not exceed 10 percent where human habitation is present in the volume to be flooded
    B. minimum concentration of FE 1301 used shall not be less than 10 percent

C. a discharge rate which results in attaining the design concentration in 8 seconds is acceptable
D. a central office connection must be provided for fire detection or systems operation where human habitation is present in the volume to be flooded

12. According to the Fire Prevention Code, a person who holds a permit for the manufacture of inflammable mixtures and who wishes to manufacture combustible mixtures is

   A. *required* to obtain another permit
   B. *not required* to obtain another permit
   C. *not required* to obtain another permit unless the mixtures include stove polishes or insecticides
   D. *not required* to obtain another permit unless the mixtures include medicinal and toilet preparations

13. The one of the following statements which is MOST accurate and complete is that the Fire Prevention Code permits the hanging of fresh-cut decorative greens in places of public assembly only if they do not contain

   A. pitch
   B. pitch and are hung by means of non-combustible material
   C. pitch, are hung by means of non-combustible material, and do not remain for a period in excess of 24 hours
   D. pitch, are hung by means of non-combustible material, have been treated with an approved evaporation-retarding product, and do not remain for a period in excess of 48 hours

14. In any automatic wet-pipe sprinkler system which has standard one-half inch sprinkler heads exposed to cold and subject to freezing, shut-off valves may be provided and the water supply discontinued

   A. under no circumstances
   B. from November 15 to March 15 when there are five or less such exposed heads
   C. from November 1 to April 1 when there are ten or less such exposed heads
   D. from November 15 to April 15 when there are fifteen or less such exposed heads

15. At an inspection of a building, one floor of which is used for combustible fiber storage, the following facts are revealed:
   I. The safe bearing capacity of the floor, as certified by the Department of Buildings, is 250 lbs./sq.ft. The weight of the combustible fiber is 75 lbs./sq.ft.
   II. The floor is 10,000 sq.ft. in area, of which 6,000 sq.ft. is occupied by the fiber bales.
   III. The height from floor to ceiling is 16', and the stacked bales stand 10' high.
   In this situation, _____ of the Fire Prevention Code.

   A. Item I is in
   B. Item II is in
   C. Item III is in
   D. there is no

16. Carelessness in smoking is a very common cause of fire.
   A lighted cigarette placed on top of most upholstery will GENERALLY

   A. cause no damage
   B. burn to the end without starting a fire

C. cause a gradually increasing fire
D. start a fire rapidly

17. The one of the following that is the type of automatic sprinkler system MOST commonly found in museums, art galleries, and storage places for records or valuable merchandise is the _____ system.

    A. deluge
    B. pre-action
    C. dry pipe
    D. sypho-chemical

18. The Fire Prevention Code requires that a permit be obtained for the storage of more than the equivalent of five barrels of oils and fats.
    The one of the following which is excluded from this requirement is

    A. lubricating oils
    B. grease
    C. edible oils
    D. soap stock

19. The Fire Prevention Code requires that rooms in dry cleaning establishments in which washing tanks are located be equipped with

    A. asbestos cloths or blankets
    B. carbon dioxide or dry chemical extinguishers
    C. buckets of sand
    D. automatic fire alarm device

20. The one of the following occupancies which is required to have a two-source water supply for its sprinkler system is one containing

    A. combustible fiber storage
    B. a motion picture film studio
    C. oils and fats storage
    D. a theater

21. The one of the following statements that is MOST accurate is that the Fire Prevention Code prohibits the storage of distilled liquors and alcohols in

    A. quantities aggregating more than 50 gallons, without a permit
    B. any building of wooden construction
    C. excess of one barrel for each five square feet of floor space
    D. barrels stacked more than one high

22. A special permit issued by the Fire Commissioner is required for the operation of certain businesses. Concerning parking lots, technical establishments, retail drug stores, and dry cleaning establishments, it is MOST accurate to say that special permits are required for all

    A. four of them
    B. of the above except parking lots
    C. of the above except technical establishments
    D. of the above except retail drug stores

5 (#4)

23. The one of the following chemicals which may NOT be manufactured or stored in a drug and chemical supply house in any quantity is

   A. acetone
   B. benzole
   C. chloride of nitrogen
   D. metallic magnesium

23.___

24. A permit is required for the storage of empty wooden packing boxes in buildings if the quantity stored exceeds

   A. one ton
   B. 2,000 square feet of area
   C. 2,000 cubic feet of space
   D. one ton or 2,000 square feet of area, whichever is the smaller amount

24.___

25. The MAXIMUM number of excess liquefied petroleum gas cylinders that may be stored in a single structure protected by an approved dry sprinkler system is

   A. 25   B. 50   C. 75   D. 100

25.___

KEY (CORRECT ANSWERS)

1. A
2. C
3. A
4. C
5. D

6. B
7. A
8. D
9. B
10. C

11. B
12. B
13. C
14. C
15. D

16. B
17. B
18. C
19. A
20. B

21. B
22. A
23. C
24. C
25. B

EXAMINATION SECTION
TEST 1

DIRECTIONS: Each question or incomplete statement is followed by several suggested answers or completions. Select the one that BEST answers the question or completes the statement. *PRINT THE LETTER OF THE CORRECT ANSWER IN THE SPACE AT THE RIGHT.*

1. During an inspection of a plant which manufactures paper products, the officer observes completed work being placed in paper cartons. The cartons are then stacked on wooden skids in a separate storage area awaiting shipment.
   The one of the following which is generally the MOST appropriate evaluation of the practice described in this situation is that skids

   A. are highly combustible, adding much fuel to the fire
   B. permit excess air flow to fires
   C. minimize water damage losses by raising stock off the floor
   D. provide space under the stock, thus permitting fire to be more readily extinguished

1.____

2. Assume that a three-story, Class 3 non-fireproof building has been converted to two-family use. There is one stairway to the street, 2'8" wide. The doors to the apartments all swing in. There are no fire escapes.
   The one of the following statements that is MOST accurate is that the situation as described

   A. complies with all applicable laws
   B. is illegal because the stairs are too narrow
   C. is illegal because two means of egress are required
   D. is illegal because the doors do not swing in the direction of egress

2.____

3. The flammability limits of aviation fuels are of little significance in understanding their fire hazard properties CHIEFLY because the fuels

   A. have practically the same limits
   B. form flammable vapor-air mixtures at all temperatures
   C. ignite readily under tank failure conditions
   D. resist flashing to vapor when in the gelled form

3.____

4. An inspector enters a luncheonette and discovers that the owner, the only person on duty, apparently does not understand English.
   The one of the following which would be the BEST action for the inspector to take in this situation is to attempt to

   A. make the owner understand by speaking English in a loud, clear voice
   B. make the owner understand by using sign language
   C. find a customer or passerby who can act as an interpreter
   D. question the owner closely to determine whether he really does not understand English

4.____

5. For proper protection of low flash point flammable liquid processes, automatic sprinkler protection with a strong water supply is essential.
   The BEST justification of this statement is that

5.____

A. a sprinkler system with a strong water supply will extinguish most fires involving such processes
B. water from sprinklers will reduce the intensity of burning of the liquid and the danger to exposures
C. although the sprinklers are ineffective on flammable liquid fires, they provide protection in the event of other types of fires
D. water from the sprinklers will dilute the flammable liquid and make extinguishment easier

6. According to the regulations, company commanders shall cause a thorough inspection of all schools within their administrative district.
Such inspections shall be made

   A. annually
   B. semi-annually
   C. at the beginning of each school term
   D. within 60 days after school opens for the fall term

7. While inspecting a garage, a fire inspector notices that a garage license has not been issued for the premises by the Department of Licenses.
The inspector should

   A. discontinue his inspection pending a determination by the Department of Licenses of the allowable motor vehicle occupancy
   B. complete his inspection and forward it (including a statement of the allowable motor vehicle occupancy) with a request that a copy be sent to the Department of Licenses
   C. discontinue his inspection and request that a communication (inquiry form) be sent to the Department of Licenses asking for an explanation
   D. complete his inspection and forward it with a request that the Department of Licenses be asked to determine the allowable motor vehicle occupancy

Questions 8-11.

DIRECTIONS: Questions 8 through 11 are to be answered on the basis of the information given in the following paragraph.

The principal value of inspection work is in the knowledge obtained relating to the various structural features of the building and the protective features provided. Knowledge of the location of stairways and elevators, the obstruction provided by merchandise, the danger from absorption of water by baled stock, the potential hazard of rupture of containers such as drums or cylinders, and the location of protective equipment, all are essential features to be noted and later discussed in company school and officer's college.

8. According to the above paragraph, the CHIEF value of inspection work is to gather information which will aid in

   A. fixing responsibility for fires
   B. planning firefighting operations
   C. training new firemen
   D. obtaining compliance with the Building Code

9. The one of the following objects which would be the MOST help in accomplishing the objective of the inspection as stated in the above paragraph is a

    A. copy of the Building Code
    B. chemical analysis kit
    C. plan of the building
    D. list of the building's tenants

10. An example of a *structural feature* contained in the above paragraph is the

    A. location of stairways and elevators
    B. obstruction provided by merchandise
    C. danger of absorption of water by baled stock
    D. hazard of rupture of containers such as drums or cylinders

11. Of the following, the BEST example of what is meant by a *protective feature*, as used in the above paragraph, is

    A. a fire extinguisher
    B. a burglar alarm
    C. fire insurance
    D. a medical first-aid kit

12. When a violation order is to be served and the owner or person in charge of the premises cannot readily be located, every effort shall be made to serve such order. Of the following statements concerning the attempts to serve such an order, the one that is NOT correct is:

    A. Attempt to ascertain from occupants or people in the area the name and address of the owner or management
    B. Send a member to effect service if the owner or management is located in the city but out of the company district
    C. Make an appointment by telephone for service of the order
    D. Post the violation notice prominently in or on the premises and mail a copy to the owner or management

13. Every applicant for a certificate of license to install underground gasoline storage tanks is required to

    A. be a resident of the city and maintain a place of business in the city
    B. file a bond and evidence of liability insurance
    C. be a resident of the city or maintain a place of business in the city
    D. pass a written examination given by the fire department

14. The Fire Prevention Code specifies that a special permit is required for each of the following EXCEPT

    A. refining petroleum collected from oil separators or manufacturing plants
    B. loading of small arms ammunition by hand in a retail store selling ammunition
    C. operating a wholesale drug or chemical house
    D. generating acetylene gas

15. The one of the following that is the MOST acceptable statement concerning the fire protection for the truck loading rack in a bulk oil terminal is that the rack must be equipped with a

A. water spray system, automatically controlled
B. foam system, remote manually controlled
C. water spray system, remote manually controlled
D. foam system, automatically controlled

16. The one of the following which is NOT in accord with the regulations for the use of Halon 1301, extinguishing agent, is that

    A. maximum concentration shall not exceed 10 percent where human habitation is present in the volume to be flooded
    B. minimum concentration of FE 1301 used shall not be less than 10 percent
    C. a discharge rate which results in attaining the design concentration in 8 seconds is acceptable
    D. a central office connection must be provided for fire detection or systems operating where human habitation is present in the volume to be flooded

17. Members of the uniformed force are authorized to issue summonses where fire perils exist, although it is generally preferable to first issue a violation order to correct the illegal condition.
However, members must issue a summons immediately in a licensed place of public assembly upon noting

    A. an obstructed revolving exit door in a crowded cabaret
    B. the absence of a certified standpipe system operator in a theatre
    C. an inoperative fire extinguishing system in a restaurant cooking duct
    D. standees in a motion picture theatre

18. During the course of an inspection at a blasting site, an officer notes that the magazine has been provided with electrical security devices, and that it contains eight 10-pound cartons of explosives which are to be stored overnight, overhead wires run from the magazine to the watchman's shanty, and the driller, without a C. of F., loads holes under the direct supervision of the blaster. The condition as described is generally ILLEGAL because

    A. explosives must be in original and unbroken packages of 50 or 25 pound capacity only
    B. storage of explosives between the hours of 10 P.M. and 6 A.M. is prohibited
    C. all electrical wiring must be protected by heavy wall conduit and be buried at least 12 inches deep
    D. no person may load holes in blasting operations unless they hold a certificate of fitness

19. The one of the following that is LEAST in accord with the regulations for the use of Halon 1301 extinguishing agent systems is that

    A. these systems are limited to applications as automatic total flooding systems for interior Class B and C fires and Class A fires that are not deep-seated
    B. abort systems are permitted for smoke detector activated systems which provide the manual capacity to *dump* the Halon 1301 immediately
    C. actuation of only one products-of-combustion device will fail to initiate the *dump* of Halon 1301 but will actuate the local and central office company alarms
    D. concentrations used shall not exceed 10 percent in areas where human habitation is present in the volume to be flooded

5 (#1)

20. Interstate transportation of petroleum products into and through the city in tank trucks which do NOT conform to fire department requirements is GENERALLY

    A. *not permitted* even when the pickups are all made outside the city and no pickups are made in the city
    B. *permitted* without restriction if the vehicles comply with United States Department of Transportation regulations governing interstate commerce
    C. *not permitted* where deliveries are to be made in the city
    D. *permitted* during non-business hours, along regularly established commercial routes

20.____

21. Of the following occupancies constructed and occupied in 1962, each of which accommodates less than 300 persons, the one that CANNOT be described as a *place of assembly,* according to the applicable building code, is a

    A. college assembly hall
    B. motion picture theatre
    C. courtroom
    D. legitimate theatre

21.____

22. According to the labor law, the one of the following conditions that is generally considered to be LEGAL in a 5-story building constructed and occupied as a factory since 1911 is that

    A. a single means of egress is provided from a floor of 2500 sq.ft. or less where no person is regularly employed
    B. no point on the upper floor which is equipped with an approved sprinkler system is more than 200 feet distant from an exit
    C. one of the two required stairways extends to the roof from which there is egress to an adjacent building
    D. there are double swinging doors leading to an exit on an upper floor where more than 5 persons are employed

22.____

23. Certain old factory buildings may be found to have some fire escapes which are not in accordance with the requirements of the labor law.
    It is generally CORRECT to state of these substandard factory exits that they

    A. may be used in computing occupancy exit requirements if maintained in good repair and the building is equipped with an automatic sprinkler
    B. must be provided with a counterbalanced stairway in lieu of the former drop ladder in guides
    C. shall be kept clear of all obstructions and periodically used during required fire drills
    D. may not be equipped with any exit or directional sign at the openings leading thereto

23.____

24. According to the labor law, the use of plate glass in fire windows in fireproof buildings is

    A. *prohibited,* except in buildings less than 75 feet in height
    B. *permitted,* if the fire windows are located more than 30 feet horizontally from the nearest opening in the wall of another building
    C. *prohibited* for use in all fire windows in fireproof buildings
    D. *permitted* if the fire windows are more than 30 feet above the roof of a building within a horizontal distance of 25 feet

24.____

25. Under certain conditions, a newsstand may be located in a street floor lobby which serves as an exit passageway for a building constructed after 1976.
The one of the following which is NOT one of these conditions is that the newsstand must

   A. occupy no more than 100 square feet or 5 percent of the net floor area of the lobby, whichever is greater
   B. not reduce the clear width of the lobby at any point
   C. be located at least 30 feet from an exit door
   D. be protected by at least 2 automatic sprinkler heads if constructed of combustible material

KEY (CORRECT ANSWERS)

1. C
2. A
3. C
4. C
5. B

6. A
7. D
8. B
9. C
10. A

11. A
12. D
13. C
14. D
15. C

16. B
17. C
18. D
19. D
20. D

21. C
22. B
23. A
24. B
25. B

TEST 2

DIRECTIONS: Each question or incomplete statement is followed by several suggested answers or completions. Select the one that BEST answers the question or completes the statement. *PRINT THE LETTER OF THE CORRECT ANSWER IN THE SPACE AT THE RIGHT.*

1. Suppose that a factory has stored within it a number of substances. 1.____
   If the owner asked you which of the following is MOST likely to constitute a fire hazard, you would reply

   A. sodium chloride
   B. calcium chloride
   C. chromium
   D. silicon dioxide

2. Vertical openings, such as dumbwaiters, elevators, and chutes, are the bane of a fire- 2.____
   fighting force.
   This condition arises MAINLY because the existence of such openings in a burning building facilitates

   A. accidental falls
   B. generation of gases
   C. spread of the fire
   D. the perpetration of arson

3. Suppose that a neighbor were to ask you whether there is more hazard in the use of ker- 3.____
   osene than gasoline at ordinary room temperature.
   You should reply that there is MORE hazard in the use of

   A. *kerosene,* because it gives off dangerous quantities of explosive vapors which are lighter than air
   B. *gasoline,* because gasoline vapor may flow along the floor and be ignited at a long distance from its point of origin
   C. *kerosene,* because its flash point is very low
   D. *gasoline,* particularly because when ignited it burns

4. Steel supporting beams in buildings often are surrounded by a thin layer of concrete to 4.____
   keep the beams from becoming hot and collapsing during a fire.
   The one of the following statements which BEST explains how collapse is prevented by this arrangement is that concrete

   A. becomes stronger as its temperature is increased
   B. acts as an insulating material
   C. protects the beam from rust and corrosion
   D. reacts chemically with steel at high temperatures

5. It has been suggested that property owners should be charged a fee each time the Fire 5.____
   Department is called to extinguish a fire on their property.
   Of the following, the BEST reason for *rejecting* this proposal is that

   A. delay in calling the Fire Department may result
   B. many property owners don't occupy the property they own
   C. property owners may resent such a charge as they pay real estate taxes
   D. it may be difficult to determine on whose property a fire started

6. An officer inspecting buildings in a commercial area came to one whose outside surface appeared to be of natural stone. The owner told the officer that it was not necessary to inspect his building as it was *fireproof*. The officer, however, completed his inspection of the building.
Of the following, the BEST reason for continuing the inspection is that

   A. stone buildings catch fire as readily as wooden buildings
   B. the Fire Department cannot make exceptions in its inspection procedures
   C. the building may have been built of imitation stone
   D. interiors and contents of stone buildings can catch fire

7. From the viewpoint of fire safety, the CHIEF advantage of a foam rubber mattress compared to a cotton mattress is that the foam rubber mattress

   A. is slower burning
   B. generates less heat when burning
   C. does not smolder
   D. is less subject to water damage

8. At a social gathering, a fire chief hears a man who describes himself as the owner of the XYZ factory state that he *pays off* fire department inspectors who visit his establishment. When the chief asks the man whether he will repeat his statement under oath, the man refuses with the remark, *I am not looking for trouble.*
In this situation, the chief should

   A. forget the incident since the factory owner is not willing to give evidence
   B. investigate the background and reputation of the man to determine whether he really owns the factory and has any reason for making false statements about the fire department
   C. report the incident to police authorities
   D. report the incident to higher authorities in the fire department

9. The one of the following methods of storing large piles of coal which is undesirable because it increases the danger of spontaneous heating is

   A. making the pile compact by use of a roller
   B. storing the coal on smooth, solid ground
   C. covering the sides and top of the pile with road tar
   D. mixing coal of various sizes in one pile

10. The one of the following materials which has the LEAST tendency to spontaneous heating is

    A. baled hides
    B. bagged charcoal
    C. bulk fish scrap
    D. boxed mineral wool

11. In most buildings in which lighting is provided by artificial means and an auxiliary system for emergency exit lighting is not provided, phosphorescent exit and directional signs are required.
Of the following occupancies, the one which is generally EXCLUDED from this requirement is a

    A. warehouse
    B. school dormitory
    C. hospital
    D. library

12. In determining overcrowding or adequacy of means of egress, a fire officer must be aware that the minimum number of persons to be provided for in any floor area shall be the number which can be accommodated within the net floor area at a given occupancy and area per person.
Accordingly, the GREATEST concentration of persons to be provided for will be generally found in a

    A. basement sales area
    B. high school classroom
    C. dance hall
    D. work room

13. Of the following statements, the one that is generally ACCURATE concerning the installation of combustible luminous suspended ceilings is that they may

    A. not be installed below an existing suspended ceiling
    B. be installed below existing sprinkler heads
    C. not be used in any room in occupancy group F (assembly)
    D. be installed in corridors not exceeding 100 sq.ft.

14. The building code exempts from the sprinkler requirements those floors which are generally unventilated but are equipped with a given openable area.
A fixed window will be considered openable if it is

    A. equipped with an interior heat sensitive device to actuate the automatic fire shutters
    B. of frangible glass panels and located 15 feet below grade
    C. within 8 feet of an openable window of at least 3 feet x 3 feet dimension
    D. readily broken and not more than 110 feet above grade

15. Of the following, the MOST complete and accurate statement about exit requirements is that there shall be at least two door openings, remote from each other and leading to exits from every room or enclosed space, in a business occupancy (E) in which the total occupant load *exceeds*

    A. 25   B. 50   C. 75   D. 100

16. On October 23, 1976, 25 persons died and many were injured as a result of an arson fire in an illegal social club in the Bronx.
Of the following, the MOST probable contributory cause of this multiple loss of life was the

    A. door to the club was not self-closing and was opened in the direction of egress when the fire occurred
    B. front windows had been bricked-up and prevented access by department ladders
    C. confusing layout caused many patrons to bypass the secondary means of egress and become trapped in the toilet rooms
    D. original lath and plaster had been replaced by combustible wood paneling and there had been an extensive use of highly flammable decorations

17. It is INCORRECT for a fire officer giving training on the protection of electronic data processing (EDP) units and ancillary equipment against fire damage to state that

A. the design features of EDP units make them relatively resistant to damage by temperatures under 600° F
B. smoke and acids produced by fire can adversely affect the operation of computer equipment and magnetic components
C. the heat and steam produced by a fire and its extinguishment that would not normally damage ordinary paper records may easily damage magnetic tapes
D. in cases where fire can spread throughout or beyond the computer's housing, a fixed CO_2 system may be required

18. Of the following exit and access requirements relating to dead-end corridors in various occupancy group buildings, it is generally MOST accurate to state that

    A. no more than one classroom shall be permitted on a dead-end corridor in an educational occupancy
    B. storage of combustible materials in non-combustible lockers is permitted in dead-end corridors in an institutional occupancy
    C. dead-end corridors are not permitted in an assembly occupancy
    D. no more than one patient bedroom is permitted in a dead-end corridor in an institutional occupancy

19. In the past, building marquee collapses have resulted in the injury or death of firefighters. According to the new building code, marquees are generally

    A. not permitted
    B. permitted if supported by incombustible piers at the curb line
    C. not permitted to project beyond the street line
    D. permitted on buildings of a public nature but may have to be removed if the building occupancy is changed

20. When a standpipe system is altered, extended, or extensively repaired, it must undergo certain inspections and tests.
    Of the following, it is generally MOST accurate to state that the

    A. entire system shall be subjected to the hydrostatic test pressure
    B. altered, new or repaired section shall be subjected to the pressure test and the entire system subjected to the flow test
    C. flow test shall be confined to a determination that water is available at the top outlet of each riser
    D. pressure test in buildings not exceeding 3 stories or 40 feet in height need only sustain 150 percent of the normal hydrostatic pressure at the topmost hose outlet

21. A substance which is subject to *spontaneous combustion* is one that

    A. is explosive when heated
    B. is capable of catching fire without an external source of heat
    C. acts to speed up the burning of material
    D. liberates oxygen when heated

Questions 22-25.

DIRECTIONS: Questions 22 through 25 are to be answered on the basis of the following paragraph.

For the five-year period 2006-2010, inclusive, the average annual fire loss in the United States amounted to approximately $1,354,830,000. Included in this estimate is $1,072,666,000 damage to buildings and contents, and $282,164,000 average annual loss in aircraft, motor vehicles, forest and other miscellaneous fires not involving buildings. Preliminary estimates indicate that the total United States fire loss in 2011 was $1,615,000,000. These are property damage fire losses only and do not include indirect losses resulting from fires which are just as real and sometimes far more serious than property damage losses. But because evaluation of indirect monetary losses is usually very difficult, their importance in the national fire waste picture is often overlooked.

22. According to the data in the above paragraph, the BEST of the following estimates of the total direct fire loss in the United States for the six-year period 2006-2011, inclusive, is

    A. $1,400,000,000
    B. $2,700,000,000
    C. $7,000,000,000
    D. $8,400,000,000

23. The BEST example of an indirect fire loss, as that term is used in the above paragraph, is monetary loss due to

    A. smoke or water damage to exposures
    B. condemnation of foodstuffs following a fire
    C. interruption of business following a fire
    D. forcible entry by firemen operating at a fire

24. Suppose that during the period 2011-2015 the average annual fire loss to buildings and contents increases 10 percent, and the average annual loss due to fires not involving buildings decreases 10 percent. The MOST valid of the following conclusions is that the average annual fire loss for the 2011-2015 period, compared to the losses for the 2006-2011 period,

    A. will increase
    B. will decrease
    C. will be unchanged
    D. cannot be calculated from the information given

25. If a comparison is made between total annual direct and indirect fire losses on the basis of the information given in the above paragraph, the MOST valid of the following conclusions is that

    A. generally, direct losses are higher
    B. generally, indirect losses are higher
    C. generally, direct and indirect losses are approximately equal
    D. there is not sufficient information to determine which is higher or if they are approximately equal

KEY (CORRECT ANSWERS)

1. D
2. C
3. B
4. B
5. A

6. D
7. C
8. D
9. D
10. D

11. D
12. A
13. C
14. A
15. D

16. A
17. C
18. A
19. D
20. C

21. B
22. D
23. C
24. A
25. D

TEST 3

DIRECTIONS: Each question or incomplete statement is followed by several suggested answers or completions. Select the one that BEST answers the question or completes the statement. *PRINT THE LETTER OF THE CORRECT ANSWER IN THE SPACE AT THE RIGHT.*

1. It has been suggested that companies be given additional Apparatus Field Inspection Duty and other inspectional duties as punishment for poor performance of evolutions, poor condition of equipment or quarters, etc.
   Of the following, the MOST valid objection to this proposal is that

   A. the punishment does not directly improve the skills or functions which are found to be deficient
   B. inspectional activities would be degraded by making such assignments a form of punishment
   C. the punishment is imposed on a group rather than on an individual basis
   D. scheduling of regular inspectional activities would be disrupted

2. The Administrative Code authorizes members to issue summonses in cases arising under laws relating to fires and to fire peril.
   Departmental regulations require that such summonses be returnable in the appropriate court _____ than 14 calendar days, _____ Sundays and holidays.

   A. not less; including
   B. not less; excluding
   C. not more; including
   D. not more; excluding

3. When conducting an Apparatus Field Inspection of an occupancy with a required and approved sprinkler system, it is MOST important, of the following, for firemen to make certain that

   A. feeder lines are adequate to supply the number of sprinkler heads
   B. sprinkler heads are sufficient and properly spaced
   C. stock does not interfere with the proper distribution of water from sprinkler heads
   D. records of monthly hydrostatic pressure tests are properly kept and are up to date

4. While inspecting an above-ground storage tank installation, an inspector notices leakage of the contents through *weep* holes in a tank.
   This is a sign that the

   A. tank contents are under excessive pressure
   B. strength of the entire tank may be endangered by corrosion
   C. volumetric capacity of the tank has been exceeded
   D. tank is *breathing* as intended

5. A member on inspectional duty came across, in a building under construction, a propane gas heater with its safety valve negated by means of wire and tape across the buttons at the top of the safety assembly.
   Of the following actions taken by the member in this situation, the one that is NOT in accord with departmental orders is the

A. serving of a violation order to discontinue use of devices to negate safety features on propane gas heaters on premises
B. picking up of the permits for storage and use of propane
C. notification of the Battalion Chief of the administrative district concerned
D. impounding of the propane heater

6. Of the following, the PRIMARY purpose of holding fire tests at a high-rise office building is to

   A. determine the hazard of polyurethane insulation
   B. evaluate the effectiveness of sprinklers with a limited water supply
   C. test the effectiveness of stair pressurization
   D. develop procedures for venting the fire floor by window vents

7. At the first sign of a fire, the manager of a motion picture theatre had the lights turned on and made the following announcement: *Ladies and gentlemen, the management has found it necessary to dismiss the audience. Please remain seated until it is time for your aisle to file out. In leaving the theatre, follow the directions of the ushers. There is no danger involved.*
The manager's action in this situation was

   A. *proper*
   B. *improper,* chiefly because he did not tell the audience the reason for the dismissal
   C. *improper,* chiefly because he did not permit all members of the audience to leave at once
   D. *improper,* chiefly because he misled the audience by saying that there was no danger

8. Generally, sprinkler heads must be replaced each time they are used.
The BEST explanation of why this is necessary is that the sprinkler heads

   A. are subject to rusting after discharging water
   B. may become clogged after discharging water
   C. have a distorted pattern of discharge of water after use
   D. are set off by the effect of heat on metal and cannot be reset

9. A fire insurance inspector suggested to the manager of a fireproof warehouse that bags of flour be stacked on skids (wooden platforms 6" high, 6x6 feet in area). Of the following, the BEST justification for this suggestion is that in the event of a fire, the bags on skids are less likely to

   A. topple
   B. be damaged by water used in extinguishment
   C. catch fire
   D. be ripped by fire equipment

10. Permitting piles of scrap paper cuttings to accumulate in a factory building is a bad practice CHIEFLY because they may

    A. ignite spontaneously
    B. interfere with fire extinguishment operations
    C. catch fire from a spark or smoldering match
    D. interfere with escape of occupants if a fire occurs

11. High grass and weeds should not be permitted to grow near a building CHIEFLY because, in the event of a grass fire, the weeds and grass may

   A. give off toxic fumes
   B. limit maneuverability of firemen
   C. interfere with the escape of occupants from the building
   D. bring the fire to the building and set it on fire

12. Visitors near patients in *oxygen tents* are not permitted to smoke.
   The BEST of the following reasons for this prohibition is that

   A. the flame of the cigarette or cigar may flare dangerously
   B. smoking tobacco is irritating to persons with respiratory disease
   C. smoking in bed is one of the major causes of fires
   D. diseases may be transmitted by means of tobacco smoke

13. A MAJOR difference between the building code currently in effect and the one in effect prior to it is that in the current code

   A. doors to the outside grade must be the same size as corridor doors
   B. sprinklering of a building will permit a reduction in total door width
   C. the width of an exit door is based on the width of the corridor leading to it
   D. the width of exit doors is based on both the number of persons and the type of occupancy

14. While inspecting a one-story factory building erected in 1962, you notice that an exit door has been relocated. The size, location, and lighting of all exits in the building comply with the old building code in effect before.
   To determine whether the relocated exit is a legal one, it is necessary to check the provisions of

   A. the State Labor Law and the new building code for the relocated exit *only*
   B. the State Labor Law *only*
   C. the new building code for the relocated exit *only*
   D. none of the foregoing since checking the old building code is sufficient

15. The new building code divides the construction clauses into two major construction groups.
   These two groups are called

   A. fireproof and non-fireproof
   B. rigid frame and flexible frame
   C. commercial and residential
   D. combustible and noncombustible

16. The State Labor Law requires that the balconies and stairways of outside fire escapes be able to safely sustain a live load, in pounds per square foot, of _____ with a safety factor of _____.

   A. 75; two   B. 90; four   C. 105; two   D. 120; four

17. A plant manufacturing nitro-cellulose products has 100 employees. The Fire Prevention Code requires that these premises be equipped with fire pails filled with water. The required MINIMUM number of such pails must be

    A. 25   B. 50   C. 75   D. 100

18. The MAIN purpose of an oil separator is to

    A. separate volatile inflammable oils from other oils
    B. provide a fireproof block between a spark or flame device and an oil storage tank
    C. prevent volatile inflammable oils from flowing into a sewer
    D. make it impossible for the wrong kind of oil to be delivered from a bulk storage plant

19. The MAXIMUM quantity of fuel oil permitted to be stored in an exposed tank in the cellar of a two-family dwelling is _____ gallons.

    A. 225   B. 550   C. 750   D. 875

20. According to the Fire Prevention Code, the MAXIMUM quantity of paint (other than water base) that may be stored without a permit is _____ gallons.

    A. 10   B. 15   C. 20   D. 25

21. Of the following licenses, certificates of qualification, or certificates of fitness, the Fire Department does NOT issue the one authorizing the holder to

    A. operate refrigerating machines (unlimited capacity)
    B. install underground storage tanks for gasoline
    C. operate low pressure boilers using #6 oil
    D. install oil burning equipment

22. In the course of your work in a residential area, you see a wood frame, brick veneer dwelling, two-stories and attic in height, erected in 1965. The building is occupied by two families, with a living room in the attic.
    Without special approval by the Board of Standards and Appeals, this condition could

    A. not be legal
    B. be legal provided that there is a fire escape from the attic
    C. be legal provided the stair enclosure is properly fire retarded
    D. be legal provided that the attic living room is not used as a bedroom

23. A typical occupancy falling into the Assembly occupancy group as used in the building code would be a

    A. radio station   B. library
    C. nursing home   D. tavern

24. Of the following situations, the one in which a fire escape may NOT be considered a legal means of egress is in a three-story

    A. factory building erected in 1912
    B. mixed occupancy building with a store on the first floor and one family on each of the floors above, erected in 1965
    C. multiple dwelling erected in 1971
    D. office building erected in 1950 and altered in 1972

25. A storage garage is one that has   25.____
    A. a stock room for repair parts for vehicles
    B. an area for vehicles that are not used on a daily basis
    C. a gasoline tank to supply gasoline to the vehicles
    D. room only for vehicles that are to be sold

KEY (CORRECT ANSWERS)

1.	B	11.	D
2.	A	12.	A
3.	C	13.	D
4.	B	14.	B
5.	A	15.	D
6.	C	16.	B
7.	A	17.	B
8.	D	18.	C
9.	B	19.	B
10.	C	20.	C

21. D
22. A
23. D
24. C
25. C

TEST 4

DIRECTIONS: Each question or incomplete statement is followed by several suggested answers or completions. Select the one that BEST answers the question or completes the statement. *PRINT THE LETTER OF THE CORRECT ANSWER IN THE SPACE AT THE RIGHT.*

1. A violation order is to be served requiring the immediate removal of liquefied petroleum gas cylinders when such cylinders are found on construction sites without a permit issued by the Fire Department.
   Pending removal of such cylinders,

   A. vacate procedures are to be instituted
   B. a fireman is to be detailed to the site to safeguard the illegally stored gas cylinders
   C. the contractor is to be ordered to provide a watchman to safeguard the illegally stored gas cylinders
   D. the Police Department is to be notified so that a patrolman can be assigned to the site to safeguard the illegally stored gas cylinders

   1.___

2. A four-story loft building is now occupied as follows: Street level - furniture repair and refinishing shop; 2nd story - one apartment occupied by an artist-in-residence, wife, and 5 young children; 3rd story - two apartments each occupied by an artist-in-residence and his wife; 4th story - one apartment occupied by an artist-in-residence, his wife, and his mother-in-law. The building is non-fireproof construction, 40' x 70', is 50' in height, and has an automatic wet sprinkler system protecting the furniture shop. The occupancy as described is

   A. *legal*
   B. *illegal,* because the sprinkler system does not extend throughout the building
   C. *illegal,* because the number of occupants exceeds the permissible limits
   D. *illegal,* because of the presence of the furniture repair and refinishing shop

   2.___

3. Some organizations have adopted the National Fire Protection Association diamond-shaped coding system for identifying characteristics of hazardous materials. The diamond shown in the diagram at the right has its boxes labeled W, X, Y, and Z.
   Under the National Fire Protection Association coding system, the lettered boxes represent, respectively,

   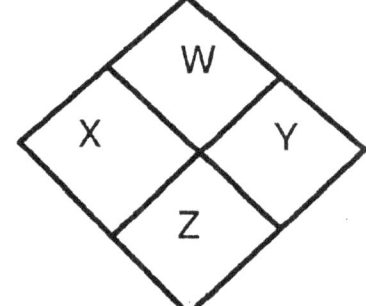

   A. X - Health, Y - Reactive, W - Flammable
   B. X - Reactive, Y - Flammable, W - Health
   C. X - Health, Y - Reactive, Z - Flammable
   D. X - Flammable, Y - Health, Z - Reactive

   3.___

4. The shut sprinkler control valve is one of industry's greatest fire hazards. When it is necessary to shut down a system for repairs or other reasons, certain precautions should be taken.
Of the following statements regarding such precautions, the LEAST acceptable is to

   A. have the system shut down during non-working hours
   B. have the system shut down during working hours while normal operations are going on
   C. notify the Fire Department of the intended shutdown
   D. prepare to supply the system through the two-inch drain in the event of an emergency or fire

Questions 5-8.

DIRECTIONS: Questions 5 through 8 are to be answered on the basis of the information given in the following paragraph.

A mixture of a combustible vapor and air will burn only when the proportion of fuel to air lies within a certain range, i.e., between the upper and lower limits of flammability. If a third, non-combustible gas is now added to the mixture, the limits will be narrowed. As increasing amounts of diluent are added, the limits come closer until, at a certain critical concentration, they will converge. This is the peak concentration. It is the minimum amount of diluent that will inhibit the combustion of any fuel-air mixture.

5. If additional diluent is added beyond the peak concentration, the flammable limits of the mixture will

   A. converge rapidly
   B. diverge slowly
   C. diverge rapidly
   D. not be affected

6. If the four numbers listed below were peak concentration values obtained in a test of four diluents, then the MOST efficient diluent would have the value of

   A. 7.5
   B. 10
   C. 12.5
   D. 15

7. The word *inhibit,* as used in the last sentence of the above paragraph, means MOST NEARLY

   A. slow the rate of
   B. prevent entirely the occurrence of
   C. reduce the intensity of
   D. retard to an appreciable extent the manifestation of

8. The one of the graphs shown below which BEST represents the process described in the paragraph is

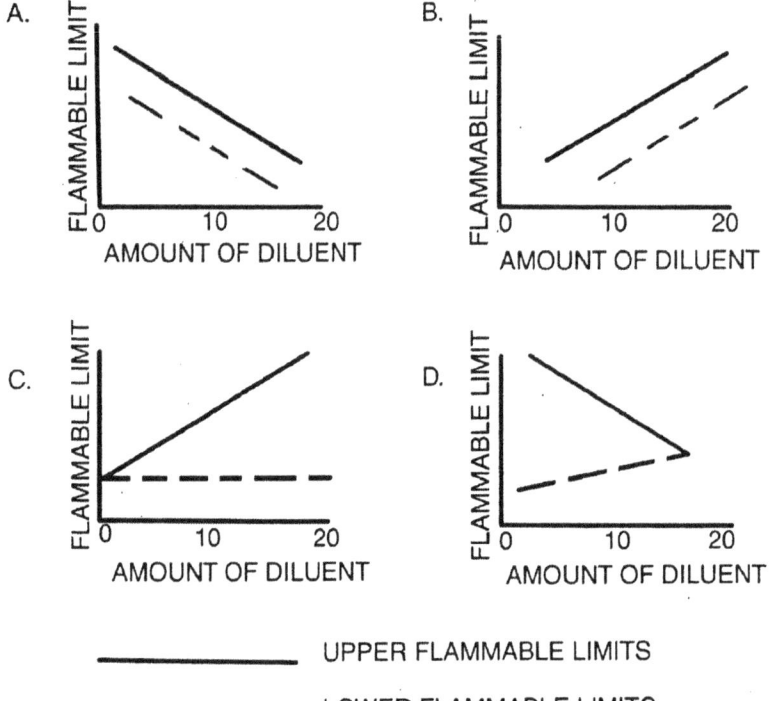

UPPER FLAMMABLE LIMITS
— — — — — LOWER FLAMMABLE LIMITS

9. Of the following metals, the one which is LEAST acceptable as a non-sparking metal for tools is

   A. hardened copper
   B. bronze
   C. brass
   D. copper alloys

10. Of the heating defects responsible for hotel fires, the MAJOR defect is

    A. defective flues
    B. overheated appliances
    C. defective appliances
    D. inadequate clearance

11. Community relations and fire prevention education efforts must be concentrated in residential neighborhoods, particularly in the depressed areas of the city.
    The one of the following which does NOT provide support for this point of view is that

    A. residential occupants are exposed to more serious occupancy hazards than industrial workers
    B. open hydrants, excessive false alarms, and hostile acts are concentrated in depressed areas
    C. rubbish fires and vacant building fires are most frequent in these areas
    D. the primary incidence of fire takes place in residential areas

12. The State Multiple Dwelling Law allows a *family* to have four boarders, and the City Multiple Dwelling Law allows a *family* to have only two boarders.
    In the city, a *family* is allowed

A. two boarders because the Multiple Dwelling Code is the more restrictive requirement
B. four boarders because the State law takes precedence over the city code
C. two or four boarders, depending upon whether the Law or Code applies to a given situation
D. two or four boarders, at the discretion of the Fire Commissioner

13. Fire Department regulations governing the issuance of city-wide permits for the use of combustible gases during temporary torch operations require fire guards to make inspections after completion of torch operations for the purpose of detecting fire. Signed inspection reports are to be filed and available for examination by the Fire Department.
The one of the following which is MOST accurate and complete is that such inspections are to be made _____ after completion of operations.

    A. every 15 minutes, for a period of one hour,
    B. one-half hour and one hour
    C. every half hour, for a period of two hours,
    D. one half hour, one hour, and two hours,

14. On an A.F.I.D., a company comes upon the following garages:
    I. Adjacent to a dwelling occupied by one family, storing two cars, one owned by the family and the other by the next door neighbor who pays a monthly rental
    II. In a dwelling outside the fire limits, occupied by one family storing three cars owned by the family
    III. In a fireproof dwelling occupied by three families in two stories above the garage, with two means of egress and no entrances to any apartment through the garage, storing two cars owned by tenants

    A Fire Department permit is required for

    A. none of these garages   B. garages I and III
    C. garages II and III   D. all three garages

15. If a building is altered under the provisions of the building code, and the building is not provided with sprinkler protection, the one of the following actions that the company officer should take is to

    A. transmit an A-8 report for referral to the Department of Buildings
    B. issue a summons to the owner of the building
    C. prepare a report on Department letterhead and send it to the Division of Fire Prevention
    D. call the Department of Buildings and notify them about the violation

16. The one of the following fibers that can be made into fabric which can be effectively treated with common water-soluble-salt flame-retardant solutions is

    A. dacron   B. nylon   C. rayon   D. nomex

17. The inspection of public assembly occupancies classified as theatres in company administrative districts should be scheduled so that each such premises is inspected AT LEAST once every

    A. 30 days, approximately one half hour before scheduled performances
    B. 30 days, at irregular time periods when premises are open to the public

C. three months, approximately one half hour before scheduled performances
D. three months, at irregular time periods when premises are open to the public

18. The one of the following automatic fire alarm detectors that works on the principle of uneven expansion of bi-metallic strips is the _____ device.

    A. rate compensation
    B. ionization type
    C. rate of rise type
    D. fixed temperature

19. The one of the following which is probably the MOST frequent source of ignition of flammable vapors in hospital operating rooms is

    A. static electricity
    B. x-ray equipment
    C. sterilizing machinery
    D. electric cauterizing devices

20. At an open demonstration, polyurethane foam, widely used in furniture, was exposed to fire.
    In this demonstration, it was shown that the foam

    A. was self-extinguishing
    B. flamed and gave off acrid smoke
    C. could not be ignited
    D. melted but would not flame

Questions 21-23.

DIRECTIONS: Questions 21 through 23 are to be answered on the basis of the following paragraph.

Shafts extending into the top story, except those stair shafts where the stairs do not continue to the roof, shall be carried through and at least two feet above the roof. Every shaft extending above the roof, except open shafts and elevator shafts, shall be enclosed at the top with a roof of materials having a fire resistive rating of one hour and a metal skylight covering at least three-quarters of the area of the shaft in the top story, except that skylights over stair shafts shall have an area not less than one-tenth the area of the shaft in the top story, but shall be not less than fifteen square feet in area. Any shaft terminating below the top story of a structure and those stair shafts not required to extend through the roof shall have the top enclosed with materials having the same fire resistive rating as required for the shaft enclosure.

21. The above paragraph states that the elevator shafts which extend into the top story are

    A. not required to have a skylight but are required to extend at least two feet above the roof
    B. neither required to have a skylight nor to extend above the roof
    C. required to have a skylight covering at least three-quarters of the area of the shaft in the top story and to extend at least two feet above the roof
    D. required to have a skylight covering at least three-quarters of the area of the shaft in the top story but are not required to extend above the roof

22. The one of the following skylights which meets the requirements of the above paragraph is a skylight measuring   22._____

    A. 4' x 4' over a stair shaft which, on the top story, measures 20' x 9'
    B. 4 1/2' x 3 1/2' over a pipe shaft which, on the top story, measures 5' x 4'
    C. 2 1/2' x 1 1/2' over a dumbwaiter shaft which, on the top story, measures 2 1/2' x 2 1/2'
    D. 4' x 3' over a stair shaft which, on the top story, measures 15' x 6'

23. Suppose that in a Class I building, a shaft which does not go to the roof is required to have a three-hour fire resistive rating.   23._____
In regard to the material enclosing the top of this shaft, the above paragraph

    A. states that a one-hour fire resistive rating is required
    B. states that a three-hour fire resistive rating is required
    C. implies that no fire resistive rating is required
    D. neither states nor implies anything about the fire resistive rating

Questions 24-25.

DIRECTIONS: Questions 24 and 25 are to be answered SOLELY on the basis of the following passage.

The four different types of building collapses are as follows:

1. <u>Building Wall Collapse</u> - An outside wall of the building collapses but the floors maintain their positions.

2. <u>Lean-to Collapse</u> - One end of a floor collapses onto the floor below it. This leaves a sheltered area on the floor below.

3. <u>Floor Collapse</u> - An entire floor falls to the floor below it but large pieces of machinery in the floor below provide spaces which can provide shelter.

4. <u>Pancake Collapse</u> - A floor collapses completely onto the floor below it, leaving no spaces. In some cases, the force of this collapse causes successive lower floors to collapse.

24. The MOST serious injuries are likely to occur at _____ collapses.   24._____

    A. pancake   B. lean-to
    C. floor   D. building wall

25. Of the following, a floor collapse is MOST likely to occur in a(n)   25._____

    A. apartment building   B. private home
    C. factory building   D. hotel

26. When using a standardized survey report during AFID, it generally is NOT advisable to make an inspection of the facilities in the strict sequence of the items on the form PRIMARILY because the   26._____

    A. sequence of the items in the form may not correspond to the physical arrangement of the occupancy or structure
    B. members performing inspection duty will be more likely to make errors of omission rather than commission on the forms

C. occupancy or structure may require a multi-inspector, multi-page form inspectional approach
D. procedure does not permit distribution of tasks among all the members participating in the inspection

27. Sparks given off by welding torches are a serious fire hazard.
The BEST of the following methods of dealing with this hazard is to conduct welding operations only

   A. in fireproof buildings protected by sprinkler systems
   B. out-of-doors on a day with little wind blowing
   C. on materials certified to be non-combustible by recognized testing laboratories
   D. after loose combustible materials have been cleared from the area and with a man standing by with a hose line

28. Two types of steel hoops are commonly found on older wooden gravity tanks - round hoops and flat ones.
The one of the following statements concerning such hoops that is MOST accurate is that hidden corrosion is a serious problem with _____ hoops.

   A. the round hoops but not with the flat
   B. the flat hoops but not with the round
   C. both types of
   D. neither type of

29. While on AFID, you come across a clothing factory which shows evidence of poor housekeeping practices.
For you to imply to the owner that the Fire Department will conduct frequent inspections of his premises until satisfactory conditions are maintained is

   A. *proper,* mainly because the owner may be persuaded by it to maintain satisfactory conditions
   B. *improper,* mainly because the owner may feel that he is being harassed
   C. *proper,* mainly because any means which result in the elimination of hazardous conditions are permissible
   D. *improper,* mainly because threats which may not be carried out should not be made

30. Generally, officers on fire prevention inspection duty do not inspect the living quarters of private dwellings unless the occupants agree to the inspection.
The BEST of the following explanations of why private dwellings are excluded from compulsory inspections is that

   A. private dwellings seldom catch fire
   B. fires in private dwellings are more easily extinguished than other types of fires
   C. people may resent such inspections as an invasion of privacy
   D. the monetary value of private dwellings is lower than that of other types of occupancies

KEY (CORRECT ANSWERS)

1.	C	11.	A	21.	A
2.	D	12.	A	22.	B
3.	A	13.	B	23.	B
4.	B	14.	B	24.	A
5.	D	15.	A	25.	C
6.	A	16.	C	26.	A
7.	B	17.	A	27.	D
8.	D	18.	D	28.	B
9.	C	19.	A	29.	A
10.	A	20.	B	30.	C

EXAMINATION SECTION
TEST 1

DIRECTIONS: Each question or incomplete statement is followed by several suggested answers or completions. Select the one that BEST answers the question or completes the statement. *PRINT THE LETTER OF THE CORRECT ANSWER IN THE SPACE AT THE RIGHT.*

1. A television receiver has a GREATER inherent fire hazard than a conventional radio receiver because

    A. of greater electrical leakage
    B. cabinets are inadequately ventilated
    C. higher voltage is used in the system
    D. they are operated for longer periods of time
    E. the coaxial cable lead-in is covered with a highly flammable coating

    1.____

2. Of the following, the MOST frequent factor contributing to conflagrations in the United States and Canada in the last 25 years has been

    A. high winds
    B. lack of exposure protection
    C. delayed alarms
    D. congestion of hazardous occupancies
    E. inadequate water distribution system

    2.____

3. If, upon reinspection of a plant which has 30 days to comply with a previous order, you find that the order has not been completely obeyed but that some work has taken place, you SHOULD

    A. report to proper authorities to obtain legal action
    B. assume the delay is unavoidable and check again in 30 days
    C. inform the person in charge that a 10-day extension will be granted and that legal action will be taken if the order has not been followed
    D. issue a summons for failure to comply
    E. none of the above

    3.____

4. An analysis of loss records in one city showed that one-third of the total loss in building fires was in residence buildings and that, of the total loss in such buildings, in the year under study, nearly 80 percent was in multiple dwelling buildings.
The one of the following courses of action for the Fire Department which should be taken IMMEDIATELY on the basis of this report is to

    A. relocate companies
    B. recommend sprinkler protection for multiple dwellings
    C. institute special training fighting multiple dwelling fires
    D. reduce the protection given to other than multiple dwelling residences
    E. inspect multiple dwellings more thoroughly

    4.____

5. It is good practice to so install heating devices that under conditions of maximum heat (long-continued exposure) they will not cause the temperature of exposed woodwork to exceed 160° F. This practice is

    5.____

A. *correct*, because of the possibility that wood and other combustible materials, after long-continued exposure to relatively moderate heat, may ignite at temperatures far below their usual ignition temperatures
B. *not correct*, because no wood in ordinary use will ignite at a temperature of less than 400°F and, consequently, the requirement is needlessly severe
C. *correct*, because oxidation proceeds much more rapidly at higher temperatures
D. *not correct*, because oxidation proceeds much more slowly at higher temperatures
E. *correct*, because under prolonged heating the temperature of the air in the room will build up until the ignition point is reached unless the applied temperature is kept sufficiently low

6. Analysis of the causes of fires is important, as only by knowing the causes of fires is it possible to effectively prevent fire.
An analysis of fires in rooms used for spraying flammable paints and finishes has shown that the MOST important of the following causes is

   A. smoking by employees
   B. defective electrical equipment
   C. spontaneous ignition of paint deposits, rubbish, and wiping rags
   D. static electricity resulting from friction
   E. cutting and welding operations

6.____

7. The flammability or combustibility of radioactive materials has little or no direct effect on the fire hazard of a laboratory PRIMARILY because

   A. the unusual structural characteristics of such a laboratory serve to limit possible fire spread from such hazards
   B. water or water spray are effective on most radioactive substances
   C. the quantities of such material in any one laboratory are usually small
   D. laboratory fire prevention and firefighting facilities usually exceed maximum fire hazards
   E. such materials are inherently of a low order of combustibility

7.____

8. Comparison of the burning qualities of foam rubber and cotton mattresses shows that GENERALLY

   A. a cotton mattress burns faster but cooler
   B. a foam rubber mattress burns slower but hotter
   C. a foam rubber mattress burns faster and hotter
   D. a cotton mattress burns faster and hotter
   E. the potential fire hazard of a foam rubber mattress is higher

8.____

9. During Christmas and other holiday shopping seasons, it is required that frequent inspections shall be made of department stores at irregular intervals. Of the following, the MOST important reason for this inspection procedure is to

   A. prevent unnecessary interference with store operations
   B. check characteristic holiday operations
   C. permit more frequent and thorough coverage of the stores in question
   D. avoid delay in urgent fire operations
   E. permit more flexible scheduling of inspection

9.____

10. The fire load computation of a building indicates, for the most part, the

    A. risk of a fire breaking out
    B. rate at which a fire is likely to grow
    C. combustibility of the various parts of the building rather than its contents
    D. amount of combustibles and the method of protection
    E. maximum fire stress to which the building might be subjected

11. It is far more important that escape routes from multistory buildings should be protected against smoke and hot gases than from direct flame or heat.
    This statement is

    A. *not correct;* resistive construction is likely to be smoke-resistive as well
    B. *correct;* adequate means for ventilation is essential to prevent cutting off escape routes
    C. *not correct;* unless corridors and escape stairs are constructed of fire resistive materials, progress of fire cannot be blocked
    D. *correct;* unless properly protected from smoke and hot gases, escape stairs would be unusable by occupants
    E. *not correct;* unless properly protected against direct flame or heat, escape routes cannot resist smoke or hot gases

12. The MINIMUM width of exit usually required for a single file of persons is MOST NEARLY _____ inches.

    A. 15-17 B. 18-20 C. 21-23
    D. 24-27 E. 27-30

13. The MOST pronounced method of reducing the fire and life hazards in public buildings is by

    A. ample exits of any type
    B. ample stairways inside the buildings
    C. the use of exit signs and panic locks
    D. fire-resisting construction suitable for the occupancy
    E. installing fire extinguishers in every hallway

14. From all viewpoints, the MOST hazardous materials that could be stored, constituting a life as well as a fire hazard, would be

    A. second-hand niter bags
    B. used motor vehicles
    C. loose or baled vegetable fibers
    D. pyroxylin and pyroxylin plastic products
    E. foam rubber mattresses

15. The CHIEF fire hazard of welding and cutting operations is

    A. flames of the torch igniting nearby material
    B. broken hose line
    C. flying sparks
    D. backfiring of torch
    E. tank explosion

16. Of the following items associated with motion picture theatres, the PRIMARY hazard is   16.____

    A. misuse of electricity
    B. heating defects
    C. smoking and matches
    D. projection booth fires
    E. improperly lit exits

17. The MOST hazardous method of fumigation is by the use of   17.____

    A. heat (125° F)
    B. carbon tetrachloride mixture with flammable fumigant
    C. carbon dioxide mixture with flammable fumigant
    D. carbon bisulphide
    E. carbon monoxide

18. The combined use of inspections, periodic reports of activities, follow-up procedures, special reports from subordinates, and a rating system comprise a system of   18.____

    A. coordination
    B. command
    C. control
    D. representation
    E. on-the-job training

19. What should be provided in air conditioning ducts to PREVENT the spread of fire and smoke through a property?   19.____

    A. Automatic dampers
    B. Intake screens
    C. Steel wool air filters
    D. Heat actuated devices
    E. Halon extinguishers

20. The OUTSTANDING fire hazard of boarding and rooming houses is   20.____

    A. misuse of electricity
    B. smoking and matches
    C. heating defects
    D. incendiary
    E. kitchen fires

21. The SIMPLEST and MOST feasible method of avoiding the overheating of woodwork near any high temperature heating appliance is by   21.____

    A. filling the intervening space with insulating material
    B. covering the woodwork with sheet metal
    C. providing an air space between the woodwork and the appliance
    D. covering the woodwork with asbestos sheets
    E. painting the woodwork with varnish

22. The PRINCIPLE source of fire hazard in connection with heating equipment in mercantile buildings comes from   22.____

    A. defective wiring
    B. insufficient clearance from combustible materials
    C. the storage and handling of fuel
    D. defective motors
    E. none of the above

23. More ink has been spilled on the item of smoking as a cause of fire than on any other, but the total result has been negligible.   23.____
    This situation is BEST accounted for by the fact that

A. smoking is generally an automatic act performed unthinkingly
B. truly effective facilities for elimination of smoking hazards are exceedingly cumbersome or expensive
C. most people regard smoking as a personal prerogative and resent control measures
D. smoking is practiced by many individuals with defective intelligence and social attitudes
E. individual behavior cannot be controlled

24. There are two basic factors in assessing building construction from the fire prevention standpoint. One is the combustibility of materials.
The other is

   A. extinguishment facilities
   B. excess structural strength
   C. ventilation control
   D. limitation of fire spread
   E. means of access and egress

25. The LEAST accurate statement concerning the protection of openings in walls and partitions is:

   A. Protection of wall openings may prevent either the horizontal or the vertical spread of fire
   B. The general features of a building have no bearing on the extent to which such protection is necessary
   C. The protection secured by fire doors and fire windows cannot be better than the fire resistant value of the walls
   D. Good solid walls are preferable to those with fire doors in restricting the spread of fire
   E. Sprinkler systems may provide adequate protection

26. The one of the following which is NOT included among the six categories in which all structures are classified by the Administrative Code with respect to type of construction is _____ structures.

   A. heavy timber   B. metal   C. wood frame
   D. fire-resistant   E. fireproof

27. All storage tanks, comprising or forming a part of an oil storage plant, shall be buried so that the tops thereof shall be a distance below the grade level of AT LEAST

   A. 1'   B. 2'   C. 3'   D. 4'   E. 6'

28. According to the Administrative Code, a Class B refrigeration system is one

   A. capable of less than 15 tons capacity
   B. containing not more than 20 lbs. of refrigerant
   C. capable of less than 30 tons capacity
   D. containing 1000 pounds or over of refrigerant
   E. capable of 40 tons capacity or over

29. According to the Administrative Code, it shall be unlawful to transport or store guncotton EXCEPT in

   A. strong wooden cases lined with liquid-proof paper
   B. strong wooden cases
   C. carboys so tinted as to exclude light
   D. water-tight metal vessels
   E. aluminum or other non-tarnishing metal

30. One purpose of building inspections is to enable the Fire Department to plan its operations before a fire starts.
    This statement is

   A. *incorrect;* no two fires are alike
   B. *correct;* many firefighting problems can be anticipated
   C. *incorrect;* fires should be prevented, not extinguished
   D. *correct;* the Fire Department should have detailed plans for every possible emergency
   E. *incorrect;* fires are not predictable

KEY (CORRECT ANSWERS)

1. C	11. D	21. C
2. A	12. C	22. B
3. A	13. D	23. A
4. E	14. D	24. D
5. A	15. C	25. B
6. C	16. D	26. D
7. C	17. D	27. B
8. C	18. C	28. C
9. B	19. A	29. D
10. E	20. C	30. B

TEST 2

DIRECTIONS: Each question or incomplete statement is followed by several suggested answers or completions. Select the one that BEST answers the question or completes the statement. *PRINT THE LETTER OF THE CORRECT ANSWER IN THE SPACE AT THE RIGHT.*

1. According to the Fire Prevention Code, an essential oil is defined as an oil   1.____

   A. needed to provide the viscosity of a given grade of oil
   B. derived from animal life and not from mineral sources
   C. which has low volatility at room temperature
   D. used for flavoring or perfuming purposes
   E. required as the base of lubricating compounds

2. According to the Fire Prevention Code, it shall be UNLAWFUL to sell or deliver for use   2.____

   A. sticks or cartridges of explosives which are packed so as to lie on their sides
   B. any explosive except in original and unbroken packages
   C. dynamite in cases of 25 and 50 lbs.
   D. nitroglycerine in liquid form under any circumstances
   E. any explosives packed in quantities in excess of 50 lbs.

3. The Fire Prevention Code requires that a storage garage containing more than four motor vehicles shall be continuously under the supervision of one or more persons, each holding a certificate of fitness.   3.____
   The MAXIMUM number of such certificated persons required for any garage shall be

   A. 7   B. 6   C. 5   D. 4   E. 3

4. According to the annual report statistics for the last years, the floor of multiple dwellings where fires started MOST frequently was the   4.____

   A. cellar   B. 1st floor   C. 2nd floor
   D. 3rd floor   E. roof

5. You are assigned to inspect buildings for fire hazards. The one of the following MOST appropriately used for fire-retardant coating of wood is   5.____

   A. varnish   B. shellac   C. wood stain
   D. lacquer   E. white wash

6. An officer taking some clothing to a dry cleaner in his neighborhood noticed that inflammable cleaning fluid was stored in a way which created a fire hazard. The officer called this to the attention of the proprietor, explaining the danger involved.   6.____
   This method of handling the situation was

   A. *bad;* the officer should not have interfered in a matter which was not his responsibility
   B. *good;* the proprietor would probably remove the hazard and be more careful in the future
   C. *bad;* the officer should have reported the situation to the fire inspector's office without saying anything to the proprietor

99

D. *good;* since the officer was a customer, he should treat the proprietor more leniently than he would treat other violators
E. *bad;* the officer should have ordered the proprietor to remove the violation immediately and issued a summons

7. Automobile fires are caused MOST frequently by

   A. overheating of the motor
   B. gasoline explosion
   C. defective carburetor
   D. defective or overheated brakes
   E. faulty ignition wiring

8. The PRINCIPAL fire hazard in connection with heating equipment in mercantile buildings comes from

   A. failure to operate and clean equipment properly
   B. insufficient clearance from combustible material
   C. use of improper types or grades of fuel
   D. defective flues
   E. exposed wiring in heating controls

9. Supermarket fires have in common the fact that MOST fires occur in the

   A. utility area
   B. sales area
   C. basement storage area
   D. check-out and packaging area
   E. shelves containing paper products

10. Of the following, the LEAST accurate statement concerning Field Violation Cards is that

    A. when all the violations listed on a Field Violation Card have been complied with, such card shall be placed in the Occupancy Folder
    B. not more than two Minor Violation Orders shall be recorded on any one card
    C. not more than two Major Violation Orders shall be recorded on any one card
    D. when the space on both sides is completely used for entries, such card is placed on file in the Occupancy Folder
    E. when subsequent violations are found for a building which previously complied with violations found, the additional entries shall be made on the same Field Violation Card

11. Of the following statements concerning coal storage, the one that is ACCEPTABLE is:

    A. Coal for storage should preferably be deposited in horizontal layers
    B. Alternate wetting and drying will prevent development of heat in the pile
    C. The desirable height of a properly stored coal pile is 25 to 30 feet
    D. Storage of mixed sizes of coal together will reduce spontaneous ignition to a minimum
    E. Standing timbers should be placed in coal piles to provide air access and circulation

12. The Multiple Dwelling Law provides that, in every multiple dwelling erected after April 18, 1929, every stair, fire stair, and fire tower beyond a specified width shall be provided with a handrail on each side.

    This specified width is

    A. 3'2"   B. 3'8"   C. 4'2"   D. 4'10"   E. 5'6"

13. The one of the following for which the Official Action Guide provides that a permit is required for storage, regardless of quantity and purpose, is

    A. shale oil
    B. heavy lubricating oil
    C. machine oil
    D. kerosene
    E. illuminating oil

Questions 14-16.

DIRECTIONS: Questions 14 through 16, inclusive, are to be answered on the basis of the following paragraph.

A flameproof fabric is defined as one which, when exposed to small sources of ignition, such as sparks or smoldering cigarettes, does not burn beyond the vicinity of the source of ignition. Cotton fabrics are the materials commonly used that are considered most hazardous. Other materials, such as acetate rayons and linens, are somewhat less hazardous, and woolens and some natural silk fabrics, even when untreated, are about equal to the average treated cotton fabric insofar as flame spread and ease of ignition are concerned. The method of application is to immerse the fabric in a flame-proofing solution. The container used must be large enough so that all the fabric is thoroughly wet and there are no folds which the solution does not penetrate.

14. According to the above paragraph, a flameproof fabric is one which

    A. is unaffected by heat and smoke
    B. resists the spread of flames when ignited
    C. burns with a cold flame
    D. cannot be ignited by sparks or cigarettes
    E. may smolder but cannot burn

15. According to the above paragraph, woolen fabrics which have not been flameproofed are as likely to catch fire as _____ fabrics.

    A. treated silk
    B. treated acetate rayon
    C. untreated linen
    D. untreated synthetic
    E. treated cotton

16. In the method described above, the flameproofing solution is BEST applied to the fabric by _____ the fabric.

    A. sponging   B. spraying   C. dipping
    D. brushing   E. sprinkling

17. The daily peak time for the number of fires in the city, in general,

    A. varies from day to day
    B. is about 9 A.M.

C. is at about 5 P.M.
D. is at about 1 A.M.
E. varies from season to season

18. According to the Multiple Dwelling Law, a part of a building is *fire-retarded* if it is protected against fire in an approved manner with materials of fire-resistive ratings of AT LEAST _____ hour(s).

    A. one   B. two   C. three   D. four   E. five

19. The Multiple Dwelling Law permits the conduct of business in any multiple dwelling EXCEPT that

    A. no space in a non-fireproof multiple dwelling may be used for a bakery or business where fat is boiled under any condition
    B. the number of persons employed in manufacturing enterprises in multiple dwellings shall be limited to a maximum of seven persons
    C. exits of the dwelling portion and the business space may be common if the number of persons employed is limited to ten persons or less
    D. when the ground story of any non-fireproof multiple dwelling is extended for business purposes, the underside of the roof of such extension shall be fire-retarded if there are fire escapes above such extension
    E. there shall be no manufacturing business conducted above the second floor of any non-fireproof multiple dwelling

20. According to the Building Code, a sprinkler system is NOT required in

    A. garages in cellars of multiple dwellings if area is less than 5,000 square feet
    B. dressing rooms and stage of auditoriums of large public high schools where seating capacity is less than 1,500
    C. furnished rooms of converted non-fireproof multiple dwellings if the public hall has sprinkler protection
    D. non-fireproof lodging houses if equipped with an automatic, closed-circuit fire alarm system
    E. department stores if each floor does not exceed 10,000 square feet

21. The Building Code requires that in all newly constructed loft buildings used for mercantile purposes,

    A. 8 inch standpipe risers shall be installed in buildings 150 feet or more in height
    B. standpipes be installed if 75 feet in height or over
    C. the minimum size of standpipe riser in a building 100 feet high be at least 3 inches
    D. when a standpipe is required, no point on a floor be more than 75 feet from a riser
    E. multiple standpipe risers may not be cross-connected

22. The proscenium of a theatre is MOST closely associated with the

    A. stage
    B. special entrance for scenery
    C. street entrance and exit
    D. passageways to boxes
    E. balcony arch over the orchestra section

23. The MAXIMUM quantity of kerosene fuel oil that may be stored for heating and cooking use without a permit from the Fire Commissioner is _____ gallons.   23.____

   A. 10   B. 25   C. 50   D. 100   E. 150

24. An ACCEPTABLE method of absorbing waste oils in a dry cleaning establishment is, according to the Fire Prevention Code,   24.____

   A. a quantity of sand spread on the floor
   B. use of thin asbestos fibre flooring
   C. non-combustible cloth on the floor
   D. diatomaceous earth or equivalent absorbent material spread on the floor
   E. woven glass fibre mats

25. Suppose you are making an inspection of a factory. During the inspection, the factory manager asks you a technical question which you cannot answer.
Of the following, the BEST procedure for you to follow is to   25.____

   A. tell him you are not there to answer his questions but to make an inspection
   B. guess at the answer so that he won't doubt your competency
   C. tell him you don't know the answer but that you will look it up and notify him
   D. give him the title of a textbook that probably would contain the information
   E. change the subject by asking him a question

26. While performing building inspections, a fireman finds a janitor in the basement checking for a gas leak by holding a lighted match to the gas pipes.
Of the following, the fireman's FIRST action should be to   26.____

   A. reprimand the janitor for endangering life and property
   B. explain the hazards of this action to the janitor
   C. report the janitor to his superior as incompetent
   D. tell the janitor to put out the match
   E. issue a summons for this action

27. According to the Administrative Code, a refrigerant is defined as the chemical agent used to produce refrigeration other than   27.____

   A. brine
   B. a chemical of the hydrocarbon clan
   C. the compressor
   D. methyl bromide
   E. ammonia

28. The Administrative Code defines as a combustible mixture any substance which, when tested in a Tagliabue open cup tester, emits an inflammable vapor at temperatures   28.____

   A. below 100° F   B. above 300° F
   C. between 100° F and 300° F   D. below 125° F
   E. above 125° F

29. A partially filled gasoline drum is a more dangerous fire hazard than a full one. 29.___
Of the following, the BEST justification for this statement is that

    A. a partially filled gasoline drum contains relatively little air
    B. gasoline is difficult to ignite
    C. when a gasoline drum is full, the gasoline is more explosive
    D. gasoline vapors are more explosive than gasoline itself
    E. air is not combustible

30. The tendency of this substance to spontaneous heating is very slight. It is usually 30.___
shipped in bulk. This substance should be kept dry, and storing or loading in hot wet piles should be avoided.
This description applies MOST closely to

    A. metal powder   B. soft coal   C. charcoal
    D. scrap film   E. jute

KEY (CORRECT ANSWERS)

1. D	11. A	21. B
2. B	12. B	22. A
3. E	13. A	23. A
4. A	14. B	24. A
5. E	15. E	25. C
6. B	16. C	26. D
7. E	17. C	27. A
8. B	18. A	28. C
9. A	19. E	29. D
10. E	20. E	30. E

TEST 3

DIRECTIONS: Each question or incomplete statement is followed by several suggested answers or completions. Select the one that BEST answers the question or completes the statement. *PRINT THE LETTER OF THE CORRECT ANSWER IN THE SPACE AT THE RIGHT.*

1. An inspector is denied access to a building by the building manager after presenting his identification. Of the following actions, it would be MOST appropriate for the captain to

   A. post an official notice of inspection on the premises
   B. notify the enforcement unit of the division of fire prevention
   C. give orders to have three routine inspections of premises made before taking special measures to gain access
   D. contact the building owner by telephone to request access

1._____

Questions 2-5.

DIRECTIONS: Questions 2 through 5 are to be answered on the basis of the information given in the following paragraph.

Old buildings are liable to possess a special degree of fire risk merely because they are old. Outmoded electrical wiring systems and installation of new heating appliances for which the building was not designed may contribute to the increased hazard. Old buildings have often been altered many times; parts of the structure may antedate building codes; dangerous defects may have been covered up. On the average, old buildings contain more lumber than comparable new buildings which, in itself, makes old buildings more susceptible to fire. It is not true, though, that sound lumber in old buildings is drier than new lumber. Moisture content of lumber varies with that of the atmosphere to which it is exposed.

2. According to the above paragraph, old buildings present a special fire hazard CHIEFLY because of the

   A. poor planning of the buildings when first designed
   B. haphazard alteration of the buildings
   C. failure to replace worn out equipment
   D. inadequate enforcement of the building codes

2._____

3. We may conclude from the above paragraph that lumber

   A. should not be used in buildings unless absolutely necessary
   B. should not be used near electrical equipment
   C. is more inflammable than newer types of building materials
   D. tends to lose its moisture at a constant rate

3._____

4. According to the above paragraph, the amount of moisture in the wooden parts of a building depends upon the

   A. age of the building
   B. moisture in the surrounding air

4._____

C. type of heating equipment used in the building
D. quality of lumber used

5. In regard to building codes, the above paragraph implies that

    A. old buildings are exempt from the provisions of building codes
    B. some buildings now in use were built before building codes were adopted
    C. building codes usually don't cover electrical wiring systems
    D. building codes generally are inadequate

6. According to Department Regulations, the *Monthly Statistical Report - Field Inspection Activity* should include company field inspection duty of all

    A. types
    B. types except re-inspection duty on violation orders
    C. types except surveillance inspection duty
    D. types except inspectional duty relative to complaints

7. During field inspection of a building containing an automatic sprinkler system, you note that the shut-off valves are located where they are not readily accessible. The one of the following procedures to follow in this situation, according to department regulations, is to

    A. write an order to the owner or occupant requiring correction of the physical defect
    B. require no action by the owner or occupant but make special note of the valve location in the building record file
    C. bring to the attention of the owner or occupant the potential water damage hazard inherent in this situation
    D. write an order to the owner or occupant for a sign indicating valve location

8. The difficulties encountered in fighting fire in the cellar of a pool supply occupancy were compounded by bulk storage of calcium hypochlorite.
   This bleaching and sanitizing agent is LEAST likely to

    A. be unstable and highly combustible when finely divided
    B. form a mixture that spontaneously bursts into flame on contact with oxidizable material
    C. decompose when involved in fire, by liberating oxygen and intensifying the fire
    D. have an increased fire and explosion potential when pre-mixed with algaecides and fungicides as an all-purpose water treatment

9. Acetylene is a particularly hazardous flammable gas because, in addition to its flammability, it is reactive and unstable. Consequently, its storage and handling in some respects differs from other flammable gases. The following statements may be pertinent to acetylene and its storage:
    I. Acetylene is not toxic but can have an anesthetic effect
    II. Copper must be avoided in most acetylene piping and equipment
    III. Acetylene gas can explode if subjected to more than 15 psi
   Which one of the following choices lists only those of the abovementioned statements that are generally CORRECT?
    A. I, II   B. II, III   C. I, III   D. I, II, III

10. Before leaving quarters to perform apparatus field inspection duty (AFID) at a hospital, a company officer holds a drill on institutional fire safety.
It would be MOST appropriate for the officer to tell the members that the MAJORITY of fires in hospitals generally occur in

   A. storage rooms
   B. lounges
   C. patients' rooms
   D. corridors

11. Special fire hazards in industry are sometimes diminished by automatic carbon dioxide fixed-pipe extinguishing systems. While difficult to check an existing system for compliance with design and installation standards, certain of the following conditions can be noted during a building inspection to determine whether it is apparently operative and in good order:
   I. Have cylinders been weighed within the past five years and is there a visible record of such weighing?
   II. Are automatic-closing doors and shutters unobstructed and free to close upon actuation?
   III. Are there means accessible during a fire of manually actuating the system?
   Which of the following choices contains only those of the above conditions that are generally VALID?

   A. I, II   B. II, III   C. I, III   D. I, II, III

12. A considerable number of serious burn injuries and fatalities result from fires involving clothing being worn. The following may or may not be correct statements concerning Fire Department experience gained from such fires:
   I. Cotton and rayon have proved to be relatively nonflammable fibers
   II. Nylon and acetate melt and liquefy under fire exposure, thereby tending to aggravate the severity of burn injuries
   III. Victims of clothing fires are more likely to be persons over 60 years of age than children under 10
   Which of the following choices contains only those of the above-mentioned statements that are generally CORRECT?

   A. I, II   B. I, III   C. II, III   D. I, II, III

13. Some communities have a program for inspecting dwellings, conducted as a courtesy and service to householders.
    The USUAL effect of a dwelling-house inspection campaign is

   A. annoyance on the part of homeowners and their refusal to admit firemen
   B. anticipation of firemen's visits by cleaning up before their arrival
   C. avoidance of major problems found by firemen and their stressing instead the easily corrected conditions
   D. embarrassment of both firemen and homeowners by the procedure and their seeking premature termination of the visit

14. Of the following agents for transferring flammable and combustible liquids, the BEST one is

   A. air pressure
   B. hydraulic or inert gas
   C. straight gravity discharge systems
   D. positive displacement pumps

15. The effect of applying wallpaper to a new interior finish surface on the flame propagation characteristics of that surface is GENERALLY considered

    A. minimal
    B. moderate
    C. considerable
    D. severe

16. While you are on apparatus field inspection duty, one of your members reports that he has issued an order to a building owner to remedy a violation forthwith. The member states that the owner seems agitated and hostile and refuses to correct the condition. You decide to speak to the owner yourself.
    In discussing this situation with the owner, it is MOST advisable for you to

    A. inform the owner firmly but bluntly that he is incorrect in insisting the condition does not require correction
    B. try to convince the owner that you are an expert in this area and that your knowledge should not be questioned
    C. express an appropriate degree of anger at the owner's refusal to correct an unsafe condition
    D. stick to discussion of the specific violation and avoid trying to convince the owner of the importance of correcting all fire hazards

17. Experience with the city fire prevention program GENERALLY demonstrates that

    A. fires have increased in the public areas of ghetto multiple dwellings despite intensive inspections
    B. inspections are ineffective in both loft buildings and ghetto multiple dwellings
    C. the extensive educational program in the schools in the 1950's resulted in decreases in the number of fires and false alarms when the children reached adulthood
    D. fires have increased in the living areas of ghetto multiple dwellings

18. It is common to find self-closing doors kept open with wooden wedges or other fastenings. To eliminate such unsafe hazards, hooks, fitted with fusible links, have been designed to hold the doors open.
    GENERALLY, these hooks are

    A. *desirable,* if placed low enough for convenient use
    B. *undesirable,* unless placed behind doors, where they would not be subject to damage
    C. *desirable,* if used only on stair and corridor doors
    D. *undesirable* under practically all conditions

19. While supervising an inspection of a commercial building, an officer notices some wooden packing cases resting against a steam riser. He advises the owner to move the stock at least 12 inches away from the riser to permit air to circulate.
    This advice GENERALLY is

    A. *proper;* however, a clearance of 36 inches should have been suggested
    B. *improper;* steam risers do not reach the ignition temperature of wood
    C. *proper;* standard practice uses a rise of 90F above room temperature as the maximum permissible temperature on surrounding woodwork
    D. *improper;* the air space suggested may permit hidden fire to travel behind the stock

20. Realistic fire tests to determine the actual burning characteristics of several rigid foam plastic wall and roof assemblies have been conducted within recent years. Of the following conclusions, the one BEST supported by this research is that

    A. low flame spread, rigid polystyrene foam, encased in aluminum skins, required automatic sprinkler protection for satisfactory performance under fire conditions
    B. low flame spread, rigid polyurethane foam, encased in aluminum skins, required automatic sprinkler protection for satisfactory performance under fire conditions
    C. rigid, foamed polyurethane products produce minimum fire contribution when sprayed on walls
    D. materials with a small-scale flame spread rating of 25 are practically self-extinguishing

20.____

21. At a neighborhood community organization meeting and discussion on *Fire Safety in the Home*, a woman asked the officer representing the Fire Department where spot-type heat detectors should be placed in a room to give an alarm properly if fire should occur. The officer responded that the center of the ceiling was the best location. He added that any point on the ceiling was the next best, and, if it were necessary to mount the detector on a side wall, it should be placed at least 6 inches but no more than 12 inches from the ceiling. The officer's instructions to the citizen were

    A. *correct*
    B. *incorrect* in his statement of *any point on the ceiling;* spot-type detectors should not be placed on ceilings in the corner of rooms
    C. *incorrect* in his statement *at least 6 inches from the ceiling*
    D. *incorrect;* side wall locations for spot-type detectors are preferable to ceiling locations

21.____

22. Safety cans for indoor handling of small quantities of flammable liquids are approved when equipped with pouring outlets that have tight-fitting caps or valves which are normally kept closed by springs, except when manual pressure is applied to keep them open. During apparatus field inspection, a company officer finds that small unsafe containers are being utilized at a certain location. Wishing to use this discovery to convince the occupants of the premises of the superiority of the authorized container, the officer decides to explain the advantages of the approved type.
Of the following, the MOST complete and accurate explanation he could give is that the approved container

    A. prevents spillage if accidentally tipped over
    B. is self-venting if exposed to fire and prevents spillage if accidentally tipped over
    C. provides relief venting in case of explosion, is self-venting if exposed to fire, and prevents spillage if accidentally tipped over
    D. prevents a static charge from building up during pouring operations, provides relief venting in case of explosion, is self-venting if exposed to fire, and prevents spillage if accidentally tipped over

22.____

23. While inspecting a cylindrical gravity tank for an automatic sprinkler system, a chief observes that the water in the tank is 10 feet deep and that the tank has a diameter of 9 feet. He asks the building manager how many gallons are in the tank and receives the reply, *About 10,000.*
Based on his own observation and calculations, the chief should

23.____

A. *agree* that the manager's answer is probably correct
B. *disagree* with the manager's answer; the answer is more nearly 20,000 gallons
C. *disagree* with the manager's answer; the answer is more nearly 15,000 gallons
D. *disagree* with the manager's answer; the answer is more nearly 5,000 gallons

24. The one of the following that is NOT an accurate statement with respect to the findings of a survey conducted by a member of the National Commission on Fire Prevention and Control concerning the public's knowledge of fire safety is that   24.____

    A. many youngsters indicated that they were likely to do something dangerous if a frying pan caught fire
    B. many adults and most youngsters did not know that a 15-ampere fuse is the safest for ordinary household lighting circuits
    C. most youngsters and adults indicated they would make the mistake of opening a hot door
    D. most youngsters and adults did not know that carbon monoxide can rob them of their judgment and coordination

25. You are inspecting a building for violations. You must perform the following steps in the order given: 25.____
    I. Find the manager of the building and introduce yourself.
    II. Have the manager accompany you during the inspection.
    III. Start the inspection by checking the Fire Department permits which have been issued to the building. The permits are located in the office of the building.
    IV. Inspect the building for violations of the Fire Prevention Laws. Begin at the roof and work down to the basement or cellar.
    V. As you inspect, write on a piece of paper any violations you find and explain them to the building manager.

    You are inspecting a supermarket. After entering the building, you identify yourself to the store manager and ask him to come along during the inspection. Which one of the following actions should you take NEXT?

    A. Start inspecting the supermarket, beginning at the basement.
    B. Start inspecting the supermarket, beginning at the roof.
    C. Ask to see the Fire Department permits which have been issued to the supermarket.
    D. Write down any violations which are seen while introducing yourself to the manager.

26. Many fires are caused by improper use of oxyacetylene torches.   26.____
    The MAIN cause of such fires is the

    A. high pressure under which the gases are stored
    B. failure to control or extinguish sparks
    C. high temperatures generated by the equipment
    D. explosive nature of the gases used

Questions 27-29.

DIRECTIONS: Questions 27 through 29 are to be answered on the basis of the following paragraph.

The only openings permitted in fire partitions except openings for ventilating ducts shall be those required for doors. There shall be but one such door opening unless the provision of additional openings would not exceed in total width of all doorways 25 percent of the length of the wall. The minimum distance between openings shall be three feet. The maximum area for such a door opening shall be 80 square feet, except that such openings for the passage of motor trucks may be a maximum of 140 square feet.

27. According to the above paragraph, openings in fire partitions are permitted only for

    A. doors
    B. doors and windows
    C. doors and ventilation ducts
    D. doors, windows, and ventilation ducts

28. In a fire partition 22 feet long and 10 feet high, the MAXIMUM number of doors 3 feet wide and 7 feet high is

    A. 1 B. 2 C. 3 D. 4

29.

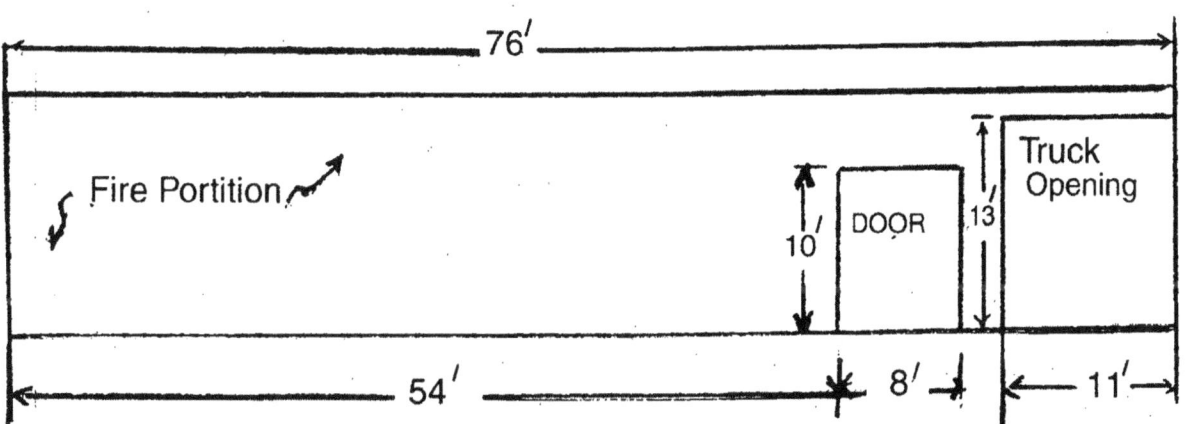

The one of the following statements about the layout shown on the preceding page that is MOST accurate is that the

    A. total width of the openings is too large
    B. truck opening is too large
    C. truck and door openings are too close together
    D. layout is acceptable

30. The Rules of the Board of Standards and Appeals provide that in a coin-operated dry-cleaning establishment spotting and sponging may be done by

    A. the general public or a qualified operator if water only is used
    B. a qualified operator if water only is used
    C. the general public if water only is used or by a qualified operator if inflammable liquids are used
    D. neither the general public nor a qualified operator

KEY (CORRECT ANSWERS)

1.	B	11.	B	21.	B
2.	B	12.	C	22.	B
3.	C	13.	B	23.	D
4.	B	14.	D	24.	C
5.	B	15.	A	25.	C
6.	A	16.	D	26.	B
7.	D	17.	D	27.	C
8.	A	18.	D	28.	A
9.	D	19.	C	29.	B
10.	C	20.	A	30.	B

TEST 4

DIRECTIONS: Each question or incomplete statement is followed by several suggested answers or completions. Select the one that BEST answers the question or completes the statement. *PRINT THE LETTER OF THE CORRECT ANSWER IN THE SPACE AT THE RIGHT.*

1. An officer is performing a routine quarterly inspection in a large motion picture theatre. Which one of the following actions taken by the officer during his inspection would generally be CORRECT?

    A. His first action is to proceed to the box office to review the theatre inspection log book.
    B. He informs the theatre owner that daily entries made by the owner in the log book should contain the name of the person designated to prevent any undue excitement or possible panic and indicate the location of the nearest street fire alarm box.
    C. Upon finding that the theatre owner has failed to maintain the log in the prescribed manner, the officer serves him with a summons.
    D. He examines the entries made since the previous inspection by an officer and records the results of this examination.

2. The owner of a building which comes under the jurisdiction of the Housing Maintenance Code would be in compliance with the Code if he

    A. installs, in a dwelling unit, a gas-fired refrigerator which is equipped with a flue assembly composed of non-metallic material
    B. obtains combustion air for the gas-fueled water heater in a bedroom in his new law tenement directly from the outer air
    C. connects each gas-fueled heater to the rigid gas piping supply line by means of a metallic flexible gas connection
    D. arranges to have the gas appliance in his old law tenement inspected by a licensed plumber on a biennial basis

3. Of the following activities, the one the code specifically permits bulk or waste oil recovery plants to do is

    A. refine waste oil for resale without a permit
    B. mix waste oil with No. 6 fuel oil for use in approved fuel oil burners
    C. transport waste oil in the vendor's container in 220 gallon quantities without a permit
    D. store waste oil in premises other than storage plants or buried tank systems in quantities greater than those restricting other combustible oils

4. A chief, visiting a company performing apparatus field inspection, is informed by the lieutenant in command of a hazardous situation just encountered in a fur processing plant. In the presence of the factory manager, the two officers discussed various sections of the Administrative Code which might be relevant and several approaches to the problem that could be taken by the fire department to abate the hazard. Finally, the chief directed the lieutenant to issue certain orders to the manager. Discussing this problem in the presence of the manager was

A. *proper,* mainly because he probably would realize that the fire department was not acting arbitrarily or unreasonably
B. *improper,* mainly because he might prefer one of the approaches which was suggested and rejected
C. *proper,* mainly because the activities of the fire department should, whenever possible, be open to the public
D. *improper,* mainly because inaccurate statements may have been made during the preliminary discussion

5. A chief supervising apparatus field inspection duty activities comes upon a company just as it is completing inspection of a clothing manufacturing plant. The lieutenant in command reports that the company has issued minor violation orders for five conditions which they discovered. The chief considers four of the conditions cited clear violations of the Administrative Code. The fifth condition he considers a borderline case which he, himself, would not have handled by issuing a violation order.
In this situation, the BEST of the following courses for the chief to take is to

   A. direct the lieutenant to cancel the violation order for the borderline situation
   B. say nothing to the lieutenant at this time but later warn him against unduly strict interpretation of the Administrative Code
   C. accept the lieutenant's findings without any comment at this time or later
   D. question the lieutenant closely about various sections of the Administrative Code to determine whether he has a proper understanding of its requirements

Questions 6-7.

DIRECTIONS: Questions 6 and 7 are to be answered SOLELY on the basis of the following passage.

Following is a list of rules for fire extinguishers which are required in different types of public buildings in the city:

Rule 1: Hospitals, nursing homes, hotels, and motels must have one 2 1/2 gallon water extinguisher for every 2,500 square feet, or part thereof, of floor area on each floor.

Rule 2: Stores with floor areas of 1,500 square feet or less must have one 2 1/2 gallon water extinguisher. Stores with floor areas of over 1,500 square feet must have one 2 1/2 gallon water extinguisher for every 2,500 square feet, or part thereof, of floor area on each floor.

Rule 3: Kitchens must have one 2 1/2 gallon foam extinguisher or one 5 pound dry chemical extinguisher for every 1,250 square feet, or part thereof, of floor area on each floor. For kitchen areas, this rule is in addition to Rules 1 and 2.

6. An inspector is inspecting a one-story nursing home which has a total of 3,000 square feet of floor area. This includes a kitchen, which is 1,500 square feet in area, in the rear of the floor.
Of the following, the inspector should conclude that the nursing home should be equipped with _____ extinguisher(s) and _____ extinguisher(s).

   A. 1 water; 1 foam
   B. 1 water; 1 dry chemical
   C. 2 water; 2 foam
   D. 2 foam; 1 dry chemical

7. An inspector is inspecting a store which has two floors. The first floor has 2,600 square feet. The second floor has 1,450 square feet.
   The store should be equipped with AT LEAST

   A. two 2 1/2 gallon water extinguishers, one for each floor
   B. three 2 1/2 gallon water extinguishers, two for the first floor and one for the second floor
   C. two 2 1/2 gallon foam extinguishers, one for each floor
   D. two 2 1/2 gallon extinguishers, either foam or water, one for each floor

7.____

8. A recycling sprinkler head called *The Aquamatic* has been developed that will turn itself off after the fire is extinguished and turn itself on again if the fire should rekindle.
   Of the following, it would generally be INACCURATE to state that this recycling sprinkler head

   A. has been approved by the Underwriters' Laboratories for installation where there is high risk of flash fires
   B. is capable of discharging 30 gpm and is approved by the Underwriters' Laboratories for use in systems engineered to make maximum use of available water
   C. eliminates the need to turn off the main valve to replace Aquamatic elements
   D. has a 165° temperature rating, the usual 1/2 inch national pipe thread, is mounted in the pendant position and is approved for installation in any sprinkler system, new or old

8.____

9. Assume that you are supervising a scheduled inspection of auxiliary fire protection equipment in a tunnel in the absence of a deputy chief.
   In supervising the inspection, it would be appropriate for you to do all of the following EXCEPT

   A. utilize the members of the Rescue Company in carrying out specific inspectional duties
   B. notify the dispatcher of the units participating, the designated radio contact, and the units which are not available for response to their assigned alarms
   C. make a written recommendation suggesting a corrective procedure to upgrade a particular piece of inadequate equipment
   D. forward referrals and recommendations through official channels to the division of fire prevention for transmittal to the various agencies concerned and for necessary follow-up

9.____

10. What was formerly known as the *spray sprinkler* is now designated as the *standard sprinkler* and is generally similar in appearance to the old type head.
    Of the following, the MOST NEARLY accurate statement about the modern one-half inch sprinkler head is that

    A. a larger area of coverage is secured by directing all the water downward and horizontally
    B. the present upright spray sprinkler operates on the direct spray principle

10.____

C. major changes in deflector design have reduced discharge capacities, but have increased particle division
D. there is increased exposure to the ceiling, but more direct discharge on the burning materials

11. The one of the following which is generally a CORRECT statement about automatic deluge sprinkler systems is that they are

    A. installed in properties when there is a danger of serious water damage due to accidental functioning
    B. equipped with quartzoid bulb type activators in lieu of fusible links
    C. controlled by a quick-opening valve known as the deluge valve
    D. ineffective where ceilings are unusually high and heads would not open quickly enough

12. An inspection of the private class 3 box cards of the computerized alarm assignment system should reveal that the cards PROPERLY list the

    A. company numbers of those engine and ladder companies responding to each terminal under the *Response Policy* column
    B. battalion number of the battalion chief assigned to respond to each terminal under the *B.C.* column
    C. company numbers of the engine and ladder companies assigned to the associated street box
    D. address of the alarm service company

13. The General Accounting Office in Washington publicized the fact that there is a possible defect in some models of a certain smoke detector.
    The one of the following which BEST describes this defect is that these detectors

    A. failed to signal an alarm under heavy smoke conditions
    B. expected battery life is only three months or less
    C. have smoke entry vents which are too narrow so that dust tends to render the detectors ineffective
    D. are overheating and, in time, tend to self-ignite

14. Assume that you are a fire officer who has been asked to address a local community group on the relative merits of smoke and heat detectors and the proper placement, operation, and maintenance of the various types of detectors. During this meeting, it would be MOST appropriate for you to point out that

    A. it is more advisable to install a smoke detector than a heat detector in the kitchen
    B. placement of a smoke detector in a room below an insulated attic should be on the ceiling towards the center of the room
    C. placing a smoke detector in the hallway near each sleeping area and on every floor level not containing a sleeping area will provide minimal protection
    D. a smoke detector installed on the ceiling near a doorway should be placed closer to the wall above the doorway than the distance from the ceiling to the top of the door

15. The basic multiple-death fire safety problem in nursing home facilities is GENERALLY considered to be the failure to

    A. confine the fire's resultant products of combustion to the room of origin
    B. conduct and properly supervise comprehensive fire exit and evacuation drills
    C. adequately service and maintain existing smoke-detection and smoke-control systems
    D. reduce the combustible contents of patients' rooms and enforcement of the no-smoking restrictions by a trained staff

15._____

16. The basic assumption of fire prevention educational programs is that people frequently

    A. must be forced into obeying fire laws
    B. are unaware of the dangers involved in some of their actions
    C. don't care whether or not their actions are dangerous
    D. assume that fire insurance protects them against all fire loss

16._____

Questions 17-19.

DIRECTIONS: Questions 17 through 19 are to be answered on the basis of the following paragraph.

Unlined linen hose is essentially a fabric tube made of closely woven linen yarn. Due to the natural characteristics of linen, very shortly after water is introduced, the threads swell after being wet, closing the minute spaces between them making the tube practically watertight. This type of hose tends to deteriorate rapidly if not thoroughly dried after use or if installed where it will be exposed to dampness or the weather. It is not ordinarily built to withstand frequent service or for use where the fabric will be subjected to chafing from rough or sharp surfaces.

17. Seepage of water through an unlined linen hose is observed when the water is first turned on.
    From the above paragraph, we may conclude that the seepage

    A. indicates that the hose is defective
    B. does not indicate that the hose is defective provided that the seepage is proportionate to the water pressure
    C. does not indicate that the hose is defective provided that the seepage is greatly reduced when the hose becomes thoroughly wet
    D. does not indicate that the hose is defective provided that the seepage takes place only at the surface of the hose

17._____

18. Unlined linen hose is MOST suitable for use

    A. as a garden hose
    B. on fire department apparatus
    C. as emergency fire equipment in buildings
    D. in fire department training schools

18._____

19. The use of unlined linen hose would be LEAST appropriate in a(n)

    A. outdoor lumber yard
    B. non-fireproof office building

19._____

C. department store
D. cosmetic manufacturing plant

20. Doors in theatres and other places of public assembly usually open outwardly. 20.____
The MAIN reason for this requirement is, in the event of fire, to

   A. provide the widest possible passageway for escape of the audience
   B. prevent panic-stricken audience from jamming the doors in a closed position
   C. indicate to the audience the safe direction of travel
   D. prevent unauthorized persons from entering the building

21. Fire prevention inspections should be conducted at irregular hours or intervals. 21.____
The BEST justification for this *irregularity* is that it permits the firemen to

   A. make inspections when they have free time
   B. see the inspected establishments in their normal condition and not in their *dressed-up* condition
   C. avoid making inspections at times which would be inconvenient for the inspected establishments
   D. concentrate their inspectional activities on those establishments which present the greatest fire hazard

22. Static electricity is a hazard in industry CHIEFLY because it may cause 22.____

   A. dangerous or painful burns
   B. chemical decomposition of toxic elements
   C. sparks which can start an explosion
   D. overheating of electrical equipment

Questions 23-25.

DIRECTIONS: Questions 23 through 25 are to be answered on the basis of the following paragraph.

   A plastic does not consist of a single substance, but is a blended combination of several. In addition to the resin, it may contain various fillers, plasticizers, lubricants, and coloring material. Depending upon the type and quantity of substances added to the binder, the properties, including combustibility, may be altered considerably. The flammability of plastics depends upon the composition and, as with other materials, upon their physical size and condition. Thin sections, sharp edges, or powdered plastics will ignite and burn more readily than the same amount of identical material in heavy sections with smooth surfaces.

23. According to the above paragraph, all plastics contain a 23.____

   A. resin
   B. resin and a filler
   C. resin, filler, and plasticizer
   D. resin, filler, plasticizer, lubricant, and coloring material

24. The one of the following conclusions that is BEST supported by the above paragraph is   24.____
    that the flammability of plastics

    A. generally is high   B. generally is moderate
    C. generally is low   D. varies considerably

25. According to the above paragraph, *plastics* can BEST be described as   25.____

    A. a trade name
    B. the name of a specific product
    C. the name of a group of products which have some similar and some dissimilar properties
    D. the name of any substance which can be shaped or molded during the production process

26. While on inspection duty, an inspector discovers the superintendent of a tenement just   26.____
    starting to remove boxes and other material which are blocking hallways. Apparently, the superintendent started removal as soon as he saw the inspector approach.
    In this situation, it is MOST important that the inspector

    A. warn the superintendent of the penalties for violation of the Fire Prevention Code
    B. help the superintendent remove the material blocking the hallways
    C. commend the superintendent for his efforts to maintain a safe building
    D. check again, after completing the inspection, to see whether the material has been removed completely

27. Persons engaged in certain hazardous activities are required to obtain a Fire Depart-   27.____
    ment permit or certificate for which a fee is charged.
    The MAIN reason for requiring permits or certificates is to

    A. obtain revenue for the city government
    B. prevent unqualified persons from engaging in these activities
    C. obtain information about these activities in order to plan for fire emergencies
    D. warn the public of the hazardous nature of these activities

28. An inspector, on his way to work, is stopped by a citizen who complains that the employ-   28.____
    ees of a nearby store frequently pile empty crates and boxes in a doorway, blocking passage.
    The one of the following which would be the MOST appropriate action for the inspector to take is to

    A. assure the citizen that the fire department's inspectional activities will eventually *catch up* with the store
    B. obtain the address of the store and investigate to determine whether the citizen's complaint is justified
    C. obtain the address of the store and report the complaint to his superior officer
    D. ask the citizen for specific dates on which this practice has occurred to determine whether the complaint is justified

29. While inspecting a business building, you discover an oil burner installation with the following features:
    I. Installed on the third story, whose floor is 40' above the street level
    II. Oil delivery lines to the burner are one and one-half inches iron pipe size, and
    III. Pressure in the oil lines to the burner is 25 lbs. per square inch

    The one of the following statements concerning this installation and the applicable sections of the rules of the Board of Standards and Appeals that is MOST accurate is that

    A. feature I is a violation of the rules
    B. feature II is a violation of the rules
    C. feature III is a violation of the rules
    D. the installation complies with the rules

30. The Fire Department now uses companies on fire duty, with their apparatus, for fire prevention inspection in commercial buildings.
    The one of the following changes which was MOST important in making this inspection procedure practicable was the

    A. reduction of hours of work of firemen
    B. use of two-way radio equipment
    C. use of enclosed cabs on fire apparatus
    D. increase in property values during the post-war period

KEY (CORRECT ANSWERS)

1. C	11. D	21. B
2. D	12. B	22. C
3. D	13. B	23. A
4. D	14. B	24. D
5. C	15. A	25. C
6. C	16. B	26. D
7. B	17. C	27. B
8. C	18. C	28. C
9. D	19. A	29. D
10. A	20. B	30. B

EXAMINATION SECTION
TEST 1

DIRECTIONS: Each question or incomplete statement is followed by several suggested answers or completions. Select the one that BEST answers the question or completes the statement. *PRINT THE LETTER OF THE CORRECT ANSWER IN THE SPACE AT THE RIGHT.*

1. Of the following, the BEST basis that an officer can use for decision making is generally

    A. consultation with other officers
    B. trying out various alternatives
    C. intuitive ideas about the problem
    D. methodical analysis of the alternatives

    1.____

2. Assume that your company commander has delegated certain authority to you and specified that you are to abide by the *exception principle* in making your decisionsy. By this is meant that you are to

    A. take action only in exceptional circumstances, leaving routine actions to be handled by your subordinates
    B. proceed with action on matters covered by standard policy, but bring to his attention any problems not so covered
    C. recommend action on the matters he delegates, and note where you take exception with the application of standard policy
    D. report to him all cases in which you find that action has been taken contrary to standard policy, so that he may review these exceptions

    2.____

3. For an officer to establish goals for his men for operations for which there are no established departmental objectives is GENERALLY considered

    A. *acceptable,* as long as his goals fit into the department's overall objectives, because it will facilitate the planning and control of work
    B. *unacceptable,* because only management is empowered to establish goals and it is the primary duty of the first-line supervisor to implement them
    C. *acceptable,* because it will increase his prestige in the eyes of his men and accentuate his authority over them
    D. *unacceptable,* even though his ideas may be constructive, because it would disturb the uniformity of operations throughout the department

    3.____

4. As an officer, you will be responsible for correcting your subordinates when they make mistakes. Of the following, the BEST way for you to deal with your men when they make errors is to

    A. find out who is at fault in each case so that records of performance can be kept and discipline administered for repeated errors
    B. overlook mistakes that do not have serious consequences so the men will not feel that you are always checking up on them
    C. warn the men that mistakes cannot be tolerated in their work and if they are unsure of how to handle something they should avoid doing it unless supervised
    D. try to find out how each mistake was made so that the men can learn to avoid making them again

    4.____

5. Studies of employee attitudes and motivation conducted by behavioral scientists during the past two decades have had a great impact on theories of management. According to these findings, a company officer is MOST likely to motivate his subordinates by

   A. providing only necessary information rather than by giving as much information as he can
   B. keeping standards low rather than by expecting superior performance
   C. encouraging them to assume responsibility rather than by protecting them from risk
   D. engaging in off-the-job social activities with his men

6. An officer has been assigned to lead a series of conferences for members of a citizens' group who want to determine what they can do in promoting public education in fire prevention. Of the following approaches, the one that should probably be used to the GREATEST extent by the officer during the course of these conferences is to

   A. allow freedom of discussion on the topic
   B. call upon each participant to give his opinion in turn
   C. enforce the rules of parliamentary procedure
   D. make the group aware of the decisions he hopes it will reach and guide them toward that goal

7. An officer should try to prevent the grapevine from inventing and spreading rumors which might result in disruption of operations. Of the following, the best way to minimize the start and spreading of undesirable rumors in quarters is for the officer to

   A. avoid giving any clues about management decisions until they are formally announced
   B. provide as much accurate information as he can and allow the men to ask questions freely
   C. insist that all communications coming into company quarters be cleared through him
   D. put all communications in writing to prevent the possibility of misinterpretation

8. When preparing to train a fireman to do a new job, the officer is urged to prepare a job breakdown. The MOST important use of such a job breakdown is to

   A. provide a narrative description of the operation for official files
   B. provide written instructions for the fireman to work from
   C. list every step, point, motion, and precaution to be taught, so that a substitute instructor will have a plan to work from if the officer is called away
   D. remind the officer of important details which he might otherwise overlook because he knows the job so well

9. The activities and duties of an officer can be classified into three groups: those which he must perform himself, those which can be delegated to others but require close supervision, and those which can be delegated with a minimum of supervision. The one of the following duties which can MOST appropriately be delegated with close supervision is the

   A. evaluation of a subordinate
   B. preparation of routine reports
   C. approval of request for leave of absence without pay
   D. determination of proper disciplinary action

10. Assume that you are an officer whose company has been called to the scene of a fire along with three other companies and you happen to see a fireman from another company violating a safety practice. For you to stop him and order him to comply with safety regulations would be

    A. *appropriate*, chiefly because any superior officer may give a command to any fireman at any time
    B. *inappropriate*, chiefly because this fireman should take orders only from his direct superior
    C. *appropriate*, chiefly because stopping a fireman from doing an unsafe act is a justifiable reason for breaking the chain of command
    D. *inappropriate*, chiefly because your main responsibility is to the members of your own company who may need you during the time it would take to correct this fireman

11. The one of the following types of loyalty which is MOST likely to create the strongest team spirit among firemen is a feeling of loyalty toward

    A. one another
    B. the Department
    C. the public they serve
    D. their commanders

12. The one of the following which is MOST likely to increase the self-confidence of new firemen is to

    A. introduce different kinds of work incentives
    B. institute an effective work follow-up program
    C. develop their speed and accuracy in work performance
    D. tell them their work duties are less difficult than in other companies

13. Assume that a fireman has asked you, an officer, for details of a reorganization that is to take place in the near future. You know some of the details but you do not know how the fireman knows anything about the reorganization since you had been told by your superior that the reorganization was strictly confidential and that nobody below your level was to be informed at this time. In such a situation, the one of the following responses which generally would be MOST suitable for you to make is:

    A. Your information is not correct
    B. Since you already know about it, let me put you straight
    C. You had better not ask any questions about that
    D. I cannot give you any information about that

14. There are several methods of instruction which can be used to train firemen recently assigned to a company. Of the following, the MAIN reason for using the lecture method in training these men is that it

   A. allows a senior man quickly to give the firemen the benefit of his knowledge and experience
   B. facilitates the learning of new procedures since the lecturer does almost all the work
   C. allows the men to apply the material they obtain to their own particular situation
   D. facilitates the learning of new material, since each fireman can learn at his own pace

14.___

15. The kind of knowledge gained by an officer from personal contacts with his men which is usually MOST important in manpower utilization is knowledge of their

   A. attitudes toward the Department
   B. attitudes toward one another
   C. interest in the affairs of the community they serve
   D. backgrounds, skills, and capabilities

15.___

16. Assume that an officer has been asked to assign one man from his company to a special detail at battalion headquarters. To make sure that the assignment will be within the capacity of the detailed member, the officer should select one who has

   A. acquired the most seniority, since his length of service assures that he has had a great deal of experience in a variety of assignments
   B. already done well on a similar job since actual performance is the best way to measure ability to handle a job
   C. acquired the least seniority, because he has had the most recent formal training in general departmental operations and also because he can be spared most easily
   D. volunteered for the job, since ability to handle a job is determined by motivation and therefore the fireman who shows interest in the job can presumably do it best

16.___

17. Although company officers are expected to play a significant role in the training of firemen, they frequently neglect training as a process and a means to an end. Of the following, the PRINCIPAL reason for company officers lacking interest in pursuing the training process is that GENERALLY they

   A. cannot adapt themselves to the training role
   B. find their firemen lack motivation to learn outside of the formal classroom situation
   C. cannot, through training, always achieve quickly enough the results expected of them
   D. find their firemen do not react to them as agents of change because of familiarity through association in the firehouse

17.___

18. Fire officers expect to have their instructions obeyed immediately and to the letter. Regardless of his skill as leader or soundness of judgment as firefighter, however, every officer occasionally will encounter resistance to his orders. Sometimes the unresponsiveness takes the form of a member's respectful questioning of certain instructions under non-emergency conditions. The BEST way for an officer to deal with such a member is to

   A. suggest that failure to follow orders may be viewed as insubordination
   B. repeat the order and request compliance
   C. tell him to do the job in any way as long as it gets done
   D. ask for his objections to see whether his reasons are valid

18.____

19. As a fire officer you may find that some of your firemen come to you for advice when they have personal problems. The BEST way for you to deal with such situations is to

   A. show your interest in your men's problems by giving advice freely
   B. advise your men that personal problems cannot be dealt with on the job
   C. make it clear that you will not discuss personal problems unless they interfere with job performance
   D. make yourself available to listen to problems and to help your men analyze possible solutions

19.____

20. From a managerial point of view, participation of subordinates in making decisions likely to affect their work is generally desirable MAINLY because these employees will

   A. appreciate a management which practices good human relations
   B. be more willing to carry out decisions they have helped to make
   C. function effectively without the need for supervision
   D. develop a broader appreciation of interpersonal relationships and thus help make even better decisions in the future

20.____

21. A company officer has an important role in maintaining effective discipline in his organization. Among the following, the BEST criterion of success in this role would be the

   A. extent to which he relies on a particular method of discipline
   B. consistency with which he applies his decisions
   C. amount of time he spends handling grievances
   D. degree to which members accept the standards he sets up

21.____

22. Assume that an officer has been presented with a personal grievance by one of his firemen. The one of the following considerations which will be MOST important in helping the officer find and implement an effective and lasting solution is

   A. developing a solution which would satisfy the fireman
   B. evaluating the opinions of all the men in the company before reaching a decision
   C. investigating the grievance thoroughly to find its underlying cause
   D. acting quickly before the situation becomes more serious

22.____

23. The mutual trust and ready cooperation that develops when individual firemen go through the process of coalescing into a tightly knit group is vital in dealing with emergencies. MOST effective among the following techniques a company officer might use in attempting to facilitate the growth of such group solidarity is

    A. pitching in to help the men to show that he considers himself a member of the group
    B. trying to unite the men in opposition to certain departmental regulations which they believe should be revised
    C. encouraging his men to compete with one another for departmental awards and other honors
    D. giving special recognition to the group as a whole when they do a good job

24. A captain interrupts a lieutenant who is instructing his platoon and tells the lieutenant he is not instructing the men properly. After the captain's departure, the lieutenant, visibly upset, informs the men that the captain is a poor supervisor. The behavior of the lieutenant in this situation would GENERALLY be considered

    A. *proper,* mainly because the captain's remark deservedly lowered the lieutenant's prestige in the eyes of his men
    B. *improper,* mainly because a lieutenant should never make derogatory remarks about a captain to his subordinates
    C. *proper,* mainly because the lieutenant should never quarrel with a captain in front of his men
    D. *improper,* mainly because the lieutenant should have responded to the captain's remark immediately

25. For which of the following purposes would it generally be MOST appropriate for a company officer to hold a conference with his subordinates?

    A. To analyze the deficiencies in a fire operation in which they were all engaged
    B. To decide what to do about excessive lateness on the part of a few men
    C. To read a new report on the firefighting techniques pertinent to operations
    D. To tell the men of several changes in assignment which he has just been informed of

KEY (CORRECT ANSWERS)

1. D
2. B
3. A
4. D
5. C

6. A
7. B
8. D
9. B
10. C

11. A
12. C
13. D
14. A
15. D

16. B
17. C
18. D
19. D
20. B

21. D
22. C
23. D
24. B
25. A

TEST 2

DIRECTIONS: Each question or incomplete statement is followed by several suggested answers or completions. Select the one that BEST answers the question or completes the statement. *PRINT THE LETTER OF THE CORRECT ANSWER IN THE SPACE AT THE RIGHT.*

1. A superior officer, visiting a company performing inspection duty, is informed by the officer in command of a hazardous situation just encountered in a fur processing plant. In the presence of the factory manager, the two officers discussed several approaches to the problem that could be taken by the fire department to abate the hazard. Finally, the superior officer directed the company officer to issue certain orders to the manager. Discussing this problem in the presence of the manager was

    A. *proper,* mainly because he probably would realize that the fire department was not acting arbitrarily or unreasonably
    B. *improper,* mainly because he might prefer one of the approaches which was suggested and rejected
    C. *proper,* mainly because the activities of the fire department should, whenever possible, be open to the public
    D. *improper,* mainly because inaccurate statements may have been made during the preliminary discussion

2. A superior officer who gives a company officer a *tongue lashing* or *bawling out* uses a dubious technique of leadership, even if done in private. Of the following, the MAIN objection to this practice is that generally the

    A. company officer does not have an adequate opportunity to defend himself
    B. point at issue tends to be obscured and the matter becomes a personal clash between individuals
    C. past records of the company officer and all the surrounding circumstances of the incident are not adequately considered
    D. incident becomes widely known and undermines the authority of the company officer

3. The one of the following which would NOT be an acceptable practice for a superior officer to observe when criticizing a subordinate is to

    A. focus attention on the act to be criticized instead of on the person
    B. express the criticism in general rather than specific terms
    C. refer to previous instances of poor performance
    D. avoid humor or sarcasm when making the criticism

4. Personal contact between the upper and lower ranks is generally recommended by students of administration as a way of maintaining good internal communications in an organization. However, the MAIN disadvantage to such personal contact between superior officers and firemen is the danger that

    A. time spent in making personal contacts will interfere with the performance of other essential activities
    B. firemen who do not receive personal attention will suspect favoritism and become resentful
    C. company officers will feel that they are being bypassed and their authority undermined
    D. the necessary distance between the ranks will be destroyed

5. At a *bull session* of officers, an officer tells of the matrimonial problems of a member with an excellent reputation as a fireman. After giving the sordid details of the situation, the officer asks a superior officer for suggestions as to how the member should handle the problem. In this situation, the MAIN error made by the officer was

   A. his failure to direct the member to an appropriate social agency
   B. consulting the superior officer before consulting the company commander
   C. discussing the member's personal affairs with other persons
   D. discussing company problems outside the confines of the company

6. The one of the following results which would be the MOST likely consequence of decentralization of authority and responsibility in an organization is

   A. improved discipline
   B. increased specialization of functions
   C. greater diversity in procedures
   D. greater interchangeability of personnel

7. A superior officer is concerned about whether a newly adopted and complicated field inspection procedure is fully understood by his company commanders. The one of the following actions which would be the MOST effective way of determinig whether or not the procedure is understood is to

   A. observe the companies as they perform inspectional duties to determine whether the new procedure is being properly applied
   B. question each of the company commanders about how he would interpret the procedure in specific situations
   C. circulate a supplementary memorandum to clarify some of the points that may be misunderstood
   D. direct all commanding officers to report any instances of misinterpretation of the procedures

8. Assume that a difficult problem developed in a battalion and the battalion commander asked all battalion chiefs and company commanders to submit detailed plans, in writing, for handling the matter. The plans were then discussed and criticized at a meeting attended by all the officers who submitted suggestions. The battalion commander then formulated his plan based upon the discussion. As a method of administration, the technique used by the battalion commander is

   A. *good,* mainly because an objective basis for evaluating the leadership potential of subordinates will be obtained
   B. *bad,* mainly because duplication of effort and waste of time results
   C. *good,* chiefly because the subordinate officers will be more receptive to the plan as a result of their participation in its formulation
   D. *bad,* chiefly because the responsibility of the battalion commander is diluted by the involvement of subordinate officers in the decision process

9. Assume that a superior officer is present during a drill involving the use of a new resuscitator. After demonstrating one of the uses of the equipment, the officer conducting the drill calls upon a fireman to operate the equipment. The fireman makes several mistakes but the officer says nothing to him until the operation is completed. Then the officer points out the mistakes and once again demonstrates the correct method of operation. The officer's teaching method was

   A. *good*, mainly because the fireman was permitted to complete the operation without frequent interruptions
   B. *bad*, mainly because the fireman's errors were not corrected immediately
   C. *good*, mainly because the officer demonstrated thorough knowledge of the equipment
   D. *bad*, mainly because the officer did not call upon other firemen to correct the errors and demonstrate the correct method of operation

10. It has been suggested that companies be given additional inspectional duties as punishment for poor performance of evolutions, poor condition of equipment or quarters, etc. Of the following, the MOST valid objection to this proposal is that

    A. the punishment does not directly improve the skills or functions which are found to be deficient
    B. inspectional activities would be degraded by making such assignments a form of punishment
    C. the punishment is imposed on a group rather than individual basis
    D. scheduling of regular inspectional activities would be disrupted

11. Some organizations, as a matter of policy, transfer their administrative staff personnel from one unit to another after stated periods of service in the unit. Of the following, the MAIN advantage of such a policy is that it

    A. helps keep the staff members abreast of the technical developments in their fields
    B. impedes the formation of personal cliques among staff members
    C. helps develop wider outlook and loyalty to the organization as a whole rather than to the unit assigned
    D. permits the more effective utilization of the individual talents of staff members

12. Leaders generally are somewhat more intelligent than their followers. The CHIEF difficulty of the leader who is markedly more intelligent than his followers is that such a leader has difficulty in

    A. overcoming the suspicion and distrust of intellectuals on the part of the group
    B. understanding the thought processes of persons who are intellectually inferior
    C. accepting the irrational and emotional basis of much of human conduct
    D. making himself understood by the group

13. Overly detailed fire prevention inspections are to be avoided CHIEFLY because they

    A. unduly interfere with the normal activities of the occupancy, causing public resentment
    B. require excessive time which could be used to better advantage inspecting other occupancies
    C. tend to result in oversight of some fundamental hazards
    D. are beyond the capabilities of many firemen who are not specifically trained in inspectional techniques

14. In a psychological study of leadership, it was found that it is possible to predict the behavior of a new man in a leadership position more accurately on the basis of the behavior of his predecessor in the post than on the behavior of the man himself in his previous job. The BEST explanation of this observation is that there is a tendency

    A. to select similar types of personalities to fill the same type of position
    B. for a newly appointed man to avoid instituting basic changes in operational procedures
    C. for a given organizational structure and set of duties to produce similar patterns of behavior
    D. for increased responsibility to impose more mature patterns of behavior on an incumbent

15. A superior officer finds that reports reaching him from his subordinates tend to exaggerate the favorable, and minimize the unfavorable, aspects of situations existing within the division. The one of the following which would be the MOST valid conclusion to draw is that

    A. the superior officer has been overly severe with subordinates and has instilled fear in them
    B. there is a normal tendency for persons to represent themselves and their actions in the best possible light
    C. members of the fire department tend to be optimists
    D. the superior officer has not been sufficiently critical of previous reports and has not been alert to conditions in the division

16. Assume that the following passage is taken from a report which you, a superior officer, receive from an officer under your command. The report relates to a fire for which the department received public criticism because of delay in response and extension of fire to neighboring buildings.
    Alarm from box _____ was received at 5:13 P.M. on Friday, October 2. All first alarm companies departed from quarters expeditiously but progress along the Vehicle-glutted arterial thoroughfares was agonizingly slow. By dint of extraordinary effort, and by virtue of great skill in maneuvering through impassable traffic, Engine Co. _____ arrived at the scene at 5:21 P.M. The sight which greeted them was a virtual Dante's INFERNO, of holocaust proportions. The hub of the conflagration was the penultimate structure of a row of houses, with extension impending to contiguous edifices....

The MAIN fault with the above report is that it

- A. contains spelling and punctuation errors
- B. contains unnecessary details
- C. uses words not in accordance with dictionary definitions
- D. uses inappropriate language and style

17. A special unit of the fire department is rife with rumors concerning plans for its future and the possibility of its abolition. As a result, morale and production of members assigned to it have suffered. To handle this situation, the superior officer in command adopts a policy of promptly corroborating factual rumors and denying false ones. This method of dealing with the problem will achieve some good results, but its CHIEF weakness is that

    - A. it gives status to the rumors by the attention paid to them
    - B. the superior officer may not have the necessary information at hand to dispose promptly of all rumors
    - C. it *chases* the rumors rather than forestalling them by giving information concerning the unit's future
    - D. the superior officer may have confidential information which he should not divulge

18. A superior officer, realizing the importance of harmonious relationships within his command, made a practice of unobtrusively intervening in any conflict situation between officers. Whenever friction seemed to be developing, he would attempt to soothe ruffled feelings, remove the source of difficulty by rescheduling activities or reassigning personnel, etc. His efforts were always behind-the-scenes, and unknown to the officers involved. Although this method of operation produces some good results, it CHIEF drawback is that it

    - A. violates the chain of command principle
    - B. involves the superior officer in personal relationships which are not properly his concern
    - C. requires confidential sources of information about relationships within the division which borders on spying
    - D. permits subordinate officers to engage in unacceptable practices without correction

19. A superior officer entered a headquarters while a regular conference was being conducted by the company commander. The major items on the agenda were a new phase of the field inspection program, unsatisfactory safety record, and improper apparatus maintenance practices. During the course of the conference, the superior officer frequently took over the discussion in order to amplify remarks of the company commander, to impart information about policies which have been adopted by headquarters but not yet disseminated, and to modify or correct possible misinterpretations of the company commander's remarks. The superior officer's actions in this situation were

    - A. *proper,* mainly because the conference members were given the latest and most accurate information concerning departmental policies
    - B. *improper,* mainly because the company commander was placed in a difficult position
    - C. *proper,* mainly because the superior officer had an obligation to support and assist the company commander
    - D. *improper,* mainly because the superior officer did not completely take over the conference

20. At a conference at which a basic change in the department's fire prevention procedures was to be announced, the conference leader started the discussion by asking the group for criticisms of the existing procedures.
    He then described the new procedures to be employed and explained the improvements in operations that were anticipated. The conference leader's method of introducing the change was

    A. *good,* mainly because the conference members would be more receptive to the new procedure if they understood the inadequacies of the old
    B. *bad,* mainly because the conference members would realize that the decision for change had been made before the discussion and without consideration of their comments
    C. *good,* mainly because the comments and criticisms of the old procedure would provide the basis for evaluating the feasibility of the new method
    D. *bad,* mainly because the focus of the discussion was on the procedure being replaced rather than on the procedure being introduced

21. A superior officer in command of a specialized unit calls a staff conference to discuss a proposed modification of some procedures. After making some introductory remarks, the superior officer wants the comments of the members of the staff. The staff consists of 8 officers ranging in rank from lieutenant to deputy chief, each officer having responsibility for a different aspect of the program. Of the following, the BEST procedure for him to follow is to call upon each member in

    A. descending order of rank mainly because the officers with the highest rank are likely to have the most experience and ability
    B. ascending order of rank mainly because the junior officers are more likely to be freer in their comments if they give their views before the senior officers speak
    C. order of their specialized knowledge and competence in the subjects under discussion mainly because those with most knowledge and competence can best lead the discussion
    D. order of seating around the table mainly because informality of procedure and democratic leadership is obtained

22. Some officers regard the preparation of reports as a routine task to be performed by subordinates without careful review. This practice is unwise CHIEFLY because the

    A. officer may appear to be shirking an unpleasant duty
    B. subordinate preparing the reports may come to regard the reports as unimportant and prepare them carelessly
    C. person preparing the reports is not responsible for their accuracy
    D. officer will not have first-hand knowledge on conditions within his command

23. An officer who observes a fireman performing an operation in an incorrect or inefficient manner should promptly correct the fireman. However, for an officer to insist that all operations, even the most trivial, be performed *his way* is undesirable CHIEFLY because

   A. an officer cannot personally supervise every operation
   B. initiative of the subordinate may be weakened
   C. the officer's way of doing things may not always be the best way
   D. officers should not concern themselves with petty details

24. An elderly man approaches you, as officer on duty, to complain that the noise of apparatus responding to alarms wakes him in the middle of the night. Of the following, the BEST way for you to handle this situation is to

   A. quickly change the subject since the man obviously is a *crank*
   B. ask the man for specific instances of apparatus making noise at night
   C. explain the need for speed in response of apparatus
   D. promise to avoid making unnecessary noise at night

25. Flexibility of operations and ability to meet emergency situations are BEST developed in firemen by stressing, during training programs,

   A. speed and proficiency in drills
   B. concepts and principles of firemanics
   C. the unusual situations which may be encountered at fires
   D. the latest developments in firefighting techniques and apparatus

KEY (CORRECT ANSWERS)

1. D	11. C
2. B	12. D
3. B	13. B
4. C	14. C
5. C	15. B
6. C	16. D
7. B	17. C
8. C	18. D
9. B	19. B
10. B	20. B

21. C
22. D
23. B
24. C
25. B

TEST 3

DIRECTIONS: Each question or incomplete statement is followed by several suggested answers or completions. Select the one that BEST answers the question or completes the statement. *PRINT THE LETTER OF THE CORRECT ANSWER IN THE SPACE AT THE RIGHT.*

1. It has been observed that the men who receive the highest grades during a training course do not always perform as well when operating in the field. Of the following, the BEST explanation of this discrepancy is that

    A. men learn only by doing
    B. training courses are theoretical rather than practical
    C. training courses do not duplicate completely field conditions
    D. most people function below their potentialities

    1.____

2. The skilled officer recognizes that he is dealing with a group and not just individuals and that the group has standards and purposes which influence the behavior of the individuals with whose work he is concerned.
   The implication of this statement for a company officer is that

    A. both individual differences and group reactions should be considered when dealing with any situation
    B. individual differences should be given less consideration than group reactions when making decisions
    C. members of a company tend to present a united front against officers
    D. cliques are inevitable in any large organization such as the fire department

    2.____

3. Public praise of a member by a company officer is an effective way of improving morale provided that it

    A. is given with some degree of uniformity among all the members
    B. appears to be spontaneous
    C. is offset by occasional public criticism
    D. is not done excessively

    3.____

4. The good leader has the capacity not only to accept responsibility and exercise initiative himself but also to develop these traits in his subordinates. Of the following, the BEST method for an officer to use to encourage firemen to use initiative and assume responsibility is to

    A. rotate routine assignments equally among all members of the company
    B. employ suggestions or implied commands rather than direct commands in other than emergency situations
    C. encourage firemen to read books and take courses in leadership
    D. ask for volunteers to perform necessary company duties

    4.____

5. An officer instructing his men on a new procedure asked at frequent intervals whether there were any questions. Asking for questions is a

   A. *good* practice, chiefly because it affords the men an opportunity to participate actively in the lesson
   B. *poor* practice, chiefly because it may result in wasting time on irrelevant matters
   C. *good* practice, chiefly because it may reveal points that are not understood by the men
   D. *poor* practice, chiefly because men generally are reluctant to ask questions

6. An officer who was assigned to deliver a talk before a civic organization first made a detailed outline of his talk. Then, with the help of two members of his company, he prepared several demonstrations and charts. The officer's procedure was

   A. *good,* chiefly because careful preparation increases the effectiveness of a talk
   B. *poor,* chiefly because a talk should be guided by the question and comments of the audience and not follow a pre-determined outline
   C. *good,* chiefly because the audience will be impressed by the care that the lieutenant has taken in preparing the talk
   D. *poor,* chiefly because the talk will appear rehearsed rather than spontaneous and natural

7. An officer who was giving a series of lectures started each talk by asking a member to summarize the points covered in the previous talk. This practice is

   A. *poor;* time is wasted in needless repetition
   B. *good;* the lieutenant is free to observe the attitude of the group while the member is speaking
   C. *poor;* the member may make erroneous statements and mislead the group
   D. *good;* the learning process is reinforced by the review

8. After giving one of his men an assignment, an officer returns to find that the member had not done the work according to instructions. The first thing that the officer should ascertain is whether the member had

   A. ever performed the work before
   B. personal problems which may be interfering with the performance of his duties
   C. previously failed to follow instructions
   D. understood the instructions

9. In training their men, officers have learned that it is rarely justifiable to stand before their company and merely lecture to them.
   Of the following, the MOST probable reason for this conclusion is that

   A. the number of persons who can be trained in this manner is severely limited
   B. most persons dislike being *talked to* constantly
   C. in order to learn, the learner must participate in the teaching process
   D. too much material is usually covered, making it difficult to memorize details

10. An officer, in an effort to improve training results, made a training progress table on which he listed the men in his group and the various skills he expected to teach in each lesson. As a member performed each task, the officer placed a check or cross on the chart which indicated satisfactory or unsatisfactory performance. The use of a training table in this manner is

   A. *desirable*, mainly because it enables the lieutenant to keep track of the members' progress and the tasks that require additional training
   B. *undesirable*, mainly because it reduces the amount of time available for teaching and observing
   C. *desirable*, mainly because it helps the lieutenant to rate his subordinates
   D. *undesirable*, mainly because the emphasis is placed on the performance of the parts of the operation rather than on the operation as a whole

11. An experienced officer teaching probationary firemen often overlooks so-called minor points because of his great familiarity with the job. When an instructor takes such points for granted, he leaves gaps in his instruction.
Of the following, the BEST way of preventing this type of oversight is to

   A. ask the probationary firemen if they have any questions during the explanation and demonstration
   B. observe the probationary firemen closely as they perform the operation for errors or misconceptions
   C. utilize visual aids in demonstrating the operation
   D. break down the operation into simple parts when planning the lesson

12. When conducting drills, an officer made an effort to devote approximately the same amount of time to each member of the group. This procedure GENERALLY is

   A. *good*, because the members will realize that they all are receiving equal treatment
   B. *bad*, because some members require more training than others
   C. *good*, because the officer is less likely to neglect any member
   D. *bad*, because the officer has to devote too much effort to keeping track of the time spent with each member

13. For an officer occasionally to devote a drill period to the use of basic tools, such as the axe or the hook, is GENERALLY

   A. *necessary*, mainly because such drills will help keep the members in good physical condition
   B. *unnecessary*, mainly because there are more important subjects requiring attention
   C. *necessary*, mainly because faulty habits may develop if fundamentals are not reviewed
   D. *unnecessary*, mainly because members have many opportunities to use these tools at fires

14. An officer conducting inspection duty enters a luncheonette and discovers that the owner, the only person on duty, apparently does not understand English. The one of the following which would be the BEST action for the officer to take in this situation is to attempt to

    A. make the owner understand by speaking English in a loud, clear voice
    B. make the owner understand by using sign language
    C. find a customer or passerby who can act as an interpreter
    D. question the owner closely to determine whether he really does not understand English

15. During the height of extinguishment operations at a fire in a taxpayer, an officer observes a newly assigned probationary fireman attempting, in an awkward and dangerous manner, to ventilate by chopping a hole in the roof with an axe. In this situation, the BEST of the following courses for the officer to follow is to

    A. briefly demonstrate the proper axe technique
    B. assign an experienced fireman to cut the hole and give the probationary fireman another assignment
    C. assign an experienced fireman to assist the probationary fireman
    D. permit the probationary fireman to finish but avoid similar assignments until after he receives additional training in the handling of axes

16. An officer who frequently changes the standard operating procedures in routine matter is PROBABLY

    A. open-minded and receptive to new ideas
    B. insecure and emotionally unstable
    C. hasty and inclined to act without careful consideration
    D. a perfectionist with very high standards

17. Although it is inevitable that on occasion an officer will have doubts about the wisdom of an order which he receives from his superior, nothing in the officer's words or manner in transmitting this order to his subordinates should betray his opinion.
    The idea expressed in this statement is

    A. *valid,* mainly because a subordinate must be sure of his grounds before criticizing the orders of his superior officer
    B. *invalid,* mainly because the officer is denied the normal outlet for his feeling which may cause psychological problems
    C. *valid,* mainly because criticism of orders to subordinates, either expressed or implied, weakens discipline
    D. *invalid,* mainly because there are established means for suggesting improvements in departmental procedures

18. The good leader encourages his men to work *with him* rather than *for him*.
The one of the following statements which MOST accurately gives the implication of this directive is that the leader should

   A. do a share of the unpleasant and hazardous tasks of the job
   B. instill the idea that he and his men have the same goals and interests
   C. maintain direct personal contact with his men whenever practicable
   D. encourage his men to exercise initiative and assume responsibility within the limits of their rank and assignment

19. On a number of occasions, an officer found it necessary to criticize the careless and untidy work of a fireman when performing housekeeping chores. After a number of incidents, the officer called the fireman into the office to discuss the problem. The officer reviewed all the previous incidents and, at the end of the discussion, said, *You have been a slob around here. If you don't improve immediately I will prefer charges against you.*
The MOST serious error made by the officer in dealing with this situation was his

   A. failure to prefer charges immediately
   B. threat to prefer charges for future incidents
   C. criticism of the member's character
   D. reference to past incidents

20. An officer in command at a fire with a high hazard of explosion made a great effort to give orders in his normal tone of voice and, generally, to conduct himself in his normal manner as though the situation were routine and without danger. In this situation, the officer's behavior was

   A. *improper,* mainly because the men under his command are not alerted to their danger
   B. *proper,* mainly because danger is part of a fireman's job and should be faced without flinching
   C. *improper,* mainly because the lieutenant is not behaving normally or honestly
   D. *proper,* mainly because the men under his command also will tend to act calmly

21. The MAIN reason for a superior officer to delegate authority to a subordinate officer is to

   A. develop the leadership potential of the subordinate
   B. make the authority equal to the responsibility of an assignment
   C. free the superior officer for more important tasks
   D. obtain new and better methods of performing the duties assigned

22. During inspection of quarters, a battalion chief criticizes the method employed in compiling a certain report and orders the officer on duty to modify the procedure. The modification is in conflict with the explicit orders of the company commander. In this situation, the officer should

   A. suggest to the battalion chief that he first discuss the matter with the company commander
   B. report the matter to the company commander before putting into effect the new method
   C. modify the record keeping method and inform the company commander of the change at the first opportunity
   D. modify the record keeping method as directed without notification to the company commander since the battalion chief usually informs the company commander of his orders

23. Fundamental to good supervision is the ability to realize and act effectively on the fact that employees' motivations, attitudes, and work output often are keyed to some aspect of their lives that is apart from their job. The officer who appreciates this

   A. expects the same performance from each man on all occasions
   B. considers the possibility of factors outside of the job influencing the poor performance of a fireman
   C. spends considerable time counseling his men on the various aspects of their personal lives
   D. refrains from consideration of the personal problems of a fireman that may affect his performance

24. When disciplinary action in the form of an oral reprimand is to be administered to a newly appointed fireman, the officer should, at the same time,

   A. warn the fireman that he'd better read up on his regulations so as not to be at fault again
   B. advise the fireman that he is required to reprimand him, but that the fireman should not worry about it
   C. ask the older men to keep a sharp eye on the new man and to notify him if additional disciplining is needed
   D. attempt to determine the reason for the fireman's error

25. Environment is like the photographer's developing chemical. It creates nothing, but it can bring out what is on the film.
   To the company officer this means MOST NEARLY that

   A. individual capacity determines what should be taught, not the predetermined course content
   B. it is necessary to provide a good environment and understandable objectives in order to make the training process effective
   C. if an individual does not have the required mental capacity, he will be unable to benefit from training to the desired degree
   D. knowledge of the developing process in photography provides key points in a productive training program

KEY (CORRECT ANSWERS)

1.	C	11.	D
2.	A	12.	B
3.	B	13.	C
4.	B	14.	C
5.	C	15.	B
6.	A	16.	C
7.	D	17.	C
8.	D	18.	B
9.	C	19.	C
10.	A	20.	D

21. C
22. C
23. B
24. D
25. C

READING COMPREHENSION
UNDERSTANDING AND INTERPRETING WRITTEN MATERIAL
EXAMINATION SECTION
TEST 1

DIRECTIONS: Each question or incomplete statement is followed by several suggested answers or completions. Select the one that BEST answers the question or completes the statement. *PRINT THE LETTER OF THE CORRECT ANSWER IN THE SPACE AT THE RIGHT.*

Questions 1-2.

DIRECTIONS: Questions 1 and 2 are to be answered on the basis of the following passage.

The firefighter who is assigned to the roof position at a fire in a brownstone building should perform the following steps in the order given:

I. Go to the roof using one of the following ways:
   (a) First choice - The aerial ladder
   (b) Second choice - An attached building of the same height as the fire building
   (c) Third choice - A rear fire escape
   (d) Fourth choice - A thirty five foot portable ladder

II. Upon arrival at the roof, look around to determine if any people are trapped who cannot be seen from the street.
   (a) If a trapped person is observed, notify the officer and the driver that a life-saving rope rescue is required. While waiting for assistance to conduct this rescue, assure the victim that help is on the way and proceed to Step III.
   (b) If no trapped persons are visible, proceed directly to Step III.

III. Remove the cover from the opening in the roof.
   (a) If there is no smoke or very little smoke coming from the opening, report to the officer for further orders.
   (b) If heavy smoke comes from the opening, proceed to Step IV.

IV. Remove the glass from the skylight.

1. Firefighters arriving at a fire in a brownstone are using the aerial ladder to make an immediate rescue. The firefighter assigned to the roof position should go to the roof of the building on fire by

   A. a 35-foot portable ladder
   B. a rear fire escape
   C. an attached building of the same height
   D. the inside stairway of the fire building

1._____

2. The firefighter assigned to the roof position at a fire in a brownstone arrives at the roof and finds that no persons are trapped. He then removes the roof cover from the opening in the roof.
Which one of the following steps should be performed NEXT?
He should _____ is coming from the roof opening.

   A. remove the glass from the skylight if heavy smoke
   B. remove the glass from the skylight if no smoke
   C. go to the top floor to assist in the search for trapped persons if heavy smoke
   D. report to the officer if heavy smoke

Questions 3-4.

DIRECTIONS: Questions 3 and 4 are to be answered on the basis of the following passage.

Firefighters are often required to remove people who are trapped in elevators. At this type of emergency, firefighters perform the following steps in the order given:

1. Upon entering the building, determine the location of the elevator involved.
2. Reassure the trapped occupants that the Fire Department is on the scene and that firefighters are attempting to free them.
3. Determine if there are any injured people in the elevator.
4. Determine if all the doors from the hallways into the elevator shaft are closed.
5. If all the doors are closed, call for an elevator mechanic.
6. Wait until a trained elevator mechanic arrives before attempting to remove any trapped persons from the elevator, unless they can be removed through the door to the hallway. However, firefighters must remove the trapped persons by any safe method if any one of the following conditions exists:
   (a) There is a fire in the building
   (b) Someone in the elevator is injured
   (c) The people trapped in the elevator are in a state of panic.

3. Firefighters arrive at an elevator emergency in an office building. When they arrive, a maintenance man directs them to an elevator which is stuck between the fourth and fifth floors. He informs the firefighters that there is a young man in the elevator who apparently is calm and unhurt.
Which one of the following steps should the firefighters perform NEXT?

   A. Determine if the young man is injured.
   B. Reassure the young man that the Fire Department is on the scene and that firefighters are attempting to free him.
   C. Check to make sure that all the doors to the elevator and hallways are closed.
   D. Call for an elevator mechanic and await his arrival.

4. Firefighters are called to an elevator emergency at a factory building. The freight elevator has stopped suddenly between floors. The sudden stop caused heavy boxes to fall on the elevator operator, breaking his arm. Upon arrival, the firefighters determine the location of the elevator. They tell the trapped operator that they are on the scene, are aware of his injury, and are attempting to free him. They determine that all the hallway doors leading into the elevator shaft are closed. The firefighters' NEXT step should be to

   A. call for an ambulance and wait until it arrives
   B. remove the trapped person through the door to the hallway

C. call for an elevator mechanic
D. remove the trapped person by any safe method

Questions 5-6.

DIRECTIONS: Questions 5 and 6 are to be answered SOLELY on the basis of the following passage.

A firefighter is responsible for a variety of duties other than fighting fires. One such duty is housewatch.

A firefighter's primary responsibility during housewatch is to properly receive alarm information. This enables firefighters to respond to alarms for fires and emergencies. The alarms are received at the firehouse by one of the following methods: computer tele-printer messages, Fire Department telephone or verbal alarm. The computer teleprinter and the telephone are used to alert the fire companies. These two types of alarms are transmitted by a dispatcher from a central communication office to the firehouse closest to the fire. The verbal alarm occurs when someone comes to the firehouse or stops the fire truck on the street to report a fire. Once an alarm has been received, the firefighter on housewatch duty alerts the rest of the firefighters to respond to the alarm.

Other housewatch responsibilities include keeping the appearance of the housewatch area neat and orderly, keeping the front of the firehouse clear of all vehicles and obstructions, and receiving telephone calls and visitors with complaints about fire hazards. The firefighter on housewatch duty also keeps an accurate and complete record of all administrative matters in a journal.

5. The methods a dispatcher uses to transmit alarms to the firehouse are the

   A. computer teleprinter, Fire Department telephone, and verbal alarm
   B. verbal alarm and computer teleprinter
   C. Fire Department telephone and verbal alarm
   D. computer teleprinter and Fire Department telephone

6. The PRIMARY responsibility of a firefighter on housewatch duty is to

   A. properly assign firefighters to specific duties
   B. properly receive alarm information
   C. keep the housewatch area neat and orderly
   D. write all important information in the company journal

Questions 7-8.

DIRECTIONS: Questions 7 and 8 are to be answered SOLELY on the basis of the following passage.

One duty of a firefighter on housewatch is to ensure that the computer teleprinter is working properly. A company officer should be notified immediately of any equipment problems. The firefighter on housewatch should check on the amount of paper in the teleprinter and should refill it when necessary. The firefighter should also check the selector panel on the computer. This selector panel has a series of buttons which are used by the firefighter to let the dispatcher know that an alarm has been received and that the fire company is responding. These buttons have lights. To check that the computer is functioning properly, the firefighter should press the button marked test and then release the button. If the computer lights go on, and then go off after the test button has been released, the computer is working properly. In addition, the light next to the test button should always be blinking.

7. In order to check that the selector panel of the computer is working properly, the firefighter on housewatch duty presses the button marked *test*, and then releases the button. The firefighter should conclude that the computer is working properly if the

   A. computer lights stay on
   B. computer lights keep blinking
   C. computer lights go on and then off
   D. test light stays on

7.___

8. A firefighter on housewatch duty notices that the teleprinter is almost out of paper. In this situation, the firefighter should

   A. test the computer panel by pushing the *test* button
   B. notify the officer to replace the paper
   C. place a new supply of paper in the teleprinter
   D. notify the dispatcher that the paper is being changed

8.___

Questions 9-10.

DIRECTIONS: Questions 9 and 10 are to be answered SOLELY on the basis of the following passage.

Following is a list of rules for fire extinguishers which are required in different types of public buildings in the city:

Rule 1: Hospitals, nursing homes, hotels, and motels must have one 2 1/2 gallon water extinguisher for every 2500 square feet, or part thereof, of floor area on each floor.

Rule 2: Stores with floor areas of 1500 square feet or less must have one 2 1/2 gallon water extinguisher. Stores with floor areas of over 1500 square feet must have one 2 1/2 gallon water extinguisher for every 2500 square feet, or part thereof, of floor area on each floor.

Rule 3: Kitchens must have one 2 1/2 gallon foam extinguisher or one 5 pound dry chemical extinguisher for every 1250 square feet, or part thereof, of floor area on each floor. For kitchen areas, this rule is in addition to Rules 1 and 2.

9. A firefighter is inspecting a one-story nursing home which has a total of 3000 square feet of floor area. This includes a kitchen, which is 1500 square feet in area, in the rear of the floor.
Of the following, the firefighter should conclude that the nursing home should be equipped with

   A. 1 water extinguisher and 1 foam extinguisher
   B. 1 water extinguisher and 1 dry chemical extinguisher
   C. 2 water extinguishers and 2 foam extinguishers
   D. 2 foam extinguishers and 1 dry chemical extinguisher

9.___

10. A firefighter is inspecting a store which has two floors. The first floor has 2600 square feet. The second floor has 1450 square feet.
The store should be equipped with AT LEAST

   A. two 2 1/2 gallon water extinguishers, one for each floor
   B. three 2 1/2 gallon water extinguishers, two for the first floor and one for the second floor
   C. two 2 1/2 gallon foam extinguishers, one for each floor
   D. two 2 1/2 gallon extinguishers, either foam or water, one for each floor

11. Firefighters from the first arriving ladder company workin teams while fighting fires in private homes. The inside team enters the building through the first floor entrance and then searches the first floor for victims. The outside team uses ladders to enter upper level windows for a quick search of the bedrooms on the second floor and above. The assignments for the members of the outside team are as follows:

    Roof person - This member places a ladder at the front porch and enters the second floor windows from the roof of the porch.

    Outside vent person and driver - These members work together and place a portable ladder at a window on the opposite side of the house from which the roof person is working. However, if the aerial ladder can be used, the outside vent person and driver climb the aerial ladder in the front of the house and the roof person places a portable ladder on the left side of the house.

    In order to search all four sides of a private home on the upper levels, firefighters from the second arriving ladder company place portable ladders at the sides of the house not covered by the first ladder company, and enter the home through the upper level windows.

    The second ladder company to arrive at a fire in a 2-story private home sees the aerial ladder being raised to the front porch roof.

    In this situation, the firefighters should place their portable ladders to the _____ sides of the house since _____.

    A. left and right; there is a front porch
    B. rear and right; the aerial ladder is being used
    C. rear and left; there is a front porch
    D. left and right; the aerial ladder is being used

12. The priority for the removal of a particular victim by aerial ladder depends on the following conditions: If two victims are at the same window and are not seriously endangered by spreading fire, the victim who is easier to remove is taken down the ladder first and helped safely to the street. In general, the term *easier to remove* refers to the victim who is more capable of being moved and more able to cooperate. After the easier removal is completed, time can be spen on the more difficult removal.

    If there are victims at two different windows, the aerial ladder is first placed to remove the victims who are the most seriously endangered by the fire. The ladder is then placed to remove the victims who are less seriously exposed to the fire.

    Assume that you are working at a fire and that there are a total of three victims at two windows. Victims #1 and #2 are at the same window, which is three floors above the fire and shows no evidence of heat or smoke. Victim #1 is a disabled, 23 year-old male, and Victim #2 is a 40 year-old woman. Victim #3, a 16 year-old male, is at a window of the apartment on fire. From your position in the street, you can see heavy smoke coming from this window and flames coming out of the window next to it. Which one of the following is the PROPER order for victim removal? Victim

    A. #3, #2, #1
    B. #1, #2, #3
    C. #1, #3, #2
    D. #3, #1, #2

Questions 13-14.

DIRECTIONS: Questions 13 and 14 are to be answered SOLELY on the basis of the following passage.

The four different types of building collapses are as follows:

1. <u>Building Wall Collapse</u> - An outside wall of the building collapses but the floors maintain their positions.
2. <u>Lean-to Collapse</u> - One end of a floor collapses onto the floor below it. This leaves a sheltered area on the floor below.
3. <u>Floor Collapse</u> - An entire floor falls to the floor below it but large pieces of machinery in the floor below provide spaces which can provide shelter.
4. <u>Pancake Collapse</u> - A floor collapses completely onto the floor below it, leaving no spaces. In some cases, the force of this collapse causes successive lower floors to collapse.

13. The MOST serious injuries are likely to occur at _____ collapses.   13.___

    A. pancake   B. lean-to
    C. floor   D. building wall

14. Of the following, a floor collapse is MOST likely to occur in a   14.___

    A. factory building   B. private home
    C. apartment building   D. hotel

Questions 15-19.

DIRECTIONS: Questions 15 through 19 are to be answered SOLELY on the basis of the following passage.

Firefighters receive an alarm for an apartment fire on the fourth floor of a 14-story housing project at 1191 Park Place. One firefighter shouts the address as the other firefighters are getting on the fire truck. Knowledge of the address helps the firefighters decide which equipment to pull off the fire truck when they reach the fire scene.

The firefighters know where the water outlets are located in the building on fire. There is an outlet in every hallway. Firefighters always attach the hose at the closest outlet on the floor below the fire.

As they arrive at 1191 Park Place, three firefighters immediately take one length of hose each and go into the building. Since an officer has been told by the dispatcher that two children are trapped in the rear bedroom, the officer and two firefighters begin searching for victims and opening windows immediately upon entering the apartment on fire.

As in all housing project fires, the roof person goes to the apartment above the apartment on fire. From this position, he attaches a tool to a rope in order to break open the windows of the apartment on fire. From this position, the roof person could also make a rope rescue of a victim in the apartment on fire.

15. A firefighter shouted the address of the fire when the alarm was received so that the firefighters would

   A. know which equipment to take from the truck at the fire scene
   B. be more alert when they arrived at the fire
   C. be prepared to make a rope rescue
   D. know that two children were reported to be trapped

15.____

16. The hose should be attached to an outlet on the

   A. floor above the fire
   B. ground floor
   C. fire floor
   D. floor below the fire

16.____

17. Because of the information given to the officer by the dispatcher, the officer and two firefighters

   A. entered the apartment above the fire for a rope rescue
   B. began immediately to search for victims and to open windows
   C. opened all the windows before the hose was moved in
   D. attached a hose and moved to the origin of the fire

17.____

18. The roof person broke the windows of the apartment on fire with a(n)

   A. axe while leaning out of the windows
   B. axe attached to the end of a rope
   C. tool while standing on the roof
   D. tool attached to a rope

18.____

19. The PROPER location for a rescue by the roof person at a fire in a housing project is the

   A. hallway
   B. apartment below the apartment on fire
   C. apartment above the apartment on fire
   D. fire escape

19.____

Questions 20-21.

DIRECTIONS: Questions 20 and 21 are to be answered SOLELY on the basis of the following passage.

Engine company firefighters are responsible for putting water on a fire and extinguishing it. To do this properly, they should perform their tasks in the following order:

1. Once an apartment door has been forced open, the engine company officer orders the driver to start the flow of water through the hose.
2. As the water starts to flow into the hose, it pushes trapped air ahead of it. To clear this air from the hose, the nozzle is pointed away from the fire area, opened, and then closed before water starts to flow from it. This is done to prevent a rush of fresh air from the hose which will intensify the fire.
3. When the fire is found, the nozzle is directed at the ceiling to allow water to rain down on the fire. As the fire becomes smaller, the nozzle is aimed directly at the burning object.

20. When engine company firefighters enter an apartment where there is a fire, the occupant takes the firefighters to a fire in the bedroom.
Once air has been cleared from the hose, the firefighter operating the nozzle should

    A. wait for the ladder company to open the door
    B. aim water directly onto the bed
    C. spray the water across the floor
    D. direct the water at the ceiling and allow it to rain down on the fire

21. After the locked door at an apartment fire has been forced open and water starts to flow into the hose, the firefighter operating the nozzle sees an intense fire just inside the apartment doorway.
She should then point the nozzle

    A. away from the fire
    B. directly at the fire
    C. at any burning object
    D. at the apartment floor

Questions 22-23.

DIRECTIONS: Questions 22 and 23 are to be answered on the basis of the following passage.

A newly appointed firefighter is studying the proper use of foam, water, or dry chemicals to extinguish a fire. The firefighter looks over past fire reports to see whether any patterns exist.

- Fire 1: Gasoline fire near a car was extinguished by foam.
- Fire 2: Fire in a television set with a disconnected power cord was extinguished by water.
- Fire 3: Fire in a fuse box of a private home was extinguished by dry chemicals.
- Fire 4: Oil fire near an oil burner in a private home was extinguished by foam.
- Fire 5: Fire near the electrical rail at a subway was extinguished by dry chemicals.
- Fire 6: Fire involving an electric range was extinguished by dry chemicals.
- Fire 7: Fire in the front seat of an automobile was extinguished by water.

22. The firefighter should conclude that dry chemicals are used to extinguish fires which involve

    A. automobiles
    B. private homes
    C. oil and gasoline
    D. live electrical equipment

23. The firefighter should conclude that foam is used to extinguish _____ fires.

    A. car
    B. oil and gasoline
    C. stove
    D. electrical

Questions 24-25.

DIRECTIONS: Questions 24 and 25 are to be answered SOLELY on the basis of the following passage.

Firefighters inspect many different kinds of places to find fire hazards and have them reviewed. During these inspections, the firefighters try to learn as much as possible about the place. This knowledge is useful should the firefighters have to fight a fire at some later date at that location. When inspecting subways, firefighters are much concerned with the effects a fire might have on the passengers because, unless they have been trapped in a subway car during a fire, most subway riders do not think about the dangers involved in a fire in the subway. During a fire, the air in cars crowded with passengers may become intensely hot. The cars may fill with dense smoke. Lights may dim or go out altogether, leaving the passengers in darkness. Ventilation from fans and air conditioning may stop. The train may be stuck and unable to be moved through the tunnel to a station. Fear may send the trapped passengers into a panic. Firefighters must protect the passengers from the fire, heat, and smoke, calm them down, get them out quickly to a safe area, and put out the fire. To do this, firefighters may have to climb from street level down into the subway tunnel to reach a train stopped inside the tunnel. Before actually going on the tracks, they must be sure that the 600 volts of live electricity carried by the third rail is shut off. They may have to stretch the hose a long distance down subway stairs, on platforms, and along the subway tracks to get the water to the fire and put it out. Subway fires are difficult to fight because of these special problems, but preparing for them in advance can help save the lives of both firefighters and passengers.

24. During a subway fire, a train is stuck in a tunnel. Firefighters have been ordered into the tunnel.
    Before firefighters actually step down on the tracks, they must be sure that

    A. all the passengers have been removed from the burning subway cars to a safe place
    B. they have stretched their fire hose a long distance to put water on the fire
    C. live electricity carried by the third rail is shut off
    D. the train is moved from the tunnel to the nearest station

25. According to the above passage, fire in the subway may leave passengers in subway cars in darkness. This occurs MAINLY because

    A. the lights may go out
    B. air in the cars may become very hot
    C. ventilation may stop
    D. people may panic

KEY (CORRECT ANSWERS)

1.	C	11.	B
2.	A	12.	A
3.	B	13.	A
4.	C	14.	A
5.	D	15.	A
6.	B	16.	D
7.	C	17.	B
8.	C	18.	D
9.	C	19.	C
10.	B	20.	D

21. A
22. D
23. B
24. C
25. A

TEST 2

DIRECTIONS: Each question or incomplete statement is followed by several suggested answers or completions. Select the one that BEST answers the question or completes the statement. *PRINT THE LETTER OF THE CORRECT ANSWER IN THE SPACE AT THE RIGHT.*

Questions 1-4

DIRECTIONS: Questions 1 through 4 are to be answered SOLELY on the basis of the following passage.

    Fires in vacant buildings are a major problem for firefighters. People enter vacant buildings to remove building material or they damage stairs, floors, doors, and other parts of the building. The buildings are turned into dangerous structures with stairs missing, holes in the floors, weakened walls and loose bricks. Children and arsonists find large amounts of wood, paper, and other combustible materials in the buildings and start fires which damage and weaken the buildings even more. Firefighters have been injured putting out fires in these buildings due to these dangerous conditions. Most injuries caused while putting out fires in vacant buildings could be eliminated if all of these buildings were repaired. All such injuries could be eliminated if the buildings were demolished. Until then, firefighters should take extra care while putting out fires in vacant buildings.

1. The problem of fires in vacant buildings could be solved by

    A. repairing buildings
    B. closing up the cellar door and windows with bricks and cement
    C. arresting suspicious persons before they start the fires
    D. demolishing the buildings

1._____

2. Firefighters are injured putting out fires in vacant buildings because

    A. there are no tenants to help fight the fires
    B. conditions are dangerous in these buildings
    C. they are not as careful when nobody lives in the buildings
    D. the water in the buildings has been turned off

2._____

3. Vacant buildings often have

    A. occupied buildings on either side of them
    B. safe empty spaces where neighborhood children can play
    C. combustible materials inside them
    D. strong walls and floors that cannot burn

3._____

4. While firefighters are putting out fires in vacant buildings, they should

    A. be extra careful of missing stairs
    B. find the children who start the fires
    C. learn the reasons why the fires are set
    D. help to repair the buildings

4._____

Questions 5-9.

DIRECTIONS: Questions 5 through 9 are to be answered SOLELY on the basis of the following passage.

Sometimes a fire engine leaving the scene of a fire must back out of a street because other fire engines have blocked the path in front of it. When the fire engine is backing up, each firefighter is given a duty to perform to help control automobile traffic and protect people walking nearby. Before the driver starts to slowly back up the fire engine, all the other firefighters are told the route he will take. They walk alongside and behind the slowly moving fire engine, guiding the driver, keeping traffic out of the street, and warning people away from the path of the vehicle. As the fire engine, in reverse gear, approaches the intersection, the driver brings it to a full stop and waits for his supervisor to give the order to start moving again. If traffic is blocking the intersection, two firefighters enter the intersection to direct traffic. They clear the cars and people out of the intersection, making way for the fire engine to back into it. The driver then goes forward, turning into the intersection. Two other firefighters keep cars and people away from the front of the fire engine as it moves. Because of the extra care needed to control cars and protect people in the streets when a fire engine is backing up, it is better to drive a fire engine forward whenever possible.

5. A fire engine is leaving the scene of a fire. The street in front of it is blocked by people and other fire engines. Of the following, it would be BEST for the driver to

    A. put on the siren to clear a path
    B. back out of the street slowly
    C. drive on the sidewalk around the other fire engines
    D. move the other fire engines out of the way

6. Firefighters walk alongside and behind the fire engine when it is backing up in order to

    A. strengthen their legs and stay physically fit
    B. look around the neighborhood for fires
    C. insure that the engine moves slowly
    D. control traffic, protect people, and assist the driver

7. A fire engine going in reverse approaches an intersection blocked with cars and trucks. The driver should

    A. go forward and then try to back into the intersection at a different angle
    B. slowly enter the intersection as the firefighters guiding the driver give the signal to move
    C. back up through the intersection without stopping
    D. stop, then enter the intersection only when the supervisor gives the signal to move

8. The above passage states that the two firefighters who first enter the Intersection

    A. clear the intersection of cars and people
    B. direct the cars past the fire engine when the engine is in forward gear
    C. see if the traffic signal is working properly
    D. set up barriers to block any traffic

9. The following diagram shows a fire engine backing slowly out of Jones Street. The letters indicate where fire-fighters are standing. Which firefighter is NOT in the correct position? Firefighter

    A. D
    B. E
    C. A
    D. C

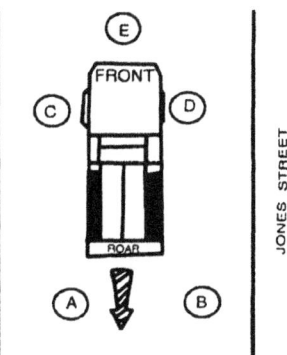

Questions 10-13.

DIRECTIONS: Questions 10 through 13 are to be answered SOLELY on the basis of the following passage.

About 48% of all reported fires are false alarms. False alarms add more risk of danger to firefighters, citizens, and property as well as waste the money and time of the fire department. When the first firefighters are called to a reported fire, they do not know if the alarm is for a real fire or is a false alarm. Until they have made sure that the alarm is false, they must not respond to a new alarm even if a real fire is burning and people's lives and property are in danger. If they do not find a fire or an emergency at the original location, then the firefighters radio the fire department that they have been called to a false alarm. The fire department radios back and tells the firefighters that they are in active service again and tells them where to respond for the next alarm. If that location is far from that of the false alarm, then the distance and the time it takes to get to the new location are increased. This means that firefighters will arrive later to help in fighting the real fire and the fire will have more time to burn. The fire will be bigger and more dangerous just because someone called the firefighters to a false alarm. In addition, each time the firefighters ride to the location of a false alarm, there is additional risk of unnecessary accidents and injuries to them and to citizens.

10. The MAIN point of the above passage is that false alarms

    A. seldom interrupt other activities in the firehouse
    B. occur more often during the winter
    C. are rarely turned in by children
    D. add more risk of danger to life and property

11. When firefighters are called to a false alarm, they must NOT respond to other alarms until they

    A. turn in a written report to the fire department
    B. take a vote and all agree to go
    C. are put back into active service by the fire department
    D. decide on the quickest route

12. Before firefighters get to the location of a reported fire, they 12.___

    A. finish eating their lunch at the firehouse
    B. do not know if the alarm is real or false
    C. search the neighborhood for the person who made the report
    D. do not know if the alarm is from an alarm box or telephone Questions 16-17.

13. The above passage states that false alarms 13.___

    A. shorten travel time to real fires
    B. give firefighters needed driving practice
    C. save money on fuel for the fire department
    D. account for about 48% of reported fires

Questions 14-15.

DIRECTIONS: Questions 14 and 15 are to be answered SOLELY on the basis of the following passage.

The Fire Department uses a firehose nozzle with an automatically adjusting tip. The automatically adjusting nozzle tip keeps the water pressure at the tip constant even though the amount of water being pumped through the hose from the fire engine may vary. A partial loss of water in the hoseline does not result in the stream of water from the nozzle falling short of the target. A partial loss of water is caused by a kink in the hose somewhere between the fire engine pumping the water and the nozzle or by insufficient pressure being supplied by the fire engine pumping water into the hoseline.

The danger of this automatic nozzle is that as the nozzle tip adjusts to maintain constant water pressure, the number of gallons of water per minute flowing out of the nozzle is reduced. When the number of gallons of water per minute flowing from the nozzle is reduced, the nozzle is easier to handle and the stream of water coming from the nozzle appears to be adequate. However, since the number of gallons of flow is reduced, the cooling power of the hose stream will probably not be enough to fight the fire. If a firefighter can physically handle the hoseline alone, the nozzle is not discharging enough water, even though the stream coming out of the nozzle appears adequate. An adequate fire stream requires two firefighters to handle the hoseline.

14. An officer tells a firefighter to check why enough water is not coming out of a hoseline equipped with an automatic nozzle. The firefighter follows the hoseline from the nozzle back to the fire engine pumping the water into the hose but finds no kinks in the hose. The firefighter should inform the officer that the inadequate flow of water is PROBABLY due to 14.___

    A. a defective automatic nozzle
    B. the nozzle stream being aimed in the wrong direction
    C. insufficient pressure being supplied by the fire engine pumping water into the hoseline
    D. the fire engine not being connected to a hydrant

15. One firefighter alone is easily handling a hoseline equipped with an automatic nozzle. The hoseline's stream is reaching the fire. 15.___
    According to the above passage, the firefighter should PROPERLY conclude that

A. being able to handle the hoseline alone indicates extreme strength and excellent physical condition
B. the stream of water coming from the nozzle is probably not an acceptable firefighting stream because not enough water is flowing
C. the stream of water coming from the nozzle is adequate and is helping to save water
D. the automatic nozzle has adjusted itself to provide the proper amount of water to fight the fire

Questions 16-17.

DIRECTIONS: Questions 16 and 17 are to be answered SOLELY on the basis of the following passage.

Firefighters at times are required to work in areas where the atmosphere contains contaminated smoke. To protect the firefighter from breathing the harmful smoke, a self-contained breathing mask is worn. The mask will supply the firefighter with a limited supply of pure breathing air. This will allow the firefighter to enter the smoke-filled area. The mask is lightweight and compact, which makes it less tiring and easier to move around with. The face mask is designed to give the firefighter the maximum visibility possible. The supply of breathing air is limited, and the rate of air used depends upon the exertion made by the firefighter. Although the mask will protect the firefighter from some types of contaminated smoke, it gives no protection from flame, heat, or heat exhaustion.

16. The rate at which the firefighter breathes the air from the mask will depend upon the   16.____

    A. amount of energy used by the firefighter
    B. amount of smoke the firefighter will breathe
    C. color of the flames that the firefighter will enter
    D. color of the heat that the firefighter will enter

17. According to the above passage, the mask will protect the firefighter from some types of   17.____

    A. flames   B. smoke
    C. heat   D. heat exhaustion

Questions 18-21.

DIRECTIONS: Questions 18 through 21 are to be answered SOLELY on the basis of the following passage.

In each firehouse, one firefighter is always on housewatch duty. Each 24-hour housewatch tour begins at 9 A.M. each day and is divided into eight 3-hour periods. The firefighter on housewatch is responsible for the correct receipt, acknowledgement, and report of every alarm signal from any source. Firefighters on housewatch are required to enter in the Company Journal the receipt of all alarms, as well as other matters required by Department regulations. All entries by the firefighter on housewatch should be written in blue or black ink. Any entries made by firefighters not on housewatch are made in red ink. Most entries, including receipt of alarms, are recorded in order, starting in the front of the Company Journal on Page 1. Certain types of entries are recorded in special places in the Journal. When high level officers visit the company, those visits are recorded on Page 500. Company training drills and instruction periods are recorded on Page 497. The monthly meter readings of the utility companies which serve the firehouse are recorded on Page 493.

18. A firefighter is asked by the company officer to find out what alarms were received the previous day, August 25, between 1 A.M. and 2 A.M.
    Where in the Company Journal should the firefighter look to obtain this information?

    A. On Page 493
    B. Between Page 1 and Page 492, on the page for August 25
    C. On Page 500
    D. Between Page 497 and Page 500 on the page for August 25

19. A firefighter on housewatch is asked to find out how much electricity was used in the firehouse between the last two meter readings taken by Con Edison. On which one of the following pages of the Company Journal should the firefighter look to find the last two electrical meter readings entered?

    A. 253   B. 493   C. 497   D. 500

20. A firefighter on housewatch duty is notified by a passing civilian of a rubbish fire around the block. The company responds, extinguishes the rubbish fire, and returns to the firehouse.
    The firefighter on housewatch should

    A. make no entry in the Company Journal of the receipt of the alarm because it was received orally from the civilian
    B. record the alarm in red ink in the Company Journal
    C. record the alarm in blue ink in the Company Journal
    D. ask the civilian to record the alarm in red ink in the Company Journal

21. The company officer asks the firefighter on housewatch to find out the last date on which the company had a training drill on high-rise building fire operations. On which one of the following pages of the Company Journal should the firefighter on housewatch look to find the date of the training drill?

    A. 36   B. 493   C. 497   D. 500

Questions 22-23.

DIRECTIONS: Questions 22 and 23 are to be answered SOLELY on the basis of the following passage.

Fire Department regulations require that upon receiving an alarm while in the firehouse, the officer of the fire company directs the firefighters to take positions in front of the firehouse. The firefighters warn pedestrians and vehicles that the fire engine is leaving the firehouse. The officer directs the driver of the fire engine to move the fire engine to the front of the firehouse and to stop to check for vehicles and pedestrian traffic. While the fire engine is stopped, the firefighters will get on, and the officer will signal the driver to go to the alarm location.

22. When do the firefighters who were sent to the front of the firehouse actually get on the fire engine? 22.____

    A. As the fire engine turns into the street leaving the firehouse
    B. As the fire engine slows down while leaving the firehouse
    C. Inside the firehouse, before the fire engine is moved
    D. After the fire engine has been moved to the front of the firehouse and Stopped

23. When responding to an alarm, why are the firefighters sent out of the firehouse before the fire engine? 23.____
    To

    A. make sure that the firehouse doors are fully opened
    B. go to the nearest corner to change the traffic signal
    C. warn pedestrians and vehicles that the fire engine is coming out of the firehouse
    D. give the firefighters time to put on their helmets and boots

Questions 24-25.

DIRECTIONS: Questions 24 and 25 are to be answered SOLELY on the basis of the following information and the diagram which appears below.

An 8-story apartment building has scissor stairs beginning on the first floor and going to the roof. Scissor stairs are two separate stairways (Stairway A and Stairway B) that criss-cross each other and lead to opposite sides of the building on each floor. Once a person has entered either stairway, the only way to cross over to the other stairway on any floor is by leaving the stairway and using the hallway on that floor. A person entering Stairway A, which starts on the east side of the building on the first floor, would end up on the west side of the building on the second floor, and back on the east side on the third floor. Similarly, a person entering Stairway B, which starts on the west side of the building on the first floor, would end up on the east side of the building on the second floor, and back on the west side on the third floor.

The apartment building has one water pipe for fighting fires. This pipe runs in a straight line near the stairway on the east side of the building from the first floor to the roof. There are water outlets for this pipe on each floor.

Both of the following questions involve a fire in an apartment on the west side of the 6th floor.

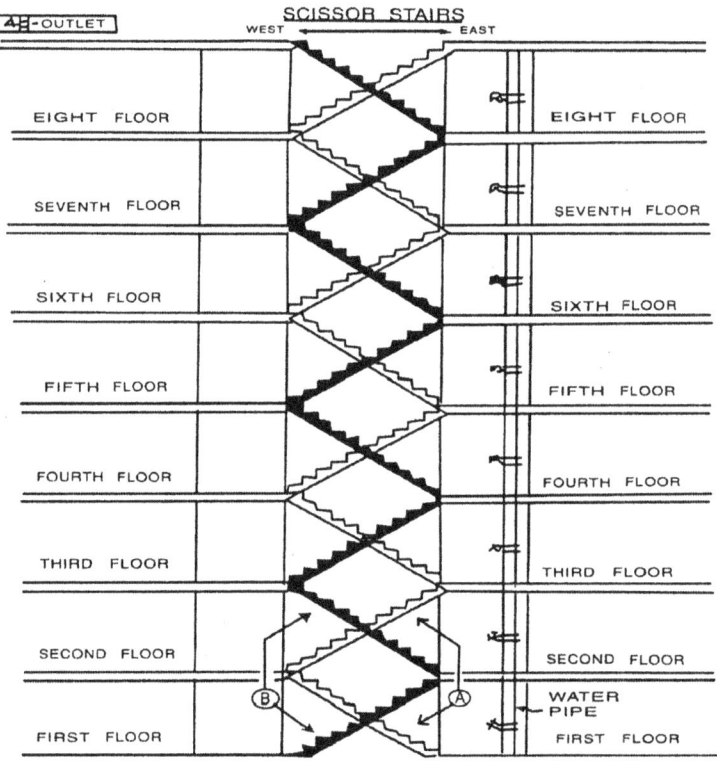

24. Firefighters are ordered to connect a hose to the nearest outlet below the fire. Upon reaching this outlet, they find that it is not usable. Where is the next available outlet? _____ floor near Stairway _____.

    A. 5th; B   B. 3rd; A   C. 4th; B   D. 4th; A

25. A firefighter working on the west side of the 7th floor is ordered to search for victims on the west side of the 8th floor. The door leading to the stairway on the west side of the 7th floor is jammed shut. To reach the victims, the firefighter should take

    A. Stairway A to the 8th floor, and then go across the hallway to the west side of the floor
    B. Stairway B to the 8th floor, and then go across the hallway to the west side of the floor
    C. the hallway to the east side of the 7th floor and go up Stairway A
    D. the hallway to the east side of the 7th floor and go up Stairway B

KEY (CORRECT ANSWERS)

1. D
2. B
3. C
4. A
5. B

6. D
7. D
8. A
9. B
10. D

11. C
12. B
13. D
14. C
15. B

16. A
17. B
18. B
19. B
20. C

21. C
22. D
23. C
24. C
25. C

TEST 3

DIRECTIONS: Each question or incomplete statement is followed by several suggested answers or completions. Select the one that BEST answers the question or completes the statement. *PRINT THE LETTER OF THE CORRECT ANSWER IN THE SPACE AT THE RIGHT.*

Questions 1-3.

DIRECTIONS: Questions 1 through 3 are to be answered SOLELY on the basis of the following passage.

When there is a fire in a subway train, it may be necessary for firefighters to evacuate people from the trains by way of the tunnels. In every tunnel, there are emergency exit areas which have stairways that can be used to evacuate people to the street from the track area. All emergency exits can be recognized by an exit sign near a group of five white lights.

There is a Blue Light Area which is located every 600 feet in the tunnel. These areas contain a power removal box, a telephone, and a fire extinguisher. Removal of power from the third rail is the first step firefighters must take when evacuating people through tunnels. When a firefighter uses the power removal box to turn off electrical power during evacuation procedures, the firefighter must immediately telephone the trainmaster and explain the reason for the power removal. Communication between the firefighter and the trainmaster is essential. If the trainmaster does not receive a phone call within four minutes after power removal, the power will be restored to the third rail.

1. When evacuating passengers through the subway tunnel, firefighters must FIRST   1.___

    A. telephone the trainmaster for assistance
    B. remove electrical power from the third rail
    C. locate the emergency exit in the tunnel
    D. go to the group of five white lights

2. Immediately after using the power removal box to turn off the electrical power, a firefighter should   2.___

    A. wait four minutes before calling the trainmaster
    B. begin evacuating passengers through the tunnel
    C. call the trainmaster and explain why the power was turned off
    D. touch the third rail to see if the electrical power has been turned off

3. A group of five white lights in a subway tunnel indicates that   3.___

    A. a telephone is available
    B. the electrical power is off in the third rail
    C. a fire extinguisher is available
    D. an emergency exit is located there

Questions 4-6.

DIRECTIONS: Questions 4 through 6 are to be answered SOLELY on the basis of the following passage.

Firefighters often know the appearance and construction features of apartments by recognizing the general features on the outside of the building. The following are some general features of different types of buildings in the city.

1. OLD LAW TENEMENTS:
   Height - 5 to 7 stories Width - 25 feet
   Fire Escapes - There will be a rear fire escape if there are two apartments per floor. There will be front and rear fire escapes if there are four apartments per floor.

2. ROW FRAMES:
   Height - 2 to 5 stories
   Width - 20 feet to 30 feet
   Fire Escapes - There will be a rear fire escape if the building is higher than 2 stories.

3. BROWNSTONES:
   Height - 3 to 5 stories
   Width - 20 feet to 25 feet
   Fire Escapes - If the brownstone has been changed from a private home to a multiple dwelling, there will be a rear fire escape. Unchanged brownstones have no fire escapes.

4. Upon arrival at a fire, a firefighter observes that the building is 3 stories high and 25 feet wide. There are fire escapes only in the rear of the building. The firefighter should conclude that the building is either a

   A. Row Frame or an unchanged Brownstone
   B. Row Frame or an Old Law Tenement with two apartments per floor
   C. changed Brownstone or an Old Law Tenement with four apartments per floor
   D. Row Frame or a changed Brownstone

   4.____

5. At another fire, the building is 5 stories high and 25 feet wide. There is a front fire escape. The firefighters should conclude that this building has _____ fire escape because the building _____.

   A. a rear; is a Row Frame higher than two stories
   B. a rear; is an Old Law Tenement with four apartments per floor
   C. no rear; is a Brownstone that has been changed into a multiple dwelling
   D. no rear; has a front fire escape

   5.____

6. At another fire, the building is 4 stories high and 30 feet wide. The building has no front fire escape.
   The firefighter should conclude that the building is a(n)

   A. Row Frame which has no rear fire escape
   B. Old Law Tenement which has four apartments per floor
   C. Row Frame which has a rear fire escape
   D. Brownstone which has been changed from a private home to a multiple dwelling

   6.____

Questions 7-9.

DIRECTIONS: Questions 7 through 9 are to be answered SOLELY on the basis of the following passage.

Firefighters use 2-way radios to alert other firefighters of dangerous conditions and of the need for help. Messages should begin with *MAY DAY or URGENT. MAY DAY* messages have priority over *URGENT* messages. Following is a list of specific emergencies and the messages which should be sent.

MAY DAY Messages:
    1. When a collapse is probable in the area where the firefighters are working: *MAY DAY - MAY DAY, collapse probable, GET OUT.*
    2. When a collapse has occurred in the area where the firefighters are working: *MAY DAY- MAY DAY, collapse occurred.* The firefighter should also give the location of the collapse. If there are trapped victims, the number and condition of the trapped victims is also given.
    3. When a firefighter appears to be a heart attack victim: *MAY DAY - MAY DAY, CARDIAC.* The location of the victim is also given.
    4. When anyone has a serious, life-threatening injury: *MAY DAY - MAY DAY.* The firefighter also describes the injury and gives the condition and the location of the victim.

URGENT Messages:
    1. When anyone has a less serious injury which requires medical attention (for example, a broken arm): *URGENT - URGENT.* The firefighter also gives the type of injury and the location of the victim.
    2. When the firefighters should leave the building and fight the fire from the outside: *URGENT - URGENT, back out.* The firefighter also indicates the area to be evacuated.
    3. *URGENT* messages should also be sent when firefighters' lives are endangered due to a drastic loss of water pressure in the hose.

7. Firefighters are ordered to extinguish a fire on the third floor of an apartment building. As the firefighters are operating the hose on the third floor, the stairway collapses and cuts the hose.
What message should the firefighters send?

    A. URGENT - URGENT, back out
    B. URGENT - URGENT, we have a loss of water on the third floor
    C. MAY DAY - MAY DAY, collapse occurred on third floor stairway
    D. MAY DAY - MAY DAtY, collapse probable, GET OUT

8. Two firefighters on the second floor of a vacant building are discussing the possibility of the floor's collapse. One of the firefighters clutches his chest and falls down. What message should the other firefighter send?

    A. MAY DAY - MAY DAY, firefighter collapse on the second floor
    B. MAY DAY - MAY DAY, CARDIAC on the second floor
    C. URGENT - URGENT, firefighter unconscious on the second floor
    D. URGENT - URGENT, collapse probable on the second floor

9. A firefighter has just decided that a collapse of the third floor is probable when he falls and breaks his wrist.
   What is the FIRST message he should send?

   A. URGENT - URGENT, broken wrist on the third floor
   B. MAY DAY - MAY DAY, broken wrist on the third floor
   C. MAY DAY - MAY DAY, collapse probable, GET OUT
   D. URGENT - URGENT, back out, third floor

Questions 10-14.

DIRECTIONS: Questions 10 through 14 are to be answered SOLELY on the basis of the following passage.

The most important activities which firefighters perform at fires are search, rescue, ventilation, and extinguishment. Ventilation is a vital part of firefighting because it prevents fire from spreading to other areas and because it enables firefighters to search for victims and to bring hoses closer to the fire area. Two types of ventilation used by firefighters are natural venting and mechanical venting. Both types permit the vertical and horizontal movement of smoke and gas from a fire building.

Natural vertical ventilation is generally performed on the roof of the building on fire by making an opening. This allows the heat and smoke to travel up and out of the fire building. Opening windows in the fire area is an example of natural horizontal ventilation. This allows the heat and smoke to travel out of the windows.

Mechanical ventilation takes place when mechanical devices, such as smoke ejectors or hoses with nozzles, are used to remove heated gases from an area. A smoke ejector might be used in a cellar fire when smoke has traveled to the far end of the cellar, creating a heavy smoke condition that cannot be removed naturally. The smoke ejector would be brought into the area to draw the smoke out of the cellar. A nozzle is used with a hose to create a fine spray of water. When directed towards an open window, the water spray pushes smoke and heated gases out of the window.

Extinguishment means bringing a hose to the fire and operating the nozzle to put water on the fire. The proper positioning of hoses is essential to firefighting tactics. Most lives are saved at fires by the proper positioning of hoses.

At each fire, firefighters must use the quickest and best method of extinguishment. There are times when an immediate and direct attack on the fire is required. This means that the hose is brought directly to the fire itself. A fire in a vacant lot, or a fire in the entrance of a building, calls for an immediate and direct attack on the fire. It is generally the ladder company that is assigned the tasks of venting, search, and rescue while the engine company performs the task of extinguishment.

10. Ventilation performed at the roof is GENERALLY _____ ventilation.

    A. mechanical vertical   B. natural vertical
    C. natural horizontal   D. mechanical horizontal

11. When an immediate and direct attack on the fire is required, the hose is 11.___

   A. positioned between the building on fire and the building which the fire might spread to
   B. brought to a window in order to push smoke and gases out
   C. brought to the roof to push the smoke and gases out
   D. brought directly to the fire itself

12. Ladder companies are GENERALLY assigned the tasks of 12.___

   A. extinguishment, rescue, and search
   B. extinguishment, venting, and search
   C. venting, search, and rescue
   D. venting, rescue, and extinguishmen

13. MOST lives are saved at fires by 13.___

   A. a systematic search
   B. the proper positioning of hoses
   C. the proper performance of ventilation
   D. the use of nozzles for ventilation and extinguishment

14. Ventilation enables firefighters to 14.___

   A. bring hoses to the fire and search for victims
   B. create a fine spray of water
   C. use a nozzle to remove smoke and gases
   D. use an ejector to draw smoke out of an area

Questions 15-16.

DIRECTIONS: Questions 15 and 16 are to be answered SOLELY on the basis of the following passage.

A new firefighter learns the following facts about his company's response area: All the factories are located between 9th Avenue and 12th Avenue, from 42nd Street to 51st Street; all the apartment buildings are located between 7th Avenue and 9th Avenue, from 47th Street to 51st Street; all the private houses are located between 5th Avenue and 9th Avenue, from 42nd Street to 47th Street; and all the stores are located between 5th Avenue and 7th Avenue, from 47th Street to 51st Street.

The firefighter also learns that the apartment buildings are all between 4 and 6 stories; the private houses are all between 1 and 3 stories; the factories are all between 3 and 5 stories; and the stores are all either 1 or 2 stories.

15. An alarm is received for a fire located on 8th Avenue between 46th Street and 47th Street. 15.___
    A firefighter should assume that the fire is in a _____ between _____ stories.

   A. private house; 1 and 3   B. private house; 4 and 6
   C. factory; 3 and 5   D. factory; 4 and 6

16. The company responds to a fire on 47th Street between 6th Avenue and 7th Avenue. The firefighter should assume that he would be responding to a fire in a(n)	16._____

   A. store of either 1 or 2 stories
   B. factory between 3 and 5 stories
   C. apartment building between 4 and 6 stories
   D. private house between 4 and 6 stories

Questions 17-22.

DIRECTIONS: Questions 17 through 22 are to be answered SOLELY on the basis of the following passage.

The portable power saw lets the firefighter cut through various materials so that a fire can be reached. It can be dangerous, however, if it is not properly used or if it has not been inspected and tested to insure that it is in serviceable condition. The parts of the saw should be clean and free of foreign material, especially the exhaust port and spark arrestor, the carburetor enclosure, the cooling fins, the spark plugs, and the V-belt pulley if the saw has one.

The saw should be checked to make sure it has both air and fuel filters. It should never be run without an air filter. The V-belt pulley, if present, must be checked to make sure it is not too tight or too loose. If too loose, it could cause slipping. If too tight, the blade might turn when the engine idles, there might be damage to the clutch bearing, or the motor might stall when the blade is stopped. All nuts, bolts, and screws should be checked for tightness.

The saw may use carbide-tipped blades, aluminum oxide blades, or silicon carbide blades. Carbide-tipped blades should be returned for replacement when two or more tips are broken or missing or when the tips are worn down to the circumference of the blade. Aluminum oxide and silicon carbide blades should be replaced when they are cracked, badly nicked, or when worn down to an eight-inch diameter or less.

17. The PRINCIPAL reason for inspecting power saws is to make sure that	17._____

   A. they are clean
   B. they are in serviceable condition
   C. the pulley is not too tight or too loose
   D. the blades are replaced

18. What does the above passage mean when it says the saw should be kept free of foreign material?	18._____

   A. Only American-made parts should be used.
   B. The saw should not be used on material that might damage it.
   C. Both air and fuel filters should be used.
   D. Anything that does not belong on the saw or in it should be removed.

19. Some saws are made to work WITHOUT which one of the following items?	19._____

   A. An air filter	B. A fuel filter
   C. A V-belt pulley	D. Blades

20. If the V-belt pulley on a power saw is too loose, it is MOST likely to cause

   A. the blade to turn when the engine idles
   B. damage to the clutch bearing
   C. the motor to stall when the blade is stopped
   D. slipping

21. The above passage says that a power saw should NEVER be run without a(n)

   A. air filter   B. fuel filter
   C. V-belt pulley   D. blade

22. Which of the following blades should be replaced when two or more tips are missing?

   A. Both aluminum oxide and carbide-tipped blades
   B. Carbide-tipped blades *only*
   C. Both silicon carbide and aluminum oxide blades
   D. Silicon carbide blades *only*

Questions 23-25.

DIRECTIONS: Questions 23 through 25 are to be answered SOLELY on the basis of the following passage.

Automatic sprinkler systems are installed in many buildings. They extinguish or keep from spreading 96% of all fires in areas they protect. Sprinkler systems are made up of pipes which hang below the ceiling of each protected area and sprinkler heads which are placed along the pipes. The pipes are usually filled with water, and each sprinkler head has a heat sensitive part. When the heat from the fire reaches the sensitive part of the sprinkler head, the head opens and showers water upon the fire in the form of spray. The heads are spaced so that the fire is covered by overlapping showers of water from the open heads.

23. Automatic sprinkler systems are installed in buildings to

   A. prevent the build-up of dangerous gases
   B. eliminate the need for fire insurance
   C. extinguish fires or keep them from spreading
   D. protect 96% of the floor space

24. If more than one sprinkler head opens, the area sprayed will be

   A. flooded with hot water
   B. overlapped by showers of water
   C. subject to less water damage
   D. about 1 foot per sprinkler head

25. A sprinkler head will open and shower water when

   A. it is reached by heat from a fire
   B. water pressure in the pipes gets too high
   C. it is reached by sounds from a fire alarm
   D. water temperature in the pipes gets too low

KEY (CORRECT ANSWERS)

1.	B	11.	D
2.	C	12.	C
3.	D	13.	B
4.	D	14.	A
5.	B	15.	A
6.	C	16.	A
7.	C	17.	B
8.	B	18.	D
9.	C	19.	C
10.	B	20.	D

21. A
22. B
23. C
24. B
25. A

PREPARING WRITTEN MATERIAL

PARAGRAPH REARRANGEMENT
COMMENTARY

The sentences that follow are in scrambled order. You are to rearrange them in proper order and indicate the letter choice containing the correct answer at the space at the right.

Each group of sentences in this section is actually a paragraph presented in scrambled order. Each sentence in the group has a place in that paragraph; no sentence is to be left out. You are to read each group of sentences and decide upon the best order in which to put the sentences so as to form a well-organized paragraph.

The questions in this section measure the ability to solve a problem when all the facts relevant to its solution are not given.

More specifically, certain positions of responsibility and authority require the employee to discover connection between events sometimes, apparently, unrelated. In order to do this, the employee will find it necessary to correctly infer that unspecified events have probably occurred or are likely to occur. This ability becomes especially important when action must be taken on incomplete information.

Accordingly, these questions require competitors to choose among several suggested alternatives, each of which presents a different sequential arrangement of the events. Competitors must choose the MOST logical of the suggested sequences.

In order to do so, they may be required to draw on general knowledge to infer missing concepts or events that are essential to sequencing the given events. Competitors should be careful to infer only what is essential to the sequence. The plausibility of the wrong alternatives will always require the inclusion of unlikely events or of additional chains of events which are NOT essential to sequencing the given events.

It's very important to remember that you are looking for the best of the four possible choices, and that the best choice of all may not even be one of the answers you're given to choose from.

There is no one right way to solve these problems. Many people have found it helpful to first write out the order of the sentences, as they would have arranged them, on their scrap paper before looking at the possible answers. If their optimum answer is there, this can save them some time. If it isn't, this method can still give insight into solving the problem. Others find it most helpful to just go through each of the possible choices, contrasting each as they go along. You should use whatever method feels comfortable and works for you.

While most of these types of questions are not that difficult, we've added a higher percentage of the difficult type, just to give you more practice. Usually there are only one or two questions on this section that contain such subtle distinctions that you're unable to answer confidently. And you then may find yourself stuck deciding between two possible choices, neither of which you're sure about.

EXAMINATION SECTION
TEST 1

DIRECTIONS: The sentences that follow are in scrambled order. You are to rearrange them in proper order and indicate the letter choice containing the CORRECT answer. *PRINT THE LETTER OF THE CORRECT ANSWER IN THE SPACE AT THE RIGHT.*

1. Fire Marshal Adams has arrested a man for pulling a false alarm. He has recorded the following items of information about the incident in his notebook for use in his subsequent report:
    I. I was on surveillance at a frequently pulled false alarm box located at Edison Street and Harvard Road.
    II. At 1605 hours, I observed the white male, with long brown hair and a mustache, wearing black pants and a red shirt, pull the fire alarm box.
    III. I interviewed the officer of the first due ladder company, Lt. Morgan - L-37, who informed me that a search of the area disclosed no cause for an alarm to be transmitted.
    IV. A man wearing a red shirt, black pants, with long brown hair and a mustache came out of Ryan's Pub, located at Edison Street and Harvard Road, and walked directly to the alarm box.
    V. I stopped the man about five blocks away at 33rd Street and Harvard Road and asked him why he pulled the fire alarm box, and he replied, *Because I felt like it.*

    The MOST logical order for the above sentences to appear in the report is

    A. I, IV, II, III, V
    B. I, II, III, IV, V
    C. I, IV, III, II, V
    D. I, IV, V, II, III

    1.____

2. A fire marshal is preparing a report regarding Tom Jones, who was a witness to an arson fire at his apartment building. Following are five sentences which will be included in the report:
    I. On July 16, I responded to the fire building, address 2020 Elm Street, to interview Tom Jones.
    II. Tom Jones described the *super* (name unknown) as a middle-aged male with beard, six feet tall, wearing a blue jumpsuit.
    III. Tom Jones stated that he saw the *super* of the building next door set the fire.
    IV. After being advised of his constitutional rights at the 44th Precinct detective's squad room, the *super* confessed.
    V. I interviewed the *super* and took him to the precinct for further investigation.

    The MOST logical order for the above sentences to appear in the report is

    A. I, II, III, V, IV
    B. I, II, III, IV, V
    C. I, III, II, IV, V
    D. I, III, II, V, IV

    2.____

3. A fire marshal is preparing a report on a shooting incident which will include the following five sentences:
    I. I ran around the corner and observed a man pointing a gun at another man.
    II. I informed the man I was a police officer and that he should drop his gun.
    III. I was on the corner of 4th Avenue and 43rd Street when I heard a gunshot coming from around the corner.
    IV. The man turned around and pointed his gun at me.
    V. I fired once, shooting him in the chest and causing him to fall to the ground.
The MOST logical order for the above sentences to appear in the report is

   A. I, III, IV, II, V
   B. IV, V, II, I, III
   C. III, I, II, IV, V
   D. III, I, V, II, IV

3.____

4. Fire Marshal Smith is writing a report. The report will include the following five sentences:
    I. I asked the woman for a description of the man and his location in the building.
    II. When I said, *Don't move, Five Marshal,* the man dropped the can containing a flammable liquid.
    III. I transmitted on my handie-talkie for fire companies to respond.
    IV. A woman approached our car and said there was a man pouring a liquid, which she thought to be gasoline, on a staircase at 123 East Street.
    V. Upon entering that location, I observed a man spilling a liquid on the floor.
The MOST logical order for the above sentences to appear on the interview sheet is

   A. IV, I, V, II, III
   B. I, IV, III, V, II
   C. V, II, IV, I, III
   D. IV, III, I, V, II

4.____

5. Fire Marshal Fox is completing an interview report for a fire in the kitchen of an apartment at 1700 Clayton Road. The following five sentences will be included in the interview report:
    I. This is the first fire in which Mrs. Brown has ever been involved.
    II. A neighbor smelled the food burning and called the Fire Department.
    III. Mrs. Brown has been a tenant in Apt. 4C for 7 years.
    IV. Mrs. Brown was very tired and laid down to rest and fell asleep.
    V. Mrs. Brown was cooking beef stew in the kitchen after coming home from work.
The MOST logical order for the above sentences to appear in the report is

   A. II, III, I, IV, V
   B. III, V, IV, II, I
   C. I, III, II, V, IV
   D. III, V, I, IV, II

5.____

6. A fire marshal is completing a report of an arson fire. The report will contain the following five statements made by a witness:
    I. I heard the sound of breaking glass; and when I looked out my window, I saw orange flames coming from the building across the street.
    II. I saw two young men on bicycles rapidly riding away, one with long blond hair, the other had long brown hair.
    III. He made a threat to get even when he was being evicted.
    IV. The young man with long blond hair was evicted from the fire building last week.
    V. The two young men rode in the direction of Flowers Avenue.
The MOST logical order for the above statements to appear in the report is

6.____

A. I, II, V, IV, III	B. I, II, IV, V, III
C. III, I, V, II, IV	D. III, I, II, IV, V

7. A fire marshal is preparing a report regarding an eleven-year-old who was burned in a fire at the Midtown School for Boys. The report will include the following five sentences:

    I. The child described the fire-setter as a male with glasses, five feet tall, wearing a blue uniform.
    II. On December 12, I responded to Hill Top Hospital to interview a child who was burned in a fire at the Midtown School for Boys.
    III. The male perpetrator made a full confession in front of the Assistant District Attorney at the precinct.
    IV. I responded to the school, after interviewing the boy, and found a security guard who fit the description.
    V. I interviewed the security guard and took him to the precinct for further questioning.

    The MOST logical order for the above sentences to appear in the fire report is

A. I, IV, V, II, III	B. IV, III, II, I, V
C. II, I, IV, V, III	D. II, IV, I, V, III

8. A fire marshal is preparing a report concerning a fire in an auto body shop. The report will contain the following five sentences:

    I. The shop owner stated that he argued with a customer about the cost of a repair job.
    II. The shop owner will be the complainant in the arson case.
    III. While on surveillance, my partner and I saw the fire and called it in over the Department radio.
    IV. The customer paid the bill and left saying, *I'll fix you for charging so much.*
    V. According to witnesses, the customer returned to the shop and threw a Molotov cocktail on the floor.

    The MOST logical order for the above sentences to appear in the report is

A. I, IV, V, II, III	B. III, I, IV, V, II
C. V, I, IV, III, II	D. III, V, I, IV, II

9. Security Officer Mace is completing an entry in her memo-book. The entry has the following five sentences:

    I. I observed the defendant removing a radio from a facility vehicle.
    II. I placed the defendant under arrest and escorted him to the patrolroom.
    III. I was patrolling the facility parking lot.
    IV. I asked the defendant to show identification. V. I determined that the defendant was not authorized to remove the radio.

    The MOST logical order for these sentences to be entered in Officer Mace's memo-book is

A. I, III, II, IV, V	B. II, V, IV, I, III
C. III, I, IV, V, II	D. IV, V, II, I, III

10. Security Officer Riley is completing an entry in his memo-book. The entry has the following five sentences:
    I. Anna Jones admitted that she stole Mary Green's wallet.
    II. I approached the women and asked them who they were and why they were arguing.
    III. I arrested Anna Jones for stealing Mary Green's wallet.
    IV. They identified themselves and Mary Green accused Anna Jones of stealing her wallet.
    V. I was in the lobby area when I observed two women arguing about a wallet.
    The MOST logical order for these sentences to be entered in Officer Riley's memo-book is

    A. II, IV, I, III, V
    B. III, I, IV, V, II
    C. IV, I, V, II, III
    D. V, II, IV, I, III

11. Assume that Security Officer John Ryan is completing an entry in his memobook. The entry has the following five sentences:
    I. I then cleared the immediate area of visitors and staff.
    II. I noticed smoke coming from a broom closet outside Room A71.
    III. Sergeant Mueller arrived with other officers to assist in clearing the area.
    IV. Upon investigation, I determined the smoke was due to burning material in the broom closet.
    V. I pulled the corridor fire alarm and notified Sergeant Mueller of the fire.
    The MOST logical order for these sentences to be entered in Officer Ryan's memo-book is

    A. II, III, IV, V, I
    B. II, IV, V, I, III
    C. IV, I, II, III, V
    D. V, III, II, I, IV

12. Security Officer Hernandez is completing an entry in his memobook. The entry has the following five sentences:
    I. I asked him to leave the premises immediately.
    II. A visitor complained that there was a strange man loitering in Clinic B hallway.
    III. I went to investigate and saw a man dressed in rags sitting on the floor of the hallway.
    IV. As he walked out, he started yelling that he had no place to go.
    V. I asked to see identification, but he said that he did not have any.
    The MOST logical order for these sentences to be entered in Officer Hernandez's memobook is

    A. II, III, V, I, IV
    B. III, I, II, IV, V
    C. IV, I, V, II, III
    D. III, I, V, II, IV

13. Officer Hogan is completing an entry in his memobook. The entry has the following five sentences:
    I. When the fighting had stopped, I transmitted a message requesting medical assistance for Mr. Perkins.
    II. Special Officer Manning assisted me in stopping the fight.
    III. When I arrived at the scene, I saw a client, Adam Finley, strike a facility employee, Peter Perkins.
    IV. As I attempted to break up the fight, Special Officer Manning came on the scene.
    V. I received a radio message from Sergeant Valez to investigate a possible fight in progress in the waiting room.

    The MOST logical order for these sentences to be entered in Officer Hogan's memobook is

    A. II, I, IV, V, III
    B. III, V, II, IV, I
    C. IV, V, III, I, II
    D. V, III, IV, II, I

14. Police Officer White is preparing a crime report concerning the burglary of Mr. Smith's home. The report will contain the following five sentences:
    I. Upon entering the house, Mr. Smith noticed that the mortgage money, which had been left on the kitchen table, had been taken.
    II. An investigation by the reporting Officer determined that the burglar had left the house through the first floor rear door.
    III. Further investigation revealed that there were no witnesses to the burglary.
    IV. In addition, several pieces of jewelry were missing from a first floor bedroom.
    V. After arriving at home, Mr. Smith discovered that someone had broken into the house by jimmying the front door.

    The MOST logical order for the above sentences to appear in the report is

    A. V, IV, II, III, I
    B. V, I, III, IV, II
    C. V, I, IV, II, III
    D. V, IV, II, I, III

15. Police Officer Jenner responds to the scene of a burglary at 2106 La Vista Boulevard. He is approached by an elderly man named Richard Jenkins, whose account of the incident includes the following five sentences:
    I. I saw that the lock on my apartment door had been smashed and the door was open.
    II. My apartment was a shambles; my belongings were everywhere and my television set was missing.
    III. As I walked down the hallway toward the bedroom, I heard someone opening a window.
    IV. I left work at 5:30 P.M. and took the bus home.
    V. At that time, I called the police.

    The MOST logical order for the above sentences to appear in the report is

    A. I, V, IV, II, III
    B. IV, I, II, III, V
    C. I, V, II, III, IV
    D. IV, III, II, V, I

16. Police Officer LaJolla is writing an Incident Report in which back-up assistance was required. The report will contain the following five sentences:
    I. The radio dispatcher asked what my location was and he then dispatched patrol cars for back-up assistance.
    II. At approximately 9:30 P.M., while I was walking my assigned footpost, a gunman fired three shots at me.
    III. I quickly turned around and saw a White male, approximately 5'10", with black hair, wearing blue jeans, a yellow T-shirt, and white sneakers, running across the avenue carrying a handgun.
    IV. When the back-up officers arrived, we searched the area but could not find the suspect.
    V. I advised the radio dispatcher that a gunman had just fired a gun at me, and then I gave the dispatcher a description of the man.

    The MOST logical order for the above sentences to appear in the report is

    A. III, V, II, IV, I
    B. II, III, V, I, IV
    C. III, II, IV, I, V
    D. II, V, I, III, IV

17. Police Officer Engle is completing a Complaint Report of a burglary which occurred at Monty's Bar. The following five sentences will be included in the Complaint Report:
    I. The owner said that approximately $600 was taken, along with eight bottles of expensive brandy.
    II. The burglar apparently gained entry to the bar through the window and exited through the front door.
    III. When Mr. Barrett returned to reopen the bar at 1:00 P.M., he found the front door open and items thrown all over the bar.
    IV. Mr. Barrett, the owner of Monty's Bar, said he closed the bar at 4:00 M. and locked all the doors.
    V. After interviewing the owner, I conducted a search of the bar and found that a window in the back of the bar was broken.

    The MOST logical order for the above sentences to appear in the report is

    A. II, IV, III, V, I
    B. IV, III, I, V, II
    C. IV, II, III, I, V
    D. II, V, IV, III, I

18. Police Officer Revson is writing a report concerning a vehicle pursuit. His report will include the following five sentences:
    I. I followed the vehicle for several blocks and then motioned to the driver to pull the car over to the curb and stop.
    II. I informed the radio dispatcher that I was in a high-speed pursuit.
    III. When the driver ignored me, I turned on my siren and the driver increased his speed.
    IV. The vehicle hit a tree, and I was able to arrest the driver.
    V. While on patrol in Car #4135, I observed a motorist driving suspiciously.

    The MOST logical order for the above sentences to appear in the report is

    A. V, I, III, II, IV
    B. II, V, III, I, IV
    C. V, I, II, IV, III
    D. II, I, V, IV, III

19. Crime Reports are completed by Police Officers. One section of a report contains the following five sentences:
    I. The man, seeing that the woman had the watch, pushed Mr. Lugano to the ground.
    II. Frank Lugano was walking into the Flame Diner on Queens Boulevard when he was jostled by a man in front of him.
    III. A few minutes later, Mr. Lugano told a police officer on foot patrol about a man and a woman taking his watch.
    IV. As soon as he was jostled, a woman reached toward Mr. Lugano's wrist and removed his expensive watch.
    V. The man and woman, after taking Mr. Lugano's watch, ran around the corner.

    The MOST logical order for the above sentences to appear in the report is

    A. II, IV, I, III, V
    B. II, IV, I, V, III
    C. IV, I, III, II, V
    D. IV, II, I, V, III

20. Detective Adams completed a Crime Report which includes the following five sentences:
    I. I arrived at the scene of the crime at 10:20 A.M. and began to question Mr. Sands about the security devices he had installed.
    II. Several clearly identifiable fingerprints were found.
    III. A Fingerprint Unit specialist arrived at the scene and immediately began to dust for fingerprints.
    IV. After questioning Mr. Sands, I called the Fingerprint Unit.
    V. On Friday morning at 10 A.M., Mr. Sands, the owner of the High Fashion Fur Store on Fifth Avenue, called the precinct to report that his safe had been broken into.

    The MOST logical order for the above sentences to appear in the Crime Report is

    A. I, V, IV, III, II
    B. I, V, III, IV, II
    C. V, I, IV, II, III
    D. V, I, IV, III, II

KEY (CORRECT ANSWERS)

1. A
2. D
3. C
4. A
5. B

6. A
7. C
8. B
9. C
10. D

11. B
12. A
13. D
14. C
15. B

16. B
17. B
18. A
19. B
20. D

TEST 2

DIRECTIONS: The sentences that follow are in scrambled order. You are to rearrange them in proper order and indicate the letter choice containing the CORRECT answer. *PRINT THE LETTER OF THE CORRECT ANSWER IN THE SPACE AT THE RIGHT.*

1. Police Officer Ling is preparing a Complaint Report of a missing person. His report will contain the following five sentences:
    I. I was greeted by Mrs. Miah Ali, who stated her daughter Lisa, age 17, did not return from school.
    II. I questioned Mrs. Ali as to what time her daughter left for school and what type of clothing she was wearing.
    III. I notified the Patrol Sergeant, searched the building and area, and prepared a Missing Person Complaint Report.
    IV. I received a call from the radio dispatcher to respond to 9 Maple Street, Apartment 1H, on a missing person complaint.
    V. Mrs. Ali informed me that Lisa was wearing a grey suit and black shoes, and departed for school at 7:30 A.M.
    The MOST logical order for the above sentences to appear in the report is

    A. IV, I, V, II, III B. I, IV, V, III, II
    C. IV, I, II, V, III D. III, I, IV, II, V

    1.___

2. Police Officer Dunn is preparing a Complaint Report which will include the following five sentences:
    I. Mrs. Field screamed and fought with the man.
    II. A man wearing a blue ski mask grabbed Mrs. Field's purse.
    III. Mrs. Field was shopping on 34th Street and Broadway at 1 o'clock in the afternoon.
    IV. The man then ran around the corner.
    V. The man was white, five feet six inches tall with a medium build.
    The MOST logical order for the above sentences to appear in the report is

    A. I, V, II, IV, III B. III, II, I, IV, V
    C. III, IV, V, I, II D. V, IV, III, I, II

    2.___

3. Police Officer Davis is preparing a written report concerning child abuse. The report will include the following five sentences:
    I. I responded to the scene and was met by an adult and a child who was approximately four years old.
    II. I was notified by an unidentified pedestrian of a possible case of child abuse at 325 Belair Terrace.
    III. The adult told me that the child fell and that the police were not needed.
    IV. I felt that this might be a case of child abuse, and I requested that a Sergeant respond to the scene.
    V. The child was bleeding from the head and had several bruises on the face.
    The MOST logical order for the above sentences to appear in the report is

    A. II, I, V, III, IV B. I, II, IV, III, V
    C. I, III, IV, II, V D. II, IV, I, V, III

    3.___

4. The following five sentences will be part of a memobook entry concerning found property:

   I. Mr. Gustav said that while cleaning the lobby he found six credit cards and a passport.
   II. The credit cards and passport were issued to Manuel Gomez.
   III. I went to the precinct to give the property to the Desk Officer.
   IV. I prepared a receipt listing the property, gave the receipt to Mr. Gustav, and had him sign my memobook.
   V. While on foot patrol, I was approached by Mr. Gustav, the superintendent of 50-12 Maiden Parkway.

   The MOST logical order for the above sentences to appear in the memobook is

   A. V, I, II, IV, III B. I, II, IV, III, V
   C. V, I, III, IV, II D. I, IV, III, II, V

5. Police Officer Thomas is making a memobook entry that will include the following five sentences:

   I. My partner obtained a brief description of the suspects and the direction they were heading when they left the store.
   II. Edward Lemkin was asked to come with us to search the immediate area.
   III. I transmitted this information over the radio.
   IV. At the corner of 72nd Street and Broadway, our patrol car was stopped by Edward Lemkin, the owner of PJ Records.
   V. He told us that a group of teenagers stole some merchandise from his record store.

   The MOST logical order for the above sentences to appear in the report is

   A. V, IV, I, III, II B. IV, V, I, III, II
   C. V, I, III, II, IV D. IV, I, III, II, V

6. Police Officer Caldwell is completing a Complaint Report. The report will include the following five sentences:

   I. When I yelled, *Don't move, Police,* the taller man dropped the bat and ran.
   II. I asked the girl for a description of the two men.
   III. I called for an ambulance.
   IV. A young girl approached me and stated that a man with a baseball bat was beating another man in front of 1700 Grande Street.
   V. Upon approaching the location, I observed the taller man hitting the other man with the bat.

   The MOST logical order for the above sentences to appear in the report is

   A. IV, V, I, II, III B. V, IV, II, III, I
   C. V, I, III, IV, II D. IV, II, V, I, III

7. Police Officer Moore is writing a memobook entry concerning a summons he issued. The entry will contain the following five sentences:
    I. As I was walking down the platform, I heard music coming from a radio that a man was holding on his shoulder.
    II. I asked the man for some identification.
    III. I was walking in the subway when a passenger complained about a man playing a radio loudly at the opposite end of the station.
    IV. I then gave the man a summons for playing the radio. V. As soon as the man saw me approaching, he turned the radio off.
    The MOST logical order for the above sentences to appear in the memobook entry is

    A. III, V, II, I, IV
    B. I, II, V, IV, III
    C. III, I, V, II, IV
    D. I, V, II, IV, III

8. Police Officer Kashawahara is completing an Incident Report regarding fleeing suspects he had pursued earlier. The report will include the following five sentences:
    I. I saw two males attempting to break into a store through the front window.
    II. On Myrtle Avenue, they ran into an alley between two abandoned buildings.
    III. I yelled to them, *Hey, what are you guys doing by that window?*
    IV. At that time, I lost sight of the suspects and I returned to the station house.
    V. They started to run south on Wycoff Avenue heading towards Myrtle Avenue.
    The MOST logical order for the above sentences to appear in the report is

    A. I, V, II, IV, III
    B. III, V, II, IV, I
    C. I, III, V, II, IV
    D. III, I, V, II, IV

9. Police Officer Bloom is completing an entry in his memo-book regarding a confession made by a perpetrator. The entry will include the following five sentences:
    I. I went towards the dresser and took $400 in cash and a jewelry box with rings, watches, and other items in it.
    II. There in the bedroom, lying on the bed, a woman was sleeping.
    III. It was about 1:00 A.M. when I entered the apartment through an opened rear window.
    IV. I spun around, punched her in the face with my free hand, and then jumped out the window into the street.
    V. I walked back to the window carrying the money and the jewelry box and was about to go out when all of a sudden I heard the woman scream.
    The MOST logical order for the above sentences to appear in the memobook entry is

    A. I, III, II, V, IV
    B. I, V, IV, III, II
    C. III, II, I, V, IV
    D. III, V, IV, I, II

10. Police Officer Webster is preparing an Arrest Report which will include the following five sentences:
    I. I noticed that the robber had a knife placed at the victim's neck.
    II. I told the robber to drop the knife.
    III. While on patrol, I observed a robbery which was in progress.
    IV. I grabbed the robber, placed him in handcuffs, and took him to the precinct.
    V. The robber dropped the knife and tried to flee.
    The MOST logical order for the above sentences to appear in the report is

    A. I, II, V, IV, III
    B. III, I, II, V, IV
    C. III, II, IV, I, V
    D. I, III, IV, V, II

11. Police Officer Lee is preparing a report regarding someone who apparently attempted to commit suicide with a gun. The report will include the following five sentences:
    I. At the location, the woman pointed to the open door of Apartment 7L.
    II. I called for an ambulance to respond.
    III. The male had a gun in his hand and a large head wound.
    IV. A call was received from the radio dispatcher regarding a woman who heard a gunshot at 936 45th Avenue.
    V. Upon entering Apartment 7L, I saw the body of a male on the kitchen floor.
    The MOST logical order for the above sentences to appear in the report is

    A. IV, I, V, III, II
    B. I, III, V, IV, II
    C. I, V, III, II, IV
    D. IV, V, III, II, I

12. Police Officer Modrak is completing a memobook entry which will include the following five sentences:
    I. The victim, a male in his thirties, told me that the robbery occurred a few minutes ago.
    II. My partner and I jumped out of the patrol car and arrested the suspect.
    III. We responded to an armed robbery in progress at Billings Avenue and 59th Street.
    IV. On Chester Avenue and 68th Street, the victim spotted and identified the suspect.
    V. I told the victim to get into the patrol car and that we would drive him around the area.
    The MOST logical order for the above sentences to appear in the memobook is

    A. III, I, V, IV, II
    B. I, III, V, II, IV
    C. I, IV, III, V, II
    D. III, V, I, II, IV

13. Police Officer Rodriguez is preparing a report concerning an incident in which she used her revolver. Her report will include the following five sentences:
    I. Upon seeing my revolver, the robber dropped his gun to the ground.
    II. At about 10:55 P.M., I was informed by a passerby that several people were being robbed at gunpoint on 174th Street and Walton Avenue.
    III. I was assigned to patrol on 174th Street and Ghent Avenue during the evening shift.
    IV. I saw a man holding a gun on three people, took out my revolver, and shouted, *Police, don't move!*
    V. After calling for assistance, I went to 174th Street and Walton Avenue and took cover behind a car.
    The MOST logical order for the above sentences to appear in the report is

    A. II, III, IV, V, I
    B. IV, V, I, III, II
    C. III, II, V, IV, I
    D. II, IV, I, V, III

14. Police Officer Davis is completing an Activity Log entry which will include the following five sentences:
    I. A radio car was dispatched and the male was taken to Greenville Hospital.
    II. Several people saw him and called the police.
    III. A naked man was running down the street waving his arms above his head and screaming, *Insects are all over me!*
    IV. I arrived on the scene and requested an ambulance.
    V. The dispatcher informed me that no ambulances were available.

    The MOST logical order for the above sentences to appear in the Activity Log is

    A. III, IV, V, I, II
    B. II, III, V, I, IV
    C. III, II, IV, V, I
    D. II, IV, III, V, I

15. Police Officer Peake is completing an entry in his Activity Log. The entry contains the following five sentences:
    I. He went to his parked car only to find he was blocked in.
    II. The owner of the vehicle refused to move the van until he had finished his lunch.
    III. Approximately 30 minutes later, I arrived on the scene and ordered the owner of the van to remove the vehicle.
    IV. Mr. O'Neil had an appointment and was in a hurry to keep it.
    V. Mr. O'Neil entered a nearby delicatessen and asked if anyone in there drove a dark blue van, license plate number BUS 265.

    The MOST logical order for the above sentences to appear in the Activity Log is

    A. II, III, I, IV, V
    B. IV, I, V, II, III
    C. V, IV, I, III, II
    D. II, I, III, IV, V

16. Police Officer Harrison is preparing a report regarding a 10-year-old who was sexually abused at school. The report will include the following five sentences:
    I. The child described the perpetrator as a white male with a mustache, six feet tall, wearing a green uniform.
    II. On September 10, I responded to General Hospital to interview a child who was sexually abused.
    III. He later confessed at the station house.
    IV. After I interviewed the child, I responded to the school and found a janitor who fit the description.
    V. I interviewed the janitor and took him to the station house for further investigation.

    The MOST logical order for the above sentences to appear in the report is

    A. II, IV, I, V, III
    B. I, IV, V, II, III
    C. II, I, IV, V, III
    D. V, III, II, I, IV

17. Police Officer Madden is completing a report of a theft. The report will include the following five sentences:
    I. I followed behind the suspect for two blocks.
    II. I saw a man pass by the radio car carrying a shopping bag.
    III. I looked back in the direction he had just come from and noticed that the top of a parking meter was missing.
    IV. As he saw me, he started to walk faster, and I noticed a red piece of metal with the word *violation* drop out of the shopping bag.
    V. When I saw a parking meter in the shopping bag, I apprehended the suspect and placed him under arrest.

    The MOST logical order for the above sentences to appear in the report is

    A. I, IV, II, III, V
    B. II, I, IV, V, III
    C. II, IV, III, I, V
    D. III, II, IV, I, V

18. Police Officer McCaslin is preparing a report of disorderly conduct which will include the following five sentences:
    I. Police Officer Kenny and I were on patrol in a radio car when we received a dispatch to go to the Hard Rock Disco on Third Avenue.
    II. We arrived at the scene and found three men arguing loudly and obviously intoxicated.
    III. The dispatcher had received a call from a bartender regarding a dispute.
    IV. Two of the men left the disco shortly before we did.
    V. We calmed the men down after managing to separate them.

    The MOST logical order for the above sentences to appear in the report is

    A. I, II, V, III, IV
    B. III, I, IV, II, V
    C. II, I, III, IV, V
    D. I, III, II, V, IV

19. Police Officer Langhorne is completing a report of a murder. The report will contain the following five statements made by a witness:
    I. The noise created by the roar of a motorcycle caused me to look out of my window.
    II. I ran out of the house and realized the man was dead, which is when I called the police.
    III. I saw a man driving at high speed down the dead-end street on a motorcycle, closely followed by a green BMW.
    IV. The motorcyclist then parked the bike and approached the car, which was occupied by two males.
    V. Two shots were fired and the cyclist fell to the ground; then the car made a u-turn and sped down the street.

    The MOST logical order for the above sentences to appear in the report is

    A. I, II, IV, III, V
    B. V, II, I, IV, III
    C. I, III, IV, V, II
    D. III, IV, I, II, V

20. Police Officer Murphy is preparing a report of a person who was assaulted. The report will include the following five sentences:
    I. I responded to the scene, but Mr. Jones had already fled.
    II. She was bleeding profusely from a cut above her right eye.
    III. Mr. and Mrs. Jones apparently were fighting in the street when Mr. Jones punched his wife in the face.
    IV. I then applied pressure to the cut to control the bleeding.
    V. I called the dispatcher on the radio to send an ambulance to respond to the scene.

    The MOST logical order for the above sentences to appear in the report is

    A. III, II, IV, I, V
    B. III, I, II, IV, V
    C. I, V, II, III, IV
    D. II, V, IV, III, I

KEY (CORRECT ANSWERS)

1. C
2. B
3. A
4. A
5. B

6. D
7. C
8. C
9. C
10. B

11. A
12. A
13. C
14. C
15. B

16. C
17. C
18. D
19. C
20. B

PHILOSOPHY, PRINCIPLES, PRACTICES, AND TECHNICS OF SUPERVISION, ADMINISTRATION, MANAGEMENT, AND ORGANIZATION

TABLE OF CONTENTS

	Page
MEANING OF SUPERVISION	1
THE OLD AND THE NEW SUPERVISION	1
THE EIGHT (8) BASIC PRINCIPLES OF THE NEW SUPERVISION	1
I. Principle of Responsibility	1
II. Principle of Authority	2
III. Principle of Self-Growth	2
IV. Principle of Individual Worth	2
V. Principle of Creative Leadership	2
VI. Principle of Success and Failure	2
VII. Principle of Science	3
VIII. Principle of Cooperation	3
WHAT IS ADMINISTRATION?	3
I. Practices Commonly Classed as "Supervisory"	3
II. Practices Commonly Classed as "Administrative"	3
III. Practices Commonly Classed as Both "Supervisory" and "Administrative"	4
RESPONSIBILITIES OF THE SUPERVISOR	4
COMPETENCIES OF THE SUPERVISOR	4
THE PROFESSIONAL SUPERVISOR-EMPLOYEE RELATIONSHIP	4
MINI-TEXT IN SUPERVISION, ADMINISTRATION, MANAGEMENT, AND ORGANIZATION	5
I. Brief Highlights	5
A. Levels of Management	6
B. What the Supervisor Must Learn	6
C. A Definition of Supervision	6
D. Elements of the Team Concept	6
E. Principles of Organization	6
F. The Four Important Parts of Every Job	7
G. Principles of Delegation	7
H. Principles of Effective Communications	7
I. Principles of Work Improvement	7
J. Areas of Job Improvement	7
K. Seven Key Points in Making Improvements	8

	L.	Corrective Techniques for Job Improvement	8
	M.	A Planning Checklist	8
	N.	Five Characteristics of Good Directions	9
	O.	Types of Directions	9
	P.	Controls	9
	Q.	Orienting the New Employee	9
	R.	Checklist for Orienting New Employees	9
	S.	Principles of Learning	10
	T.	Causes of Poor Performance	10
	U.	Four Major Steps in On-the-Job Instructions	10
	V.	Employees Want Five Things	10
	W.	Some Don'ts in Regard to Praise	11
	X.	How to Gain Your Workers' Confidence	11
	Y.	Sources of Employee Problems	11
	Z.	The Supervisor's Key to Discipline	11
	AA.	Five Important Processes of Management	12
	BB.	When the Supervisor Fails to Plan	12
	CC.	Fourteen General Principles of Management	12
	DD.	Change	12
II.	Brief Topical Summaries		13
	A.	Who/What is the Supervisor?	13
	B.	The Sociology of Work	13
	C.	Principles and Practices of Supervision	14
	D.	Dynamic Leadership	14
	E.	Processes for Solving Problems	15
	F.	Training for Results	15
	G.	Health, Safety, and Accident Prevention	16
	H.	Equal Employment Opportunity	16
	I.	Improving Communications	16
	J.	Self-Development	17
	K.	Teaching and Training	17
		1. The Teaching Process	17
		a. Preparation	17
		b. Presentation	18
		c. Summary	18
		d. Application	18
		e. Evaluation	18
		2. Teaching Methods	18
		a. Lecture	18
		b. Discussion	18
		c. Demonstration	19
		d. Performance	19
		e. Which Method to Use	19

PHILOSOPHY, PRINCIPLES, PRACTICES, AND TECHNICS
OF
SUPERVISION, ADMINISTRATION, MANAGEMENT, AND ORGANIZATION

MEANING OF SUPERVISION

The extension of the democratic philosophy has been accompanied by an extension in the scope of supervision. Modern leaders and supervisors no longer think of supervision in the narrow sense of being confined chiefly to visiting employees, supplying materials, or rating the staff. They regard supervision as being intimately related to all the concerned agencies of society, they speak of the supervisor's function in terms of "growth," rather than the "improvement" of employees.

This modern concept of supervision may be defined as follows: Supervision is leadership and the development of leadership within groups which are cooperatively engaged in inspection, research, training, guidance, and evaluation.

THE OLD AND THE NEW SUPERVISION

TRADITIONAL
1. Inspection
2. Focused on the employee
3. Visitation
4. Random and haphazard
5. Imposed and authoritarian
6. One person usually

MODERN
1. Study and analysis
2. Focused on aims, materials, methods, supervisors, employees, environment
3. Demonstrations, intervisitation, workshops, directed reading, bulletins, etc.
4. Definitely organized and planned (scientific)
5. Cooperative and democratic
6. Many persons involved (creative)

THE EIGHT (8) BASIC PRINCIPLES OF THE NEW SUPERVISION

I. Principle of Responsibility
   Authority to act and responsibility for acting must be joined.
   A. If you give responsibility, give authority.
   B. Define employee duties clearly.
   C. Protect employees from criticism by others.
   D. Recognize the rights as well as obligations of employees.
   E. Achieve the aims of a democratic society insofar as it is possible within the area of your work.
   F. Establish a situation favorable to training and learning.
   G. Accept ultimate responsibility for everything done in your section, unit, office, division, department.
   H. Good administration and good supervision are inseparable.

II. Principle of Authority
The success of the supervisor is measured by the extent to which the power of authority is not used.
   A. Exercise simplicity and informality in supervision
   B. Use the simplest machinery of supervision
   C. If it is good for the organization as a whole, it is probably justified.
   D. Seldom be arbitrary or authoritative.
   E. Do not base your work on the power of position or of personality.
   F. Permit and encourage the free expression of opinions.

III. Principle of Self-Growth
The success of the supervisor is measured by the extent to which, and the speed with which, he is no longer needed.
   A. Base criticism on principles, not on specifics.
   B. Point out higher activities to employees.
   C. Train for self-thinking by employees to meet new situations.
   D. Stimulate initiative, self-reliance, and individual responsibility
   E. Concentrate on stimulating the growth of employees rather than on removing defects.

IV. Principle of Individual Worth
Respect for the individual is a paramount consideration in supervision.
   A. Be human and sympathetic in dealing with employees.
   B. Don't nag about things to be done.
   C. Recognize the individual differences among employees and seek opportunities to permit best expression of each personality.

V. Principle of Creative Leadership
The best supervision is that which is not apparent to the employee.
   A. Stimulate, don't drive employees to creative action.
   B. Emphasize doing good things.
   C. Encourage employees to do what they do best.
   D. Do not be too greatly concerned with details of subject or method.
   E. Do not be concerned exclusively with immediate problems and activities.
   F. Reveal higher activities and make them both desired and maximally possible.
   G. Determine procedures in the light of each situation but see that these are derived from a sound basic philosophy.
   H. Aid, inspire, and lead so as to liberate the creative spirit latent in all good employees.

VI. Principle of Success and Failure
There are no unsuccessful employees, only unsuccessful supervisors who have failed to give proper leadership.
   A. Adapt suggestions to the capacities, attitudes, and prejudices of employees.
   B. Be gradual, be progressive, be persistent.
   C. Help the employee find the general principle; have the employee apply his own problem to the general principle.
   D. Give adequate appreciation for good work and honest effort.
   E. Anticipate employee difficulties and help to prevent them.
   F. Encourage employees to do the desirable things they will do anyway.
   G. Judge your supervision by the results it secures.

VII. Principle of Science
Successful supervision is scientific, objective, and experimental. It is based on facts, not on prejudices.
   A. Be cumulative in results.
   B. Never divorce your suggestions from the goals of training.
   C. Don't be impatient of results.
   D. Keep all matters on a professional, not a personal, level.
   E. Do not be concerned exclusively with immediate problems and activities.
   F. Use objective means of determining achievement and rating where possible.

VIII. Principle of Cooperation
Supervision is a cooperative enterprise between supervisor and employee.
   A. Begin with conditions as they are.
   B. Ask opinions of all involved when formulating policies.
   C. Organization is as good as its weakest link.
   D. Let employees help to determine policies and department programs.
   E. Be approachable and accessible—physically and mentally.
   F. Develop pleasant social relationships.

WHAT IS ADMINISTRATION

Administration is concerned with providing the environment, the material facilities, and the operational procedures that will promote the maximum growth and development of supervisors and employees. (Organization is an aspect and a concomitant of administration.)

There is no sharp line of demarcation between supervision and administration; these functions are intimately interrelated and, often, overlapping. They are complementary activities.

I. Practices Commonly Classed as "Supervisory"
   A. Conducting employees' conferences
   B. Visiting sections, units, offices, divisions, departments
   C. Arranging for demonstrations
   D. Examining plans
   E. Suggesting professional reading
   F. Interpreting bulletins
   G. Recommending in-service training courses
   H. Encouraging experimentation
   I. Appraising employee morale
   J. Providing for intervisitation

II. Practices Commonly Classified as "Administrative"
   A. Management of the office
   B. Arrangement of schedules for extra duties
   C. Assignment of rooms or areas
   D. Distribution of supplies
   E. Keeping records and reports
   F. Care of audio-visual materials
   G. Keeping inventory records
   H. Checking record cards and books

4

    I.   Programming special activities
    J.   Checking on the attendance and punctuality of employees

III.   Practices Commonly Classified as Both "Supervisory" and "Administrative"
    A.   Program construction
    B.   Testing or evaluating outcomes
    C.   Personnel accounting
    D.   Ordering instructional materials

RESPONSIBILITIES OF THE SUPERVISOR

A person employed in a supervisory capacity must constantly be able to improve his own efficiency and ability. He represent the employer to the employees and only continuous self-examination can make him a capable supervisor.

Leadership and training are the supervisor's responsibility. An efficient working unit is one in which the employees work with the supervisor. It is his job to bring out the best in his employees. He must always be relaxed, courteous, and calm in his association with his employees. Their feelings are important, and a harsh attitude does not develop the most efficient employees.

COMPETENCES OF THE SUPERVISOR

    I.   Complete knowledge of the duties and responsibilities of his position.
    II.   To be able to organize a job, plan ahead, and carry through.
    III.   To have self-confidence and initiative.
    IV.   To be able to handle the unexpected situation and make quick decisions.
    V.   To be able to properly train subordinates in the positions they are best suited for.
    VI.   To be able to keep good human relations among his subordinates.
    VII.   To be able to keep good human relations between his subordinates and himself and to earn their respect and trust.

THE PROFESSIONAL SUPERVISOR-EMPLOYEE RELATIONSHIP

There are two kinds of efficiency: one kind is only apparent and is produced in organizations through the exercise of mere discipline; this is but a simulation of the second, or true, efficiency which springs from spontaneous cooperation. If you are a manager, no matter how great or small your responsibility, it is your job, in the final analysis, to create and develop this involuntary cooperation among the people whom you supervise. For, no matter how powerful a combination of money, machines, and materials a company may have, this is a dead and sterile thing without a team of willing, thinking, and articulate people to guide it.

The following 21 points are presented as indicative of the exemplary basic relationship that should exist between supervisor and employee:

1.   Each person wants to be liked and respected by his fellow employee and wants to be treated with consideration and respect by his superior.
2.   The most competent employee will make an error. However, in a unit where good relations exist between the supervisor and his employees, tenseness and fear do not exist. Thus, errors are not hidden or covered up, and the efficiency of a unit is not impaired.

3. Subordinates resent rules, regulations, or orders that are unreasonable or unexplained.
4. Subordinates are quick to resent unfairness, harshness, injustices, and favoritism.
5. An employee will accept responsibility if he knows that he will be complimented for a job well done, and not too harshly chastised for failure; that his supervisor will check the cause of the failure, and, if it was the supervisor's fault, he will assume the blame therefore. If it was the employee's fault, his supervisor will explain the correct method or means of handling the responsibility.
6. An employee wants to receive credit for a suggestion he has made, that is used. If a suggestion cannot be used, the employee is entitled to an explanation. The supervisor should not say "no" and close the subject.
7. Fear and worry slow up a worker's ability. Poor working environment can impair his physical and mental health. A good supervisor avoids forceful methods, threats, and arguments to get a job done.
8. A forceful supervisor is able to train his employees individually and as a team, and is able to motivate them in the proper channels.
9. A mature supervisor is able to properly evaluate his subordinates and to keep them happy and satisfied.
10. A sensitive supervisor will never patronize his subordinates.
11. A worthy supervisor will respect his employees' confidences.
12. Definite and clear-cut responsibilities should be assigned to each executive.
13. Responsibility should always be coupled with corresponding authority.
14. No change should be made in the scope or responsibilities of a position without a definite understanding to that effect on the part of all persons concerned.
15. No executive or employee, occupying a single position in the organization, should be subject to definite orders from more than one source.
16. Orders should never be given to subordinates over the head of a responsible executive. Rather than do this, the officer in question should be supplanted.
17. Criticisms of subordinates should, whoever possible, be made privately, and in no case should a subordinate be criticized in the presence of executives or employees of equal or lower rank.
18. No dispute or difference between executives or employees as to authority or responsibilities should be considered too trivial for prompt and careful adjudication.
19. Promotions, wage changes, and disciplinary action should always be approved by the executive immediately superior to the one directly responsible.
20. No executive or employee should ever be required, or expected, to be at the same time an assistant to, and critic of, another.
21. Any executive whose work is subject to regular inspection should, wherever practicable, be given the assistance and facilities necessary to enable him to maintain an independent check of the quality of his work.

MINI-TEXT IN SUPERVISION, ADMINISTRATION, MANAGEMENT, AND ORGANIZATION

I. Brief Highlights

Listed concisely and sequentially are major headings and important data in the field for quick recall and review.

A. Levels of Management
Any organization of some size has several levels of management. In terms of a ladder, the levels are:

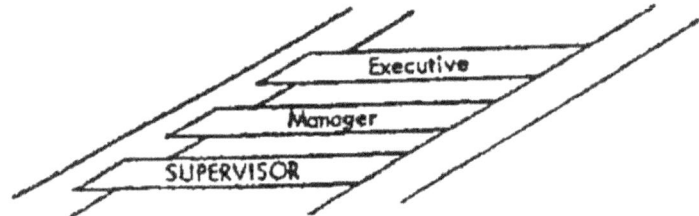

The first level is very important because it is the beginning point of management leadership.

B. What the Supervisor Must Learn
A supervisor must learn to:
1. Deal with people and their differences
2. Get the job done through people
3. Recognize the problems when they exist
4. Overcome obstacles to good performance
5. Evaluate the performance of people
6. Check his own performance in terms of accomplishment

C. A Definition of Supervisor
The term supervisor means any individual having authority, in the interests of the employer, to hire, transfer, suspend, lay-off, recall, promote, discharge, assign, reward, or discipline other employees or responsibility to direct them, or to adjust their grievances, or effectively to recommend such action, if, in connection with the foregoing, exercise of such authority is not of a merely routine or clerical nature but requires the use of independent judgment.

D. Elements of the Team Concept
What is involved in teamwork? The component parts are:
1. Members
2. A leader
3. Goals
4. Plans
5. Cooperation
6. Spirit

E. Principles of Organization
1. A team member must know what his job is.
2. Be sure that the nature and scope of a job are understood.
3. Authority and responsibility should be carefully spelled out.
4. A supervisor should be permitted to make the maximum number of decisions affecting his employees.
5. Employees should report to only one supervisor.
6. A supervisor should direct only as many employees as he can handle effectively.
7. An organization plan should be flexible.

8. Inspection and performance of work should be separate.
9. Organizational problems should receive immediate attention.
10. Assign work in line with ability and experience.

F. The Four Important Parts of Every Job
1. Inherent in every job is the *accountability* for results.
2. A second set of factors in every job is *responsibilities*.
3. Along with duties and responsibilities one must have the *authority* to act within certain limits without obtaining permission to proceed.
4. No job exists in a vacuum. The supervisor is surrounded by key *relationships*.

G. Principles of Delegation
Where work is delegated for the first time, the supervisor should think in terms of these questions:
1. Who is best qualified to do this?
2. Can an employee improve his abilities by doing this?
3. How long should an employee spend on this?
4. Are there any special problems for which he will need guidance?
5. How broad a delegation can I make?

H. Principles of Effective Communications
1. Determine the media.
2. To whom directed?
3. Identification and source authority.
4. Is communication understood?

I. Principles of Work Improvement
1. Most people usually do only the work which is assigned to them.
2. Workers are likely to fit assigned work into the time available to perform it.
3. A good workload usually stimulates output.
4. People usually do their best work when they know that results will be reviewed or inspected.
5. Employees usually feel that someone else is responsible for conditions of work, workplace layout, job methods, type of tools/equipment, and other such factors.
6. Employees are usually defensive about their job security.
7. Employees have natural resistance to change.
8. Employees can support or destroy a supervisor.
9. A supervisor usually earns the respect of his people through his personal example of diligence and efficiency.

J. Areas of Job Improvement
The areas of job improvement are quite numerous, but the most common ones which a supervisor can identify and utilize are:
1. Departmental layout
2. Flow of work
3. Workplace layout
4. Utilization of manpower
5. Work methods
6. Materials handling

7. Utilization
8. Motion economy

K. Seven Key Points in Making Improvements
1. Select the job to be improved
2. Study how it is being done now
3. Question the present method
4. Determine actions to be taken
5. Chart proposed method
6. Get approval and apply
7. Solicit worker participation

l. Corrective Techniques of Job Improvement
Specific Problems
1. Size of workload
2. Inability to meet schedules
3. Strain and fatigue
4. Improper use of men and skills
5. Waste, poor quality, unsafe conditions
6. Bottleneck conditions that hinder output
7. Poor utilization of equipment and machine
8. Efficiency and productivity of labor

General Improvement
1. Departmental layout
2. Flow of work
3. Work plan layout
4. Utilization of manpower
5. Work methods
6. Materials handling
7. Utilization of equipment
8. Motion economy

Corrective Techniques
1. Study with scale model
2. Flow chart study
3. Motion analysis
4. Comparison of units produced to standard allowance
5. Methods analysis
6. Flow chart and equipment study
7. Down time vs. running time
8. Motion analysis

M. A Planning Checklist
1. Objectives
2. Controls
3. Delegations
4. Communications
5. Resources
6. Manpower

7. Equipment
8. Supplies and materials
9. Utilization of time
10. Safety
11. Money
12. Work
13. Timing of improvements

N. Five Characteristics of Good Directions
In order to get results, directions must be:
1. Possible of accomplishment
2. Agreeable with worker interests
3. Related to mission
4. Planned and complete
5. Unmistakably clear

O. Types of Directions
1. Demands or direct orders
2. Requests
3. Suggestion or implication
4. volunteering

P. Controls
A typical listing of the overall areas in which the supervisor should establish controls might be:
1. Manpower
2. Materials
3. Quality of work
4. Quantity of work
5. Time
6. Space
7. Money
8. Methods

Q. Orienting the New Employee
1. Prepare for him
2. Welcome the new employee
3. Orientation for the job
4. Follow-up

R. Checklist for Orienting New Employees   Yes   No
1. Do you appreciate the feelings of new employees when they first report for work? ___ ___
2. Are you aware of the fact that the new employee must make a big adjustment to his job? ___ ___
3. Have you given him good reasons for liking the job and the organization? ___ ___
4. Have you prepared for his first day on the job? ___ ___
5. Did you welcome him cordially and make him feel needed? ___ ___

		Yes	No
6.	Did you establish rapport with him so that he feels free to talk and discuss matters with you?	___	___
7.	Did you explain his job to him and his relationship to you?	___	___
8.	Does he know that his work will be evaluated periodically on a basis that is fair and objective?	___	___
9.	Did you introduce him to his fellow workers in such a way that they are likely to accept him?	___	___
10.	Does he know what employee benefits he will receive?	___	___
11.	Does he understand the importance of being on the job and what to do if he must leave his duty station?	___	___
12.	Has he been impressed with the importance of accident prevention and safe practice?	___	___
13.	Does he generally know his way around the department?	___	___
14.	Is he under the guidance of a sponsor who will teach the right way of doing things?	___	___
15.	Do you plan to follow-up so that he will continue to adjust successfully to his job?	___	___

S. Principles of Learning
 1. Motivation
 2. Demonstration or explanation
 3. Practice

T. Causes of Poor Performance
 1. Improper training for job
 2. Wrong tools
 3. Inadequate directions
 4. Lack of supervisory follow-up
 5. Poor communications
 6. Lack of standards of performance
 7. Wrong work habits
 8. Low morale
 9. Other

U. Four Major Steps in On-The-Job Instruction
 1. Prepare the worker
 2. Present the operation
 3. Tryout performance
 4. Follow-up

V. Employees Want Five Things
 1. Security
 2. Opportunity
 3. Recognition
 4. Inclusion
 5. Expression

W. Some Don'ts in Regard to Praise
1. Don't praise a person for something he hasn't done.
2. Don't praise a person unless you can be sincere.
3. Don't be sparing in praise just because your superior withholds it from you.
4. Don't let too much time elapse between good performance and recognition of it

X. How to Gain Your Workers' Confidence
Methods of developing confidence include such things as:
1. Knowing the interests, habits, hobbies of employees
2. Admitting your own inadequacies
3. Sharing and telling of confidence in others
4. Supporting people when they are in trouble
5. Delegating matters that can be well handled
6. Being frank and straightforward about problems and working conditions
7. Encouraging others to bring their problems to you
8. Taking action on problems which impede worker progress

Y. Sources of Employee Problems
On-the-job causes might be such things as:
1. A feeling that favoritism is exercised in assignments
2. Assignment of overtime
3. An undue amount of supervision
4. Changing methods or systems
5. Stealing of ideas or trade secrets
6. Lack of interest in job
7. Threat of reduction in force
8. Ignorance or lack of communications
9. Poor equipment
10. Lack of knowing how supervisor feels toward employee
11. Shift assignments

Off-the-job problems might have to do with:
1. Health
2. Finances
3. Housing
4. Family

Z. The Supervisor's Key to Discipline
There are several key points about discipline which the supervisor should keep in mind:
1. Job discipline is one of the disciplines of life and is directed by the supervisor.
2. It is more important to correct an employee fault than to fix blame for it.
3. Employee performance is affected by problems both on the job and off.
4. Sudden or abrupt changes in behavior can be indications of important employee problems.
5. Problems should be dealt with as soon as possible after they are identified.
6. The attitude of the supervisor may have more to do with solving problems than the techniques of problem solving.
7. Correction of employee behavior should be resorted to only after the supervisor is sure that training or counseling will not be helpful.

8. Be sure to document your disciplinary actions.
9. Make sure that you are disciplining on the basis of facts rather than personal feelings.
10. Take each disciplinary step in order, being careful not to make snap judgments, or decisions based on impatience.

AA. Five Important Processes of Management
1. Planning
2. Organizing
3. Scheduling
4. Controlling
5. Motivating

BB. When the Supervisor Fails to Plan
1. Supervisor creates impression of not knowing his job
2. May lead to excessive overtime
3. Job runs itself—supervisor lacks control
4. Deadlines and appointments missed
5. Parts of the work go undone
6. Work interrupted by emergencies
7. Sets a bad example
8. Uneven workload creates peaks and valleys
9. Too much time on minor details at expense of more important tasks

CC. Fourteen General Principles of Management
1. Division of work
2. Authority and responsibility
3. Discipline
4. Unity of command
5. Unity of direction
6. Subordination of individual interest to general interest
7. Remuneration of personnel
8. Centralization
9. Scalar chain
10. Order
11. Equity
12. Stability of tenure of personnel
13. Initiative
14. Esprit de corps

DD. Change

Bringing about change is perhaps attempted more often, and yet less well understood, than anything else the supervisor does. How do people generally react to change? (People tend to resist change that is imposed upon them by other individuals or circumstances.

Change is characteristic of every situation. It is a part of every real endeavor where the efforts of people are concerned.

1. Why do people resist change?
   People may resist change because of:
   a. Fear of the unknown
   b. Implied criticism
   c. Unpleasant experiences in the past
   d. Fear of loss of status
   e. Threat to the ego
   f. Fear of loss of economic stability

2. How can we best overcome the resistance to change?
   In initiating change, take these steps:
   a. Get ready to sell
   b. Identify sources of help
   c. Anticipate objections
   d. Sell benefits
   e. Listen in depth
   f. Follow up

II. Brief Topical Summaries

   A. Who/What is the Supervisor?
      1. The supervisor is often called the "highest level employee and the lowest level manager."
      2. A supervisor is a member of both management and the work group. He acts as a bridge between the two.
      3. Most problems in supervision are in the area of human relations, or people problems.
      4. Employees expect: Respect, opportunity to learn and to advance, and a sense of belonging, and so forth.
      5. Supervisors are responsible for directing people and organizing work. Planning is of paramount importance.
      6. A position description is a set of duties and responsibilities inherent to a given position.
      7. It is important to keep the position description up-to-date and to provide each employee with his own copy.

   B. The Sociology of Work
      1. People are alike in many ways; however, each individual is unique.
      2. The supervisor is challenged in getting to know employee differences. Acquiring skills in evaluating individuals is an asset.
      3. Maintaining meaningful working relationships in the organization is of great importance.
      4. The supervisor has an obligation to help individuals to develop to their fullest potential.
      5. Job rotation on a planned basis helps to build versatility and to maintain interest and enthusiasm in work groups.
      6. Cross training (job rotation) provides backup skills.

7. The supervisor can help reduce tension by maintaining a sense of humor, providing guidance to employees, and by making reasonable and timely decisions. Employees respond favorably to working under reasonably predictable circumstances.
8. Change is characteristic of all managerial behavior. The supervisor must adjust to changes in procedures, new methods, technological changes, and to a number of new and sometimes challenging situations.
9. To overcome the natural tendency for people to resist change, the supervisor should become more skillful in initiating change.

C. Principles and Practices of Supervision
1. Employees should be required to answer to only one superior.
2. A supervisor can effectively direct only a limited number of employees, depending upon the complexity, variety, and proximity of the jobs involved.
3. The organizational chart presents the organization in graphic form. It reflects lines of authority and responsibility as well as interrelationships of units within the organization.
4. Distribution of work can be improved through an analysis using the "Work Distribution Chart."
5. The "Work Distribution Chart" reflects the division of work within a unit in understandable form.
6. When related tasks are given to an employee, he has a better chance of increasing his skills through training.
7. The individual who is given the responsibility for tasks must also be given the appropriate authority to insure adequate results.
8. The supervisor should delegate repetitive, routine work. Preparation of recurring reports, maintaining leave and attendance records are some examples.
9. Good discipline is essential to good task performance. Discipline is reflected in the actions of employees on the job in the absence of supervision.
10. Disciplinary action may have to be taken when the positive aspects of discipline have failed. Reprimand, warning, and suspension are examples of disciplinary action.
11. If a situation calls for a reprimand, be sure it is deserved and remember it is to be done in private.

D. Dynamic Leadership
1. A style is a personal method or manner of exerting influence.
2. Authoritarian leaders often see themselves as the source of power and authority.
3. The democratic leader often perceives the group as the source of authority and power.
4. Supervisors tend to do better when using the pattern of leadership that is most natural for them.
5. Social scientists suggest that the effective supervisor use the leadership style that best fits the problem or circumstances involved.
6. All four styles—telling, selling, consulting, joining—have their place. Using one does not preclude using the other at another time.

7. The theory X point of view assumes that the average person dislikes work, will avoid it whenever possible, and must be coerced to achieve organizational objectives.
8. The theory Y point of view assumes that the average person considers work to be a natural as play, and, when the individual is committed, he requires little supervision or direction to accomplish desired objectives.
9. The leader's basic assumptions concerning human behavior and human nature affect his actions, decisions, and other managerial practices.
10. Dissatisfaction among employees is often present, but difficult to isolate. The supervisor should seek to weaken dissatisfaction by keeping promises, being sincere and considerate, keeping employees informed, and so forth.
11. Constructive suggestions should be encouraged during the natural progress of the work.

E. Processes for Solving Problems
1. People find their daily tasks more meaningful and satisfying when they can improve them.
2. The causes of problems, or the key factors, are often hidden in the background. Ability to solve problems often involves the ability to isolate them from their backgrounds. There is some substance to the cliché that some persons "can't see the forest for the trees."
3. New procedures are often developed from old ones. Problems should be broken down into manageable parts. New ideas can be adapted from old one.
4. People think differently in problem-solving situations. Using a logical, patterned approach is often useful. One approach found to be useful includes these steps:
   a. Define the problem
   b. Establish objectives
   c. Get the facts
   d. Weigh and decide
   e. Take action
   f. Evaluate action

F. Training for Results
1. Participants respond best when they feel training is important to them.
2. The supervisor has responsibility for the training and development of those who report to him.
3. When training is delegated to others, great care must be exercised to insure the trainer has knowledge, aptitude, and interest for his work as a trainer.
4. Training (learning) of some type goes on continually. The most successful supervisor makes certain the learning contributes in a productive manner to operational goals.
5. New employees are particularly susceptible to training. Older employees facing new job situations require specific training, as well as having need for development and growth opportunities.
6. Training needs require continuous monitoring.
7. The training officer of an agency is a professional with a responsibility to assist supervisors in solving training problems.

8. Many of the self-development steps important to the supervisor's own growth are equally important to the development of peers and subordinates. Knowledge of these is important when the supervisor consults with others on development and growth opportunities.

G. Health, Safety, and Accident Prevention
1. Management-minded supervisors take appropriate measures to assist employees in maintaining health and in assuring safe practices in the work environment.
2. Effective safety training and practices help to avoid injury and accidents.
3. Safety should be a management goal. All infractions of safety which are observed should be corrected without exception.
4. Employees' safety attitude, training and instruction, provision of safe tools and equipment, supervision, and leadership are considered highly important factors which contribute to safety and which can be influenced directly by supervisors.
5. When accidents do occur, they should be investigated promptly for very important reasons, including the fact that information which is gained can be used to prevent accidents in the future.

H. Equal Employment Opportunity
1. The supervisor should endeavor to treat all employees fairly, without regard to religion, race, sex, or national origin.
2. Groups tend to reflect the attitude of the leader. Prejudice can be detected even in very subtle form. Supervisors must strive to create a feeling of mutual respect and confidence in every employee.
3. Complete utilization of all human resources is a national goal. Equitable consideration should be accorded women in the work force, minority-group members, the physically and mentally handicapped, and the older employee. The important question is: "Who can do the job?"
4. Training opportunities, recognition for performance, overtime assignments, promotional opportunities, and all other personnel actions are to be handled on an equitable basis.

I. Improving Communications
1. Communications is achieving understanding between the sender and the receiver of a message. It also means sharing information—the creation of understanding.
2. Communication is basic to all human activity. Words are means of conveying meanings; however, real meanings are in people.
3. There are very practical differences in the effectiveness of one-way, impersonal, and two-way communications. Words spoken face-to-face are better understood. Telephone conversations are effective, but lack the rapport of person-to-person exchanges. The whole person communicates.
4. Cooperation and communication in an organization go hand in hand. When there is a mutual respect between people, spelling out rules and procedures for communicating is unnecessary.
5. There are several barriers to effective communications. These include failure to listen with respect and understanding, lack of skill in feedback, and misinterpreting the meanings of words used by the speaker. It is also common

practice to listen to what we want to hear, and tune out things we do not want to hear.
6. Communication is management's chief problem. The supervisor should accept the challenge to communicate more effectively and to improve interagency and intra-agency communications.
7. The supervisor may often plan for and conduct meetings. The planning phase is critical and may determine the success or the failure of a meeting.
8. Speaking before groups usually requires extra effort. Stage fright may never disappear completely, but it can be controlled.

J. Self-Development
1. Every employee is responsible for his own self-development.
2. Toastmaster and toastmistress clubs offer opportunities to improve skills in oral communications.
3. Planning for one's own self-development is of vital importance. Supervisors know their own strengths and limitations better than anyone else.
4. Many opportunities are open to aid the supervisor in his developmental efforts, including job assignments; training opportunities, both governmental and non-governmental—to include universities and professional conferences and seminars.
5. Programmed instruction offers a means of studying at one's own rate.
6. Where difficulties may arise from a supervisor's being away from his work for training, he may participate in televised home study or correspondence courses to meet his self-development needs.

K. Teaching and Training
1. The Teaching Process
Teaching is encouraging and guiding the learning activities of students toward established goals. In most cases this process consists of five steps: preparation, presentation, summarization, evaluation, and application.

 a. Preparation
 Preparation is two-fold in nature; that of the supervisor and the employee. Preparation by the supervisor is absolutely essential to success. He must know what, when, where, how, and whom he will teach. Some of the factors that should be considered are:
 1) The objectives
 2) The materials needed
 3) The methods to be used
 4) Employee participation
 5) Employee interest
 6) Training aids
 7) Evaluation
 8) Summarization

 Employee preparation consists in preparing the employee to receive the material. Probably the most important single factor in the preparation of the employee is arousing and maintaining his interest. He must know the objectives of the training, why he is there, how the material can be used, and its importance to him.

b. Presentation
In presentation, have a carefully designed plan and follow it. The plan should be accurate and complete, yet flexible enough to meet situations as they arise. The method of presentation will be determined by the particular situation and objectives.

c. Summary
A summary should be made at the end of every training unit and program. In addition, there may be internal summaries depending on the nature of the material being taught. The important thing is that the trainee must always be able to understand how each part of the new material relates to the whole.

d. Application
The supervisor must arrange work so the employee will be given a chance to apply new knowledge or skills while the material is still clear in his mind and interest is high. The trainee does not really know whether he has learned the material until he has been given a chance to apply it. If the material is not applied, it loses most of its value.

e. Evaluation
The purpose of all training is to promote learning. To determine whether the training has been a success or failure, the supervisor must evaluate this learning.
In the broadest sense, evaluation includes all the devices, methods, skills, and techniques used by the supervisor to keep himself and the employees informed as to their progress toward the objectives they are pursuing. The extent to which the employee has mastered the knowledge, skills, and abilities, or changed his attitudes, as determined by the program objectives, is the extent to which instruction has succeeded or failed.
Evaluation should not be confined to the end of the lesson, day, or program but should be used continuously. We shall note later the way this relates to the rest of the teaching process.

2. Teaching Methods
A teaching method is a pattern of identifiable student and instructor activity used in presenting training material.
All supervisors are faced with the problem of deciding which method should be used at a given time.

a. Lecture
The lecture is direct oral presentation of material by the supervisor. The present trend is to place less emphasis on the trainer's activity and more on that of the trainee.

b. Discussion
Teaching by discussion or conference involves using questions and other techniques to arouse interest and focus attention upon certain areas, and by doing so creating a learning situation. This can be one of the most

valuable methods because it gives the employees an opportunity to express their ideas and pool their knowledge.

    c. Demonstration

The demonstration is used to teach how something works or how to do something. It can be used to show a principle or what the results of a series of actions will be. A well-staged demonstration is particularly effective because it shows proper methods of performance in a realistic manner.

    d. Performance

Performance is one of the most fundamental of all learning techniques or teaching methods. The trainee may be able to tell how a specific operation should be performed but he cannot be sure he knows how to perform the operation until he has done so.

As with all methods, there are certain advantages and disadvantages to each method.

    e. Which Method to Use

Moreover, there are other methods and techniques of teaching. It is difficult to use any method without other methods entering into it. In any learning situation, a combination of methods is usually more effective than any one method alone.

Finally, evaluation must be integrated into the other aspects of the teaching-learning process.

It must be used in the motivation of the trainees; it must be used to assist in developing understanding during the training; and it must be related to employee application of the results of training.

This is distinctly the role of the supervisor.

www.ingramcontent.com/pod-product-compliance
Lightning Source LLC
Chambersburg PA
CBHW081808300426
44116CB00014B/2286